SMALL
CRAFT
NAVIES

▼USS *Hercules*, the second of the 'Pegasus'-class missile hydrofoils, at speed. Note the slicing effect of the hydrofoils at the surface.

SMALL CRAFT NAVIES

CHRISTOPHER CHANT

ARMS AND
ARMOUR

Arms and Armour Press
A Cassell Imprint
Villiers House, 41–47 Strand, London WC2N 5JE.

Distributed in the USA by Sterling Publishing Co. Inc., 387 Park Avenue South, New York, NY 10016-8810.

Distributed in Australia by Capricorn Link (Australia) Pty. Ltd, P.O. Box 665, Lane Cove, New South Wales 2066.

British Library Cataloguing-in-Publication Data: a catalogue record for this book is available from the British Library

ISBN 1-85409-046-1

Designed and edited by DAG Publications Ltd. Designed by David Gibbons; edited by David Dorrell; layout by Anthony A. Evans; typeset by Ronset Typesetters, Darwen, Lancashire; camerawork by M&E Reproductions, North Fambridge, Essex; printed and bound in Great Britain by The Bath Press, Avon

Author's note: the USSR, etc.

Though the collapse of Communism in eastern Europe between the late 1980s and early 1990s has rendered country names such as USSR and East Germany technically incorrect, they have been retained in this book as they reflect the *status quo* relevant to the craft and tactics described. Most of the Soviet craft were designed and built in what is now Russia within the Commonwealth of Independent States, and most of them form part of the Russian contribution to the navy of the Commonwealth of Independent States. The major exceptions are the craft based in the ports along the eastern side of the Baltic Sea proper, which now lie in the independent states of Estonia, Latvia and Lithuania, and the craft that formed part of the Black Sea Fleet based at Odessa in what is now the Ukraine, which is in dispute with Russia about the national status of the Black Sea Fleet's ships. The East German navy has now been absorbed into the navy of a reunified Germany, and most of its FACs have been deleted or otherwise scheduled for disposal. The Soviet-supplied FACs of the USSR's other erstwhile satellites within the Warsaw Pact organization are at a comparably low ebb of serviceability for shortages of spares and their lack of real utility to their now independent owners.

Photograph credits

The author extends his thanks to the manufacturers who supplied the photographs in this book.

Contents

◀A Swiftships 105ft fast
patrol craft at sea. Note the
excellent fields of fire
afforded to all guns.

◀Next up in size from the
FAC is the corvette, here
exemplified by the Iraqi
navy's *Mussa ben Hussair*.

◀Fast attack boat at speed.
Note the 'chaff' launchers
by the bridge, torpedo tube
launchers and standard
76mm gun forward.

PART ONE
Small Craft Navies Today

Many of the world's navies, including a large number without any claim to a long-standing naval or even maritime tradition, now operate forces of small but comparatively heavily armed fast combat craft. These can be defined as vessels possessing a displacement of up to 600 tons and a top speed of 25 knots or more, and fall into two basic categories: the fast patrol boat (FPB) and the fast attack craft (FAC). The FPB is generally fitted with only a light armament (generally machine-guns and cannon of up to 40mm calibre) together with minimal sensor and fire-control suites. The FAC is a considerably more formidable type, usually capable of higher speeds and carrying a heavier, longer-ranged armament that can include anti-ship guided missiles, guns of up to 3in (76mm) calibre, heavyweight anti-ship torpedoes of up to 21in (533mm) calibre and anti-submarine weapons such as lightweight homing torpedoes, rocket-propelled grenades and depth-charges, all controlled with the aid of considerably more sophisticated sensor and fire-control suites. The nature of the primary armament is generally indicated by a suffixed letter: thus the FAC(G) carries a medium-calibre gun, the FAC(M) carries anti-ship missiles, the FAC(T) carries anti-ship torpedoes, etc.

The FPB is considerably inferior to the FAC in combat capability but is still worthy of examination. Many countries use FPBs for patrol and the protection of their territorial waters and associated economic zones, which have acquired considerably greater importance in recent years as resources such as oil and gas have been discovered in such areas. In time of peace, therefore, the FPB has an important role as a type of maritime policeman that can also be used for rescue and other humanitarian purposes. Many such FPBs have been designed with upgrading in mind, however, and in times of crisis can be converted into FACs by the addition of items such as a heavier armament (usually anti-ship missiles and/or medium-calibre guns) and a more capable fire-control system.

The most important weapon carried by the FAC is the anti-ship missile, which is now a light and compact weapon carrying a potent warhead over a usefully long range with devastating accuracy. The modern anti-ship missile can destroy a major warship with a single round, as demonstrated during the Falklands War of 1982, when a French-supplied Aérospatiale Exocet (in this instance fired by a warplane, though in its basic form it is a surface-launched weapon) devastated the British Type 42 destroyer HMS *Sheffield*. The light weight and compact size of these missiles mean that even small FACs can carry four such weapons, conferring on these highly affordable craft almost the status of a capital ship.

A large part of the anti-ship missile's capability rests with its advanced guidance, self-protection and attack electronics, which have benefited greatly from advances in technology (not least miniaturization) in the last quarter of a century. Developments in electronics, including the use of digital in place of analogue processing and computing techniques, have made the guidance package considerably more capable, yet miniaturization techniques have allowed this package to be made smaller and lighter so that a missile of the same weight can carry either a greater fuel load or a larger warhead. Electronic improvements have also transformed the capabilities of the launch vessel's sensor and fire-control suites. Combined with advances in computing, technological progress has allowed modern surveillance and tracking radars, optronic sensors, sonars, electronic warfare systems, action information systems and fire-control systems to be fitted into small hulls that nonetheless carry a potent long-range armament whose destructive capabilities are maximized by the launch vessel's electronic systems. In this instance, small most certainly does mean beautiful, for it reduces procurement costs as an initial advantage and then contributes to reduced manning and maintenance costs.

A similar advance has been made in propulsion. The modern diesel engine is powerful, yet notably compact and highly reliable, and is often used in conjunction with a gas turbine. The former has been developed in turbo-charged form for great power and considerable economy of operation despite its small overall dimensions and comparatively low weight. The latter is also compact and light, yet offers a very high power-to-weight ratio at the expense of high fuel consumption. A combined propulsion arrangement therefore offers the power of the gas turbine for combat speed and the economy of the diesel for long cruising endurance.

Recent developments have tended to obscure the fact that the fast attack craft is not a wholly new development but a type with more than a century of pedigree behind it. The first small warship may be regarded as John I. Thornycroft's torpedo boat *Lightning*, built for the Royal Navy in 1876–77. About ten years earlier Robert Whitehead had demonstrated the capabilities of his new invention, the self-propelled torpedo, and since that time Thornycroft had urged the Admiralty to give him permission to develop a torpedo-armed vessel based on his successful series of fast steam launches. Displacing 32.5 tons and possessing an overall length of 87ft (26.52m), *Lightning* was powered by a compound steam engine delivering 460ihp (343kW) to one shaft for a speed of 19kt and had a complement of 15. On completion, *Lightning* was fitted with two 'torpedo frames', which were torpedo-carrying cages that could be lowered into the water on either side of the launch before the torpedo was released for its free-running attack. These frames could not be used when the launch was moving at any speed, and in 1879 they were replaced by a torpedo tube mounted over the bow; two reload torpedoes were carried on trolleys either side amidships. By the beginning of the twentieth century, the Royal Navy alone had operated more than 100 such steam-powered boats. The later units displaced some 200 tons each and could reach 25kt.

By the time of the First World War there was already a division of torpedo boats into smaller attack craft (torpedo boats) and slightly larger defensive craft (torpedo boat destroyers), and the divergence between the two types increased during the war: the small torpedo boat virtually disappeared; and the torpedo boat destroyer emerged as the multi-role destroyer, a larger and far more capable type offering high speed together with a gun and torpedo armament. The original stream of small attack craft did not disappear entirely, however, for as late as 1918 the Germans were still producing such boats. The vessels of the 'A92' class, for example, displaced 392 tons and had an overall length of 61.2m (200ft 9in), and their geared steam turbines delivered 6,000hp (4,475kW) to two shafts for a maximum speed of 26.7kt; the armament comprised two 88mm (3.46in) guns and one 450mm (17.7in) torpedo tube.

The trouble with such torpedo boats, however, was that they were too small and vulnerable for fleet operations, and at the same time too large and unhandy for coastal operations against convoys escorted by destroyers. Thus the mantle of coastal operations, now firmly established as the métier of such torpedo boats, shifted on to the shoulders of the type of smaller craft made possible by the replacement of the steam powerplant by the internal combustion engine. The main thrusting force in the development of such torpedo boats was the German Navy. The 'LM'-class units of 1917 and 1918 each displaced between 15 and 17 tons and had an overall length of between 14.6 and 17.1m (48–56ft). Each boat was powered by three Maybach petrol engines delivering a total of between 630 and 720hp (470 and 535kW) to three shafts for a maximum speed of between 28 and 32kt. The armament consisted of a single 450mm (17.7in) torpedo tube.

On the other side of the maritime front line, the British developed a similar though smaller type as the coastal motor boat (CMB), which entered service in 1916. The CMB was evolved from pre-war racing boats with a stepped, hydroplaning hull that allowed speeds in excess of 40kt. The type was too small and too light to carry a torpedo tube, so the boats were armed with a single torpedo that was launched tail-first via a stern chute, the boat then having the agility to swerve out of the torpedo's path as the latter accelerated along the boat's original course.

CMBs were built in 40, 55 and 70ft (12.2, 16.8 and 21.3m) lengths, the most numerous being the 55ft (16.8m) type, which was built in several forms with different engines and armament arrangements. The typical 55ft CMB had a displacement of 11 tons and an overall length of 60ft (18.3m) over the torpedo-launching chute. Two petrol engines delivered between 750 and 900hp (560 and 670kW) to two shafts for a maximum speed of between 34 and 42kt. The armament comprised one or two 18in (457mm) torpedoes, four 0.303in (7.7mm) Lewis machine-guns and up to four depth-charges.

The First World War combatant that made the greatest use of torpedo craft was Italy, which developed and built 422 craft of several MAS types. Although completed after the war, a class that typifies such Italian craft is the 'D' group of the SVAN Veloce type. Each unit displaced 28.9 tons and had an overall length of 22m (72.2ft). The propulsion arrangement comprised four Isotta-Fraschini petrol engines delivering 1,600hp (1,195kW) to four shafts or two Rognini electric motors delivering 10hp (7.5kW) to two shafts for silent approach, the maximum speeds for the two systems being 30kt and 4kt respectively. The armament comprised two 450mm (17.7in) torpedoes, two 6.5mm (0.26in) machine-guns and up to 20 depth-charges. Two of these MAS boats showed the potential of small attack craft by torpedoing and sinking *Wien*, a pre-dreadnought battleship of the Austro-Hungarian navy.

During the 1920s, coastal torpedo craft fell into disfavour and it was only during the late 1930s that there was something of a revival. It was Germany that effectively pioneered the renaissance, with the *S 1* of 1929, designed and built by Lürssen of Vegesack as the prototype of the new Schnellboote (fast boats) that were later called 'E-boats' by the Allies. These boats were based on a round-bilge rather than hard-chine hull for improved seaworthiness. *S 1* displaced 51.5 tons and had an overall length of 27m (88.5ft). The propulsion arrangement comprised three Daimler-Benz petrol engines delivering 3,300hp (2,460kW) to three shafts for a maximum speed of 34kt, and the armament included one 20mm cannon and two tubes for 500mm (19.7in) torpedoes.

S 1 proved seaworthy and effective, but serious doubts were raised about her propulsion arrangement, whose petrol engines provided her with a shorter range than diesel units would have done and whose fuel was known to be dangerously inflammable. This last became of particular concern, for the boat lacked armour protection and would therefore be highly vulnerable to a fire that might follow hits from conventional or, worse, incendiary projectiles. *S 6* therefore introduced the diesel-engined powerplant that remained standard in all Schnellboote up to the end of the Second World

War. *S 7* introduced the distinctive knuckled hull form, and *S 18* introduced the Daimler-Benz diesel that was used in all subsequent boats. Later boats had a raised forecastle over the torpedo tubes, and reload torpedoes were carried aft. During the Second World War, the gun armament was increased significantly, and the Schnellboote matured as exceptional fast combat craft.

Lürssen built 162 Schnellboote during the Second World War, and other yards produced about the same number to the basic Lürssen design. The craft were used extensively in the North Sea and Baltic Sea, but their undoubted technical merits were not matched by aggressive leadership, so their effect was less than that of the smaller and less capable British craft, which were handled with considerably greater flair.

During the war, the displacement of the average Schnellboot increased from 35 to 105 tons, the length from 28 to 34.9m (91ft 11in to 114ft 6in) and the speed from 37 to 42kt. Typical of the Schnellboot in fully fledged form was the 'S 186' type built in 1944 and 1945. This had a displacement of 105.5 tons and an overall length of 35.1m (114.75ft), and its propulsion arrangement was based on three Daimler-Benz diesels delivering 7,500hp (5,590kW) to three shafts for a maximum speed of 41kt. The armament included two 533mm (21in) tubes for four torpedoes, and two 30mm cannon (fore and aft), often supplemented by numbers of lighter weapons.

The British returned to the concept of torpedo-armed coastal craft in 1935, when the Admiralty placed orders for motor torpedo boat (MTB) prototypes with the British Power Boat Company. These became the precursors of several important types, most notably the British motor gun boat (MGB) and American PT (pursuit torpedo) boat, but in the event most British MTBs were built to a baseline Vosper design of hard-chine form. This was enlarged during the Second World War and fitted with greater power and armament, but the design remained essentially unchanged. A notable feature of British wartime MTBs was the frequent replacement of the 21in (533mm) heavyweight torpedo, of which only two could be shipped, with the 18in (457mm) medium-weight torpedo, of which four could be carried. In common with their German foes, the British crews added whatever gun armament they could to their fast combat craft as wartime experience revealed the need for additional cannon and machine-guns for use against enemy surface craft and aircraft.

For lack of a suitable British engine, the Italian Isotta-Fraschini petrol engine was used in early craft until Italy's entry into the war in June 1940 cut off supplies. After a problem with the final drive had been eliminated, Packard engines from the United States then became the standard type for British craft. It was notable throughout the war, however, that the petrol-engined British craft were considerably more susceptible to fires than their diesel-engined German opponents.

Typical of the British MTB late in the Second World War was the Vosper 73ft (22.25m) type, which was authorized and built in 1944. This had a displacement of 46.7 tons and an overall length of 72ft (22.3m). The propulsion arrangement was three Packard petrol engines delivering 4,050hp (3,020kW) to three shafts for a maximum speed of 39.5kt, and the armament comprised four 18in (457mm) tubes for four torpedoes, two 20mm cannon and four 0.303in (7.7mm) machine-guns.

The 'Fairmile D' class, also produced late in the Second World War, was a larger and more capable design that could be completed as an MTB or MGB. The type had a displacement of 105 tons and an overall length of 115ft (35.1m). The propulsion arrangement comprised four Packard petrol engines delivering 5,000hp (3,730kW) to four shafts for a maximum speed of 29kt. The basic armament included one 2pdr (40mm) gun, two 20mm cannon in a twin mounting, four 0.5in (12.7mm) machine-guns in two twin mountings, and four 0.303in machine-guns in two twin mountings; later in the war, the 2pdr gun was replaced by a 6pdr (57mm) gun, a second weapon of the same type being located aft in place of the 20mm twin mounting, which was moved farther forward. To this could be added two 21in (533mm) tubes for two torpedoes, although later in the war it was more common to see four 18in tubes for four torpedoes.

The British also developed dedicated MGBs that complemented the MTBs in providing a balanced offensive capability. Here the primary designer and builder was the British Power Boat Company, which produced five basic classes. The largest of these classes was the 'MGB107' type, of which 60 were built from 1942. These boats had a displacement of 37 tons and an overall length of 71ft 9in (21.9m). The propulsion arrangement comprised three Packard petrol engines delivering 4,050hp (3,020kW) to three shafts for a maximum speed of 42kt, and the armament included one 2pdr gun, two 20mm cannon in a twin mounting and four 0.303in

machine-guns in two twin mountings. In 1943 some of the craft were converted into hybrid MTB/MGB types with two 18in tubes for two torpedoes, while other boats were completed to this standard.

Early experience with the MTB and MGB showed the British that a large measure of tactical surprise could be secured by the boats' high speed and small silhouette, but that this element of surprise was often lost because of the noise which resulted from the use of unsilenced engines. In the longer term, the answer was found to lie in an effective silencing system. In the shorter term, however, the British tried to develop a quieter craft with steam propulsion. The resulting steel-hulled steam gunboat (SGB) was a large, round-bilge type that was both fast and quiet. Unfortunately, however, its machinery was also extremely vulnerable to damage from even the lightest of gunfire and its production could only be undertaken at the expense of the construction of larger warships such as destroyers, frigates, corvettes and sloops.

Plans were laid for 60 SGBs, but in the event only nine were ordered and seven actually built. To provide protection for their vulnerable machinery, the boats were fitted with 0.75in (19mm) armour over their machinery spaces, and the weight of this metal reduced speed dramatically. The SGB displaced 165 tons and had an overall length of 145ft 3in (44.3m). The propulsion arrangement comprised geared steam turbines delivering 8,000hp (5,965kW) to two shafts for a maximum speed of 35kt and the armament included two 2pdr guns in single mountings, four 0.5in machine-guns in two twin mountings and two 21in tubes for two torpedoes. The gun armament was later strengthened to one 3in (76mm) gun, two 6pdr guns in single mountings and six 20mm cannon in three twin mountings, which required the complement to be increased from 27 to 34. Together with the armour, this raised the displacement to 260 tons and reduced the speed to 30kt.

The US Navy showed little interest in fast combat craft of such coastal types until 1939, when contracts were placed with six yards, including the British Power Boat Company, for prototype craft varying in length between 54 and 80ft (16.5–24.4m). The type that found the greatest technical favour was that of the British Power Boat Company, and salient features of this design were incorporated in later American boats. Like the British craft, these American vessels were of the hard-chine type, and more than 800 were ordered before the end of the

Second World War. The three main types were the 'PT71' class ordered from Higgins Industries of New Orleans, Louisiana, the 'PT103' class ordered from Elco (Electric Boat Company) of Bayonne, New Jersey, and the 'PT368' class ordered from a number of smaller yards such as R. Jacobs, Herreshoff, the Annapolis Yacht Company and Canadian Power Boats.

The 'PT71' class displaced 46 tons and had an overall length of 78ft (23.8m). The propulsion arrangement comprised three Packard 4M2500 petrol engines delivering 4,050hp (3.020kW) to three shafts for a maximum speed of over 40kt, and the armament comprised two or four 21in tubes for two or four torpedoes, one 40mm gun, two 20mm cannon, varying numbers of 0.5in machine-guns and, in two-tube craft, twelve depth-charges or four mine racks. The 'PT103' class displaced 45 tons and had an overall length of 80.3ft (24.5m). The propulsion arrangement again comprised three Packard 4M2500 petrol engines delivering 4,050hp to three shafts for a maximum speed of more than 40kt and the armament comprised four 21in tubes for four torpedoes, two 20mm cannon and varying numbers of 0.5in machine-guns. The 'PT368' class displaced 43 tons and had an overall length of 70ft (21.3m). The propulsion arrangement comprised the standard three Packard 4M2500 petrol engines delivering 4,050hp to three shafts for a maximum speed of over 40kt and the armament comprised two 21in tubes for two torpedoes as well as varying numbers of 20mm cannon and 0.5in machine-guns.

Like the Americans, the Japanese were late in developing coastal craft. All Japanese craft of this type were developed from two British Thornycroft-built CMBs, one of which had been captured at Canton in 1938. Examination of these two types resulted in a Japanese-designed experimental boat built in 1940, and this led to the construction of at least 248 MTBs before Japan's defeat in 1945. Typical of the Japanese craft was the 'Type T-14' class, which had a displacement of 15 tons, a length of 15m (49ft 2in), a propulsion arrangement of one Type 91 petrol engine delivering 920hp (685kW) for a maximum speed of 28kt and an armament of two 457mm (18in) tubes for two torpedoes as well as one 25mm cannon or 13mm (0.51in) machine-gun. In parallel with these small and highly limited MTBs, the Japanese also developed some MGBs, typical of which was the 'Type H-2' class with a displacement of 24.5 tons, a length of 18m (59ft 1in), a propulsion arrangement of two Type 11 petrol engines deliver-

ing 2,100hp (1,565kW) to two shafts for a maximum speed of 33.5kt and an armament of two 20mm cannon, two 7.7mm (0.303in) machine-guns and two depth-charges. In general, however, the Japanese MTBs and MGBs represented a technical dead end.

After the Second World War, the development of these fast combat craft came to a virtual end in the navies of the victorious Western Allies. The United Kingdom and the United States of America decided that their fast combat craft had played only a comparatively ineffective part in the naval effort of the war and that they should therefore return to the style of the pre-war navies whose large surface combatants had dominated operations in the Atlantic and Pacific Oceans. Large numbers of fast combat craft were therefore either deleted or transferred to smaller navies. These latter used the craft mainly for the patrol role, but the navies of some middle-rank nations used them as a sort of stepping stone toward the re-creation of conventional navies out of the ashes of the Second World War. It is worth noting, however, that there were a number of interesting experimental developments in fast combat craft. The most important, one can now say with hindsight, was the re-engining of a British SGB with two Rolls-Royce RM.60 engines to create the world's first vessel powered purely by gas turbines.

The single exception to the general rule of returning to an orthodox navy was the Union of Soviet Socialist Republics. This nation had emerged in 1945 as a potential 'superpower', but Josef Stalin was totally convinced that this potential could only be realized if the USSR developed air and naval forces with strategic capabilities that matched the vast strength of the Red Army. Soon after the end of the war, therefore, Stalin ordered a massive development of the Soviet navy, at that time a part of the Red Army. It was clear that it would take several decades for the plan to reach fruition, but in the short term there remained the supposed threat of American attack. This threat seemed very real to the Soviets, for the location of the USSR in the centre of the Soviet strategic map suggested that the country was virtually encircled by the unfriendly territory and bases of the United States and her allies. The greatest threat was posed by American long-range bombers carrying strategic nuclear weapons, but another significant offensive capability was their large and superbly equipped navy, which was centred on modern aircraft-carriers and amphibious warfare vessels.

▲ A Lürssen PB-57 serving with the naval forces of Ghana. Built to the original PB-57 specifications rather than the 'F' prefix, they are useful craft with 33kt top speed and 3in and 40mm Bofors weapons capacity.

▼Lürssen FPB-45 small patrol boat, armed with 57mm gun forward and 40mm aft.

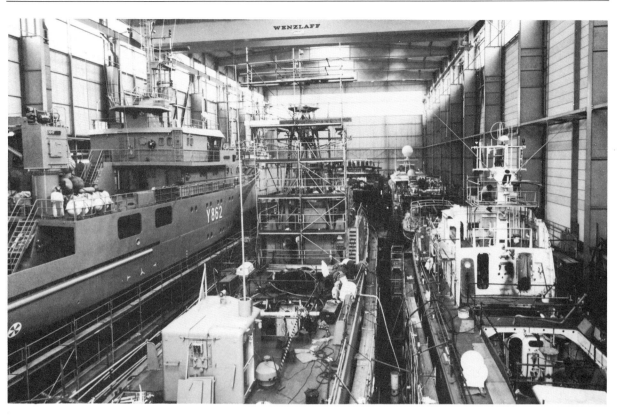

▲Construction/main-
tenance depot showing the
variety of boats tightly
packed in for attention.

▼The 'driving seat' of a
typical modern fast attack
craft, with main rudder
control and all four engine

throttles taking centre
stage.

Submarines offered the Soviets the possibility of countering an invasion force some distance from the USSR, but a way had also to be found to tackle any American warships that might evade the submarine cordon and close the Soviet shore. Here the Soviets turned once more to the concept of fast combat craft, initially armed with the heavyweight torpedo that offered the best chance of crippling or sinking American warships. In the period leading up to the Second World War, the USSR had made extensive use of stepped-hull boats derived from the Thornycroft CMB and incorporating elements of the Italian MAS; these provided the Soviets with a technical base for the development of an interim type as they prepared more ambitious craft based on the hard-chine Elco PT boats they had received from the USA under Lend-Lease during the war. In 1946 the first post-war Soviet MTB appeared as the 'P 2' class. This was based on the pre-war 'D 3' class but, probably as a result of experience with the Elco craft, introduced to Soviet service the ahead-firing torpedo tube that had been common-place in other navies for more than fifteen years. The 'P 2'-class MTBs had a displacement of 50 tons and an overall length of 24.4m (80ft 0½in) but displayed their obsolescent ancestry in their propulsion arrangement, which comprised three petrol engines delivering 3,675kW (4,930hp) to three shafts for a maximum speed which Western estimates put at between 40 and 50 kt. The type was thus very powerfully engined, if only at the expense of high inflammability, and could thus carry without degradation of performance the heavy armament of two 533mm (21in) tubes for two torpedoes and four 12.7 or 14.5mm (0.5 or 0.57in) machine-guns in two twin mountings. Production numbers are uncertain, for while some sources indicate that large numbers were supplied to China, the fact that the type was only rarely seen suggests that comparatively small numbers were produced. The 'P 2s' were deleted in 1966, a last remembrance of an older period in fast combat craft design.

The next Soviet MTB was another descendant of the pre-war concept, for though the 'P 4' class had an aluminium hull, it retained the stepped planing design. This hull-form contributes significantly to outright speed, but it is also a tactically inhibiting factor because its low stability means that tight turns can only be made at considerably lower speeds. The 'P 4' class entered production in 1950 or 1951, and about 200 units had been completed when production ended in 1956; most of these were later transferred to the navies of Soviet client and allied states. The type was made possible by the advent of the USSR's first effective marine diesel engine, the four-stroke M 503 rated at 900kW (1,210hp). The 'P 4' class had a displacement of 25 tons and an overall length of 22m (72ft 2in) and a propulsion arrangement consisting of two M 503 diesels delivering 1,800kW (2,415hp) to two shafts, providing a maximum speed of 42kt. The 'P 4' design had a length-to-beam ratio of 4.7:1 compared with the 3.65:1 of the 'P 2', and this meant only a slight reduction in speed from the preceding class despite less than half the installed power. What the 'P 4' class had to sacrifice, however, was some of its predecessor's offensive power: thus the heavy-weight firepower of the 'P 2' class was exchanged for the medium-weight punch of two smaller 457mm (18in) torpedoes. Other weapons were two 12.7 or 14.5mm machine-guns in a twin turret, and between four and eight depth-charges.

In appearance, the 'P 4' class was highly distinctive, with the bridge structure located well aft, almost amidships behind a long forecastle. Another notable feature, and one indicative of the USSR's emergence from the technological 'dark ages', was the installation of 'Skin Head' surface search radar with its antenna in a radome at the head of a separate lattice mast stepped abaft the wheelhouse. The last 'P 4'-class craft were deleted from Soviet service in the mid-1970s, but the type remains in declining service with several smaller navies up to the present day.

As these two classes were giving an interim coastal defence capability to the Soviet Navy, which became an independent service in 1953, evaluation of the Elco 80ft (24.4m) type was completed and the design finalized for what would be a new type of MTB in Soviet service. This was the 'P 6' class that entered production in 1953; the first units were completed in about 1955 and the programme ran through the 1960s and saw the construction of about 500 craft in total, including some 200 which were transferred to client and allied navies. The type adopted the hard-chine hull used in the Elco boats supplied under Lend-Lease but reverted to wooden construction, possibly as a result of salt-water corrosion in the aluminium-hulled 'P 4' class. The type proved most successful in service, for it was reliable and, compared with its predecessors, offered higher levels of seaworthiness and manoeuvrability. The greater power available in this type not only improved performance but also made possible a reversion to the heavyweight 533mm torpedo and the installation of heavier gun armament, the latter comprising four 25mm cannon in two twin mountings. The forward unit gave the class a distinctive appearance for it was offset to port, probably to give the bridge crew better vision ahead. The propulsion that gave the 'P 6' class its high performance was the quadruple arrangement of M 503 high-speed diesels, providing twice the power of the twin-engined installation in the 'P 4' class. The M 503 is a 42-cylinder engine that is in reality six seven-cylinder radial engines sandwiched together to provide 900kW (1,210hp) at the comparatively light weight of 1.76kg per kilowatt (2.9lb per horsepower). The M 503 was used in several types of Soviet fast combat craft, and, in coupled form (the M 507 driving a combining gearbox), the powerplant was also used for larger craft. The same basic design philosophy was evident in the M 504, a 56-cylinder type developing 3,700kW (4,965hp).

Mid-way through the construction life of the 'P 6' class, emerging technologies were reaching the stage where benefit could be gained from a measure of practical experience under operational conditions. One of these technologies was propulsion, where the gas turbine was beginning to mature as a power unit of exceptional capability in terms of an attractive combination of high power and low installed weight and volume. From about 1958, therefore, some twenty 'P 6'-class craft were modified into two new configurations with a combined diesel and gas turbine (CODAG) propulsion arrangement. As the price of an increase in displacement to 90 tons, the hull was lengthened by some 2m (6ft 7in), a small funnel was added abaft the bridge for the considerable quantity of exhaust gases produced by the gas turbine, and an air inlet was installed between the bridge and the funnel, offset slightly to starboard and facing to port. The propulsion arrangement was one gas turbine delivering 3,800kW (5,095hp) to a central shaft and two diesels delivering 1,800kW (2,415hp) to the two wing shafts. The 'P 8' class, a derivative of the 'P 6' class, had another addition in the form of a pair of semi-submerged hydrofoils forward, and these were designed to lift and stabilize the bow as the boat planed at high speed on its very flat bottom. The result was extended cruising endurance and a maximum speed of 45kt with the gas turbine delivering its full power. The slightly later 'P 10'-class conversions, produced from about 1960, had no hydrofoils and featured 'Pot Head'

surface search radar instead of the 'Skin Head' radar of the 'P 8' and 'P 6' types.

From the end of 1967, the funnel disappeared from both the 'P 8' and 'P 10' classes, suggesting that the turbine had been removed. The craft remained in service, however, indicating that the original diesel-engined propulsion arrangement had been restored. It was assumed that this reconversion was effected because the CODAG propulsion arrangement had proved unsatisfactory. However, given the later prominence of such propulsion arrangements in Soviet fast combat craft, it perhaps safer to say that the original conversions validated the concept of a CODAG propulsion arrangement but at the same time revealed limitations in the Soviets' current level of CODAG technology. These reconversions meant that the Soviet navy had another twenty first-line fast combat craft as the designers evaluated the lessons of the experiment and set about developing definitive CODAG propulsion arrangements.

Since the end of the Second World War, the Soviets had undertaken an intensive programme of missile development with the intention of creating a range of weapons right across the tactical and strategic spectrum. In the late 1950s, this programme began to yield useful results in the field of surface-to-surface anti-ship missiles. The first Soviet experiments had been made in the immediate aftermath of the war with captured Fieseler Fi 103 (V-1) flying bombs and led to spectacular success in the development of Soviet cruise missiles, which were placed in service some four years before the first Western equivalents. The first such type to reach operational status was the SS-N-1 'Scrubber', which entered service in 1958 as a large ship-launched weapon carrying a conventional or nuclear warhead to a maximum range of 185km (115 miles) with radar or infra-red homing. Although the 'Scrubber' was a considerable technical achievement and boded well for future Soviet developments, the missile was too large for truly practical use, and its deployment was limited to 'Kildin' and 'Krupny'-class destroyers.

Yet the 'Scrubber' did pave the way for more practical weapons of the same aeroplane-type layout, and the first of these more effective weapons was the considerably smaller SS-N-2 'Styx', a missile that can truly be regarded as a weapon that revolutionized naval warfare. Spanning 2.75m (9ft 0.25in) and measuring 6.3m (20ft 8in) in length, the 'Styx' weighed 3,000kg (6,614lb) with a 500kg (1,102lb) high-explosive warhead, and its combination of a jettisonable solid-propellant rocket booster and a storable liquid-propellant sustainer rocket provided a theoretical maximum range of 85km (52.8 miles) at a speed of 1,100km/h (684mph). The full range could only be usefully employed if mid-course updating of the guidance package were provided by a supporting helicopter (an extremely unlikely contingency in this period); so the effective range of the missile was 37km (23 miles) under the control of an autopilot with an active radar taking over for the terminal phase of the attack. A cruise altitude of anything up to 300m (985ft) was set before the missile was launched.

The missile entered production in the late 1950s as the 4K40 and reached initial operational capability in late 1958 or early 1959 as the P-15, although it remains best known in the West by its combination of American designation and NATO reporting name. By this time the process of designing a specialist fast combat craft for the type was well advanced, but as an interim measure it was decided to convert a number of 'P 6'-class torpedo craft into simple launch platforms. This resulted in a total of about 100 'Komar'-class craft which entered service probably in late 1958, although the Western powers became aware of the type only in 1960. The Soviets classified this type of craft as the 'RK', standing for Raketnyy Kater (rocket cutter), and this designation has been retained for all later Soviet FAC(M)s. Of the 100 or so 'Komar'-class craft completed in the USSR by 1961, some 78 were later transferred to the navies of satellite and client countries and about another 40 of the modified steel-hulled 'Hegu' class were built in China. The 'Komar' class was intended only as a stopgap, and the last of this type was retired from Soviet service by about 1981.

Topweight was clearly a problem in the conversion, for each 'Komar'-class craft was armed with only two 'Styx' missiles in open-ended but often tarpaulin-sealed container-launchers that provided only minimal protection against the elements. Each launcher was located on a ramp that provided a fixed elevation of about 12° at an angle of about 1.5° out from the centre-line. The missile installation was wider than the hull, so wedge-shaped sponsons, supported by struts braced against the hull, were fitted as outboard projections that helped to protect the missile installation against spray. In an effort to lighten the load on the bow, the bridge and the twin 25mm cannon mounting were moved aft.

The longer range of missiles, compared with that of the torpedoes of the 'P 6' class, dictated the use of improved radar, and this was the type designated 'Square Tie' by NATO. The equipment can see to a maximum range of about 80km (49.7 miles), but its effective range in the acquisition of surface targets is only about 28km (17.4 miles), and it was this that limited the effective range of the 'Styx' in the absence of any mid-course targeting update. The 'Komar' class had a full-load displacement of some 80 tons – compared with the 73 tons of the 'P 6' class – and this reduced maximum speed from 43 to 40kt on the same power.

The use of hulls that existed or were in production greatly sped the process of getting the 'Komar' class into service as the pioneer platform for the 'Styx' missile. By the mid-1960s there were a number of theoretically superior types in service, but the utility of the basic system was confirmed on 21 October 1967 when the Israeli destroyer *Eilat* was hit and sunk by 'Styx' missiles launched from two 'Komar'-class craft of the Egyptian navy lying in Alexandria harbour. This was the first occasion on which a ship-launched anti-ship missile had sunk another warship.

From that time on, it was clear that a new factor had entered the equation of naval power. It had been anticipated in the third quarter of the nineteenth century that the torpedo would have such an effect, giving small and comparatively impoverished navies the means to tackle and defeat the major warships of larger and more affluent navies. Such a change had never really materialized, however, because partial solutions to the torpedo and torpedo boat were provided by improved protection for larger warships and by the development of torpedo boat destroyers and quick-firing guns respectively. Even so, the threat of the torpedo remained, and this greatly conditioned the tactics of surface warfare right up to the end of the Second World War. The anti-ship missile now seemed to offer the same type of threat that had been promised by the torpedo. The 'Styx' had proved itself an effective weapon, and technical developments would inevitably yield smaller though more potent weapons of the same type. This created the possibility that smaller countries could adopt swarms of FAC(M)s to overwhelm the larger and more conventional warships of theoretically more powerful navies. As always, however, it was not long before counter-measures and counter-tactics were evolved. Thus another 'first' involving a 'Komar'-class boat occurred in April 1972, when a North Vietnamese navy craft launched a 'Styx' against the USS *Sterett*, a guided-missile cruiser that was bombarding coastal targets in North Vietnam. *Sterett* launched a Terrier surface-to-air missile that intercepted the 'Styx'; and the result was the first successful destruction of an anti-ship missile by another missile under combat conditions.

Even as the first 'Komar'-class craft were entering service, the Soviets were building an improved successor as the 'Osa' class. This was designed for excellent seakeeping qualities and full capability in coastal operations, especially in European waters. The type was therefore based on a larger hull of the displacement rather than planing variety, and was built of steel with a steel and aluminium superstructure providing citadel-type protection against the effects of nuclear, biological and chemical warfare. The gun armament of the 'Osa'-class craft comprises four 30mm cannon in two remotely controlled mountings on the centre-line forward and aft of the superstructure. These mountings are intended for use against attacking aircraft but also possess a capability against light surface attackers. The sensor fit also reflects the greater capability of the 'Osa' class in comparison with the 'Komar' class, and includes the standard 'Square Tie' search radar on the mast and 'Drum Tilt' fire-control radar for the 30mm mountings on a small pedestal mounting above the rear of the superstructure between the two after anti-ship missile-launchers. Other antennae on the mast are associated with the two 'Square Head' IFF (Identification Friend or Foe) interrogators and one 'High Pole-B' IFF responder.

The design was fully optimized for the carriage and launching of the 'Styx' missile, of which four are carried in container-launchers arranged as two on each side of the deck abaft the bridge. The launchers are angled out very slightly from the centre-line, and while the two forward container-launchers are elevated at 12° the after pair are elevated at 15° so that their missiles will clear the forward launchers. The launchers themselves are fully enclosed to provide the missiles with complete protection against the effects of the atmosphere and of salt water. The front of each launcher is hinged along its upper side to open forward and upward before missile launch, and aft of each launcher is a shield for the outward deflection of the booster rocket's exhaust plume. No spare missiles are carried, and for reloading alongside a support ship

or shore base the launcher is pulled forward from the container: the missile is installed with the aid of a crane and the launcher is then pushed back into the container.

The first unit of the 'Osa' class was laid down in 1959 or 1960 and the type entered service in 1961. Production continued up to 1966 and amounted to some 175 craft (excluding more than 100 built in China as the 'Huangfeng' class). The Soviet craft served with all four of the Soviet navy's main surface forces (the Northern, Baltic, Black Sea and Pacific Fleets), but over a period of years many of them were transferred to the navies of satellite, allied and client states as more modern craft entered Soviet service.

The first of these more modern types was an improved 'Osa II' class, which entered service in 1966 and resulted in the NATO redesignation of the initial type as the 'Osa I' class. The 'Osa II' class is notably different from the 'Osa I' class in its revised missile arrangement. This comprises four cylindrical container-launchers, with their rears supported just above deck level by short brackets and their fronts raised on twin legs, in place of the original slab-sided container-launchers. The new arrangement is considerably lighter than its predecessor, offers less windage and is associated with an improved variant of the 'Styx' missile. Succeeding what now became the SS-N-2A, this was dubbed SS-N-2B by the Americans and was a more compact weapon with folding wings and, probably, infra-red terminal homing as an alternative to the original active radar homing. The revised guidance package allows the missile to home on the heat signature of the target, and this passive terminal mode offers considerable tactical advantages over the original active system, whose emissions could be detected by the target in time for counter-measures to be implemeted. Production of the 'Osa II' class continued up to 1970 and amounted to perhaps 115 craft. Both 'Osa' classes have a three-shaft propulsion arrangement, but whereas the 'Osa I' class has three 3,000kW (4,025hp) M 503A diesels for a maximum speed of 38kt at a full-load displacement of 210 tons, the 'Osa II' class uses three 3,750kW (5,030hp) M 504 diesels for a maximum speed of 40kt at a full-load displacement of 245 tons.

In service, many of the 'Osa II'-class craft have been upgraded with superior weapons, notably the SS-N-2C version of the 'Styx' and the SA-N-5 naval version of the SA-7 'Grail' man-portable surface-to-air missile. Introduced in the early 1970s and sometimes known as the SS-N-2 (Mod), the SS-N-2C is a longer-range derivative of the SS-N-2B with the choice of active radar or infra-red terminal guidance and updated electronics, the latter permitting a sea-skimming approach to the target. This offers powerful tactical advantages, for it reduces the time available to the target for the detection of the missile and the implementation of counter-measures: it also minimizes the missile's visual and electromagnetic cross-sections, further hampering the efforts of the defences. The SA-N-5 system adds significantly to the short-range defences of the craft against attacking aircraft. The missile is basically similar to the land-based weapon with its passive infra-red homing and is installed on a traversing and elevating four-round launcher.

Craft of the 'Osa I' class have been used in combat by the navies of several countries, including that of India in 1971 when the Pakistani destroyer *Khaibar* was sunk, the Egyptian navy in 1973 against Israel, the Syrian in 1973 against Israel and the Iraqi between 1980 and 1990 against Iran. The only navy which has used craft of the 'Osa II' class in combat is that of Iraq, during the same ten-year war with Iran. The failure of Arab-operated 'Osa'-class craft against the Israeli navy during the Yom Kippur War of October 1973 highlighted the fact that the type was obsolete, not so much in its basic hull but in its primary weapon. On several occasions 'Styx' missiles were launched at Israeli targets but were defeated by Israeli electronic counter-measures. Although a pioneering weapon of its type, the 'Styx' was clearly outmoded, but the Soviets had appreciated this fact and had already introduced into service a replacement anti-ship missile carried by a new class of boat.

The new missile was the SS-N-9 'Siren', a weapon delivered from the factory in a sealed container that doubles as the launcher. This greatly improves the unserviced 'shelf life' of the weapon, and, with its basic capabilities proved by use aboard surface vessels, the type was then developed in encapsulated form for use by submarines. Weighing some 3,000kg (6,614lb), the SS-N-9 is another aeroplane-configured weapon, in this instance with a span of 2.50m (8ft 2½in) and a length of 9.2m (30ft 2in) and is powered by a solid-propellant rocket for a high subsonic speed and a range of 65km (40.4 miles), increased to 130km (80.8 miles) with the aid of mid-course update to the guidance. This comprises an autopilot for the updatable mid-course phase and a combined active radar and passive infra-red package for the terminal phase. The missile carries either a 500kg (1,102lb) high-explosive or a 200-kiloton nuclear warhead, the former being installed for general use and the latter if there is the possibility of attacking a major target such as an aircraft-carrier, battleship or cruiser.

The Soviets clearly decided that while their previous FAC(M) classes had been useful, they were perhaps based on hulls that were too small to offer a fully practical seaward defence capability. In the new type, therefore, they opted for a displacement more than three times greater than that of the 'Osa' classes. This allowed the installation of a larger and more varied armament (including a significantly improved anti-aircraft capability) in a hull that could accept greater power for improved performance, greater stability and better general seaworthiness in coastal rather than inshore applications. There are indications that the Soviets did not achieve all their objectives, however, for some reports suggest that the hull has not displayed the required seaworthiness and that the engines are somewhat unreliable.

The surface vessel designed to use the SS-N-9 was the 'Nanuchka'-class FAC(M), a type large and capable enough to be considered virtually a missile-armed corvette as it has a full-load displacement of 660 tons on a displacement-type hull possessing an overall length of 59.3m (194ft 6in) and is able to reach a speed of 36kt on the 22,500kW (30,175hp) generated by six M 504 diesels coupled to three shafts. The greater size and increased capabilities of the 'Nanuchka' class were recognized by the Soviets, who designated the type 'MRK' (Malyy Raketnyy Korabl, or small rocket ship) rather than 'RK'.

The type that entered service in 1969 was subsequently designated 'Nanuchka I' by NATO. It carries a primary armament of six SS-N-9 missiles used in conjunction with the 'Band Stand' air/surface search radar located in a large radome above and behind the bridge. The missiles are located in two triple mountings flanking the forward superstructure, whose lower parts aft of the bridge are angled out towards the sides of the craft to deflect the exhaust plumes of the missiles as they are fired. The gun armament comprises two 57mm dual-purpose weapons in a twin mounting located at the stern. Here it has excellent fields of fire under the control of its associated 'Muff Cob' radar, located above the aftermost part of the superstructure just forward of the gun mounting. The location of the gun mounting was dictated by the decision to give the new design a greater air-defence capability than preceding classes, in this instance with an inbuilt surface-to-air missile system, the medium-weight SA-N-4 'Gecko'. This missile is associated with a twin-arm launcher fed by a 20-round magazine, and is retractable system covered by a lid when lowered into its circular bin, which is located just forward of the bridge behind a breakwater that helps to keep the area at least partially dry. The associated 'Pop Group' fire-control radar is another retractable system, in this instance located just aft of the launcher in the forward part of the superstructure above and between the forward edges of the SS-N-9 missile installations.

The Soviets built seventeen 'Nanuchka I'-class units for their own use and also exported the type in downgraded form as the 'Nanuchka II' with two triple container-launcher installations for the SS-N-2C version of the 'Styx' supported by 'Square Tie' radar. Production for Soviet use then switched to an improved model, the 'Nanuchka III'. This has the aft-mounted 57mm guns replaced by a single 76mm (3in) dual-purpose gun (a fully automatic weapon that is therefore unmanned and, as a result, highly compact), and adds a 30mm close-in weapon mounting. The latter is used in conjunction with a 'Bass Tilt' fire-control radar that replaces the 'Muff Cob' system of the 'Nanuchka I'. Production of the 'Nanuchka III' class totalled fifteen units, and the later craft were complemented by a single 'Nanuchka IV'-class vessel with two sextuple container-launchers for a new and as yet undesignated type of anti-ship missile. It is still unclear whether this singleton is a trials vessel for the new missile or the first of a new sub-class.

Just ten years after they introduced the 'Nanuchka' class, the Soviets followed with the 'Tarantul' class, which is a slightly smaller type that is nonetheless large and powerful enough to encroach on corvette status and, as such, is classified as an MRK. It is still difficult to determine the origins of this class, for its design and other features are in many respects not as advanced as those of the 'Nanuchka' class. The first 'Tarantul I'-class unit was commissioned in 1978. The design is based on that of the 'Pauk' class of anti-submarine corvettes and may have been conceived for export. Exports of the 'Tarantul I' class were indeed made to four countries, but the Soviet navy also received two of the type, which has a full-load displacement of 580 tons on a hull possessing an overall length of 56m

(183ft 9in). One feature of the 'Tarantul I' class which is more modern than that of the 'Nanuchka' class, however, is the propulsion arrangement. This is of either the CODOG (Combined Diesel or Gas turbine) or COGOG (Combined Gas turbine or Gas turbine) variety in which the two shafts are driven either by two diesels or gas turbines delivering up to 4,500kW (6,035hp) for an economical cruising speed of 20kt, or by two NK-12M gas turbines delivering 18,000kW (24,140hp) for a maximum speed of 36kt.

The armament is somewhat strange. The gun armament is a potent variant of the combination that had now become the standard for Soviet fast combat craft and comprises one 76mm (3in) dual-purpose gun and two 30mm rotary six-barrel cannon in close-in weapon system mountings for short-range air defence, a task in which they are supplemented by one SA-N-5 quadruple launcher for a maximum of sixteen short-range surface-to-air missiles. But there is no medium surface-to-air missile system, and the anti-ship missile system is limited to two twin container-launchers for the SS-N-2C version of the venerable 'Styx'. The electronic suite of the 'Tarantul I' class includes one 'Plank Shave' air/surface search radar and one 'Bass Tilt' gun fire-control radar. This is considerably improved in the 'Tarantul II' class that was built exclusively for the Soviet Navy and features the more modern 'Light Bulb' radar in place of the 'Plank Shave' and adds one 'Band Stand' surface search radar. Some twenty 'Tarantul II'-class units were delivered between 1980 and 1986.

The basic 'Tarantul' design might have been conceived for a more powerful anti-ship armament whose missile then suffered development delays. Certainly the 'Tarantul III' class that appeared in 1986 is far more powerfully armed in this respect than its predecessors, with one or two twin container-launchers for SS-N-22 'Sunburn' missiles in place of the earlier variants' SS-N-2Cs. Little is known about the SS-N-22, but it is probably a development of the SS-N-9 with considerably improved electronics. These provide a 'home-on-jam' capability in conditions where the target is using electronic counter-measures and also allow a true sea-skimming approach to the target, in place of the SS-N-9's 75m (245ft) approach height, with all the tactical advantages of low optical and electromagnetic visibility. The electronic suite of the 'Tarantul II' class was retained for the 'Tarantul IIIs', which probably reflects the standard which

◄This is a 'Pahlawan'-class fast attack boat of the Royal Brunei Malay Regiment Flotilla, seen here on trials.

◄Seen here being test-fired on the Swedish minesweeper *Arko*, the Bofors 40mm is the gun most frequently installed on FACs.

◄*Pelikan*, is the 13th of the 20 'Type 148' class FACs.

the designers initially wanted but were denied by problems in the development of the radar and missiles.

The Soviets had not altogether lost interest in the RK, or smaller type of FAC(M), and during the early and mid-1970s they developed a design that retained the SS-N-2C missile but was based on a hull of higher performance. The result was the 'Matka' class that started to enter service in 1978 as another classic example of the Soviet predilection for producing hybrids combining the best features of existing craft. Thus the new class retained the basic hull and propulsion arrangement of the 'Osa II' married to the hydrofoil system developed for the 'Turya' class of torpedo craft. Complete with armament, this resulted in a full-load displacement of 260 tons and, on the power of three 3,750kW (5,030hp) M 504 diesels, a maximum speed of 40kt. The hydrofoil is located just forward of the bridge, and was designed for the dual purposes of lifting the bow and improving seaworthiness. The weapon fit of this hybrid type is also interesting, for its combines just two container-launchers for SS-N-2C missiles with the fast combat craft gun armament of one 76mm dual-purpose gun and one 30mm rotary six-barrel cannon in a close-in weapon system mounting. The gun is located on the forecastle just forward of the bridge, where the weight of the gun, its mounting and its ammunition is supported mainly by the hydrofoil, and is a medium-calibre type effective against surface and aerial targets. The close-in weapon system mounting is located just aft of the superstructure close to the stern and is a pioneering close-in weapon system designed for the last-ditch destruction of incoming missiles and/or attack aircraft under the control of an automatic fire-control system. These weapons are used with the standard but still impressive complex of electronic systems that includes one 'Plank Shave' air/surface search and tracking radar, one 'Bass Tilt' 30mm cannon fire-control radar and an IFF system with one interrogator and one responder. The 'Matka' class was built in Leningrad between 1977 and 1983 but reached a total of just sixteen units, probably reflecting the fact that it is limited in real operational terms by its obsolete missile armament.

Despite its introduction of the anti-ship missile with the 'Komar' class in 1960, the USSR did not lose its earlier enthusiasm for the torpedo-armed fast combat craft. Yet it was clear that the day of the MTB, a small torpedo-armed 'gnat' of high speed and considerable agility but little else, was past and that what was now needed was the type that matured as the FAC(T), a boat comparable in size with early FAC(M)s and as such a larger, torpedo-armed 'wasp' offering other attributes in addition to speed and agility. In Soviet terminology, the FAC(T) is designated 'TK' (Torpednyy Kater, or torpedo cutter). The tactical inspiration for the development of the Soviet FAC(T)s was possibly the West German 'Jaguar' class, but the type was derived physically from the 'Osa' class of FAC(M)s.

The craft of the resulting 'Shershen' class share the propulsion arrangement and gun armament of the 'Osa' class and use what is essentially a scaled-down version of that type's hull, with the overall length reduced from 39m (127ft 11in) to 34.7m (113ft 10in). The propulsion arrangement comprises three M 503A diesels driving three propellers, and in this application the engine has been assessed as possessing a good power/weight ratio although it is also hot and noisy. The time between overhauls is normally 600 hours, but this can be extended to 750 hours. At such an overhaul rate, the engine can be run at 1,500rpm for an unlimited time, generating 2,450kW (3,285hp), or at 1,700rpm for 15 per cent of the time, generating 2,700kW (3,620hp), or at 2,200rpm for 10 per cent of the time, generating 3,000kW (4,025hp). It normally requires one hour of warm-up before the engines can be run, and it is claimed that breakdowns (especially in the rubber joints of the fuel system) are not uncommon at anything over 1,500rpm.

Instead of the SS-N-2 anti-ship missiles carried by the 'Osa' class craft, the units of the 'Shershen' class each carry a primary armament of four 533mm (21in) torpedoes in four separate tubes located two on each side of the deck outboard of the superstructure. The provision at the stern of two racks for a maximum of twelve depth-charges was designed to provide an anti-submarine capability. However, the absence of sonar with which to detect and locate submarines means that this is not a real capability, although the depth-charges can still be used for the useful function of discouraging and indeed harassing submarines. The sensors are restricted to one 'Pot Drum' surface search radar and one 'Drum Tilt' gun fire-control radar, and the curved edges of the deck and superstructure indicate that the 'Shershen' class has citadel-type protection against the effects of nuclear, biological and chemical warfare.

The close relationship between the 'Osa' and 'Shershen' classes offered clear logistical benefits in terms of production and maintenance. The 'Shershen' type remained in production from 1962 to 1974 and some 85 units were completed. After only a comparatively short period of Soviet service, however, most of these craft were transferred to the navies of satellite, client and allied states. A variant produced specifically for the export market was the 'Mol' class, which was based on the standard 'Osa' class hull, but only a few such craft were built.

Further development and, indeed, expansion of the concept embodied in the 'Shershen' class led to the 'Turya' class. This is a FAH(T) or fast attack hydrofoil (torpedo) type analogous to the 'Matka'-class hydrofoil derivative of the 'Osa' class. The type is based on the hull of the 'Osa II'-class FAC(M) but is fitted with a single set of continuous half-submerged foils heavily braced in their centre to the hull and spanning an estimated 14m (45ft 11in). These fixed, surface-piercing foils are relatively ineffective in rough water and were installed mainly to lift the bow and improve stability when the boat is planing on the after portion of its hull, which is trimmed by an adjustable flap located on the transom. Later units of the class have semi-retractable foils to reduce the 'span' of these units and so ease the problem of coming alongside.

The foil system was also responsible for the precise nature and disposition of the gun armament. As it was important to keep the bow light, it was decided to install only a small-calibre mounting on the forecastle, in this instance the elderly mounting with two superimposed 25mm anti-aircraft cannon. Weight over the stern was a less critical factor, and so the main armament was located there in the form of two modern 57mm anti-aircraft (but actually dual-purpose) guns in a twin mounting.

It was at first assumed that the type had been conceived for the anti-ship role, but it later became clear that the 'Turya' class was in fact an anti-submarine type, with acoustic-homing, heavy-weight, anti-submarine torpedoes and a sensor suite that includes, on the starboard quarter, a dipping sonar of the same basic type as that carried by the Kamov Ka-25 'Hormone' anti-submarine helicopter. This makes the craft particularly useful in the Baltic Sea and the coastal waters of the Pacific Ocean, where the sonar can be lowered to listen for submarines lurking underneath the acoustically insulating thermal layers of these waters. This type of tactic is called 'sprint and drift', and the craft can also be used as quick-reaction types in association with anti-submarine helicopters.

As anti-submarine craft, the 'Turya' class fell outside the normal organization and tactical scheme for Soviet FAC forces. It should be noted here that, following the break-up of the USSR and subsequent creation of the Commonwealth of Independent States, the former Soviet navy has been reorganized, and apportioned, along different lines. However, it would seem likely that the doctrine and tactics evolved by the Soviets will be continued by their successors. The Soviets saw the main task of such forces as being night attacks by several units against important convoys, amphibious forces and high-value single targets operating in Soviet coastal waters. The possibility of daylight attacks was not discounted, however, despite the known vulnerability of FACs in such operational conditions. The Soviets therefore considered that daylight FAC operations demanded considerable support from tactical warplanes both for protection and for the attack itself, where the defences might be diluted by the need to counter simultaneous air and sea attacks, allowing one or other of the attacking forces to close to a decisive range.

Soviet training concentrated on the mass surface attack by several squadrons of FAC(M)s and FAC(T)s. The largest unit in the Soviet coastal forces was the brigade, which generally comprised three or four squadrons of FAC(M)s and/or FAC(T)s. Each squadron consisted of six craft divided into three two-craft units, and these pairs remained together even if one of them was undergoing repairs or a refit.

A typical attack would be delivered by three squadrons, one of FAC(M)s and two of FAC(T)s, in five phases. The first phase was the covert approach, starting from the time the craft left their base and ending with the location and identification of the target. At that point the second phase began, and that was the deployment of the craft from divisional squadron column formation into their tactical attack positions that at best avoided, or at worst reduced, the chances of mutual interference. The third phase was the run-in to the target, and before that started the craft would move into line-abreast formation or a left- or right-hand 'vee' formation. The fourth phase was the attack proper, which would last between 10 and 15 seconds as the craft of each group fired their weapons. For the FAC(T)s, this event would take place at a range of 5,000m (5,470yds), when two straight-running or passive acoustic-homing torpedoes were launched. For the FAC(M)s, it occurred at a distance of between 20,800 and 17,600m (22,750 and 19,250yds) from the target, and the missiles were generally launched in pairs (with radar and infra-red homing where possible), the exact number depending on the nature of the target. In general, Soviet doctrine called for the launch of some eight missiles against a target of cruiser size and above, four at a destroyer, two or four at an escort or FAC and two at a small transport or landing craft. The fifth and final phase was the disengagement, which was undertaken as rapidly as possible.

For the first, second and fifth phases, Soviet craft would use their highest continuous speed and for the third and fourth phases their maximum speed. The FAC(M)s were generally tasked with the engagement of warships, even those in the middle of a convoy, while the FAC(T)s were allocated the transports and any warships damaged by the FAC(M)s. The whole operation was co-ordinated by the unit commander, who was generally embarked in one of the FAC(M)s.

This represents the Soviet FAC attack in its 'classical' form in the period from 1965 until the mid-1980s, when the decline of the FAC(T) began to demand an alternative tactical arrangement reflecting the increased importance of the FAC(M) – which is now available in larger numbers and in more effective forms. The two main tactical organizations for all-FAC(M) units was one squadron of 'Nanuchka'-class craft and two or three squadrons of 'Tarantul', 'Matka' and 'Osa'-class craft, or one squadron of 'Tarantul'-class craft and two or three squadrons of 'Matkas' and 'Osas'. The rationale behind this organization was that the craft of the larger types offered superior command facilities and possessed the longer-range sensors that could optimize the capabilities of their smaller brethren; but some tactical problems were encountered in reaching the correct range for the different types of missile carried.

The considerable investment made by the Soviets in these larger classes of FAC(M)s and FAC(T)s was mirrored at a slightly lower level by a more limited but nonetheless significant programme of smaller classes of the same two basic types. These smaller classes may have been developed for purely experimental purposes, or alternatively as the first units of larger classes that were intended to replace existing types but were then found to possess one or more of the various

severe technical or tactical limitations that precluded large-scale production and deployment. It was typical of the Soviets, however, that, even when production of these types was curtailed, the existing craft were kept in service, probably as back-ups for the primary forces. The three most interesting of these types are the 'Sarancha', 'Babochka' and 'Slepen' classes.

The 'Sarancha' class is a FAH(M) type, and it seems that just a single craft was completed in 1976. The design has some similarities to the American 'Pegasus' class FAH(M) in that it has two fully submerged sets of hydrofoils for much enhanced rough-water performance, compared with the earlier classes' single set of surface-piercing hydrofoils. Fully submerged hydrofoils require a sophisticated control system, however, and the fact that no further 'Sarancha'-class craft have appeared may reflect not so much the experimental nature of the existing unit as difficulties in the development of such a system. The current unit has a full-load displacement of 330 tons and propulsion is provided by two propellers, pod-mounted on the after hydrofoil and driven by a CODOG arrangement of two diesels or two 8,250kW (11,065hp) NK-12 gas turbines, for a maximum speed of 45kt. The armament comprises two twin container-launcher installations for four SS-N-9 anti-ship missiles, one twin-arm launcher for SA-N-4 'Gecko' surface-to-air missiles and one 30mm six-barrel rotary cannon in a close-in weapon system mounting above the after portion of the high superstructure. The last is dominated by the hemispherical radomes for 'Band Stand' air search radar and 'Fish Bowl' surface search and missile-control radar.

A FAH(T) counterpart to the 'Sarancha' class is the sole 'Babochka' class unit, which was completed in 1977. This was the largest hydrofoil built for Soviet naval service, and, like the 'Sarancha' class unit, it has fully submerged hydrofoils, in this instance a substantial set just forward of the bridge. Like the 'Sarancha', it was probably designed for research and development. It has a full-load displacement of some 400 tons for a maximum speed of 50kt on the power of the three 8,750kW (11,865hp) NK-12 gas turbines that constitute the more powerful half of what is probably a CODOG arrangement with two diesels for long-endurance cruising. The gun armament is limited to two 30mm six-barrel rotary cannon in two close-in weapon system mountings (one on the forecastle and the other on the after portion of the substantial superstructure), and the type's optimization for the anti-submarine role is attested to by the rest of the armament, which comprises eight 406mm (16in) tubes for lightweight anti-submarine torpedoes. These tubes are located in two trainable installations, one on each side of the deck between the forward edge of the superstructure and the 30mm cannon mounting on the forecastle, and each installation comprises two superimposed pairs of tubes. Located near the stern is a large deckhouse, and this is probably associated with, among other things, a variable-depth or dipping sonar installation.

The third of these classes was clearly developed for the research and development role, for the single example of the 'Slepen' class is based on the hull and propulsion arrangement of the 'Osa' class and has been seen with several armament fits. The type was completed in 1970, and its main visual identifying feature is the location of the tripod mast, which is farther aft than on the 'Osa' class. As completed, the craft had a twin 57mm gun mounting on the forecastle and a 30mm six-barrel rotary cannon in a close-in weapon system mounting (complete with the prototype 'Bass Tilt' fire-control radar) over the stern for trials of the gun armament planned for the 'Grisha III' class of corvette. In 1975, the 57mm twin mounting was replaced by a 76mm (3in) gun mounting, leading to the introduction of this weapon on the 'Matka' FAH(M) and 'Nanuchka III' FAC(M) classes. More recently still, this craft has been fitted with the type of 'chaff'-launcher designed for the anti-radar protection of the 'Krivak'-class frigates and 'Nanuchka'-class FAC(M)s.

Operating in parallel with these FAC and FAH classes of the Soviet navy were large numbers of patrol vessels. These fell into two categories, which the Soviets designated 'PSK' (Pogranichnyy Storozhevoy Korabl', or border patrol ship) and 'MPK' (Malyy Protivolodochny Korabl', or small anti-submarine ship). The best known type of PSK is the 'Stenka' class of FAC(T)s, of which some 90 were built between 1976 and 1977 for the Maritime Border Guard Directorate of the KGB, with production resuming at a later date and continuing. The type is based on the hull and propulsion arrangement of the 'Osa I' class but has a different bridge and superstructure. The sensors and armament inevitably reflect the type's optimization for maritime border patrol. The sensors include 'Pot Drum' surface search radar and the same type of dipping

sonar as that used in the 'Hormone' helicopter, while the armament includes two twin 25mm cannon mountings, four 406mm (16in) tubes for lightweight anti-submarine torpedoes and racks for a probable maximum of twelve depth-charges. The torpedoes are electrically powered weapons with acoustic homing.

The best known of the MPK classes are the 'SO I' and 'Poti' classes. Production of the former, which is a steel-hulled type, totalled some 150 craft between 1957 and the late 1960s, but the boats are fast disappearing from Soviet and satellite service although they are still in extensive use by many of the USSR's allies and clients. The 'Poti' class vessels, more than 60 of which were built between 1961 and 1968, were intended as successors to the 'SO I' class, and are based on a considerably larger hull whose displacement raises the type virtually into the corvette category. The class has gas turbine propulsion, but it was ultimately built to serve as a supplement to rather than a replacement for the 'SO I' class. The 'Poti' class is now itself being replaced by the considerably more advanced 'Pauk' class, which is in essence an anti-submarine development of the 'Tarantul' class.

In the late 1940s, the 'Iron Curtain' settled across Europe to divide the continent between the Soviet-dominated Eastern Bloc and the American-led Western grouping that later became the Warsaw Pact and North Atlantic Treaty Organization respectively. On the Western side of this barrier, there was at first little enthusiasm for the fast combat craft. The major powers reasoned that any strategic aggression by the USSR would be met and eliminated by American nuclear power. At the operational level, any Soviet-led offensive would take place on land with the support of massive conventional air power, and would be countered by the conventional forces and possibly the nuclear weapons of the American-dominated alliance. The Soviet navy was known at this time to be a negligible factor, and the consensus of opinion was that the most it could attempt would be to support the minor amphibious operations that might be launched against the Allied nations' coastal flanks. Allied air and conventional naval power was more than adequate to meet this threat, so there seemed little purpose in developing fast combat craft specifically to protect the Allied coast or to carry the coastal war into Soviet territorial waters, where there would be only few and unimportant targets.

The one exception to this general rule was

Sweden, a politically neutral country which wished to preserve her position through the possession of strong armed forces that could deter aggression or, failing this, defeat an invasion that could realistically come only from across the Baltic Sea. Her navy was therefore the first line of defence for Sweden, initially with a conventional but obsolete force of coast-defence battleships, cruisers and destroyers as the core of three task forces. It soon became clear that the effectiveness of these forces was little or non-existent, and that far better value for money could be obtained from lighter forces that would also be more effective. Thus there emerged from 1958 the concept of the 'light navy' of perhaps two major surface warships, small but powerfully armed submarines, two flotillas of torpedo-armed fast combat craft and a larger number of coast-defence flotillas equipped with MTBs.

In the early 1950s, Sweden built ten 'T 32'-class MTBs with a standard displacement of 38.5 tons, an armament of one 40mm Bofors gun and two 533mm (21in) torpedoes and a maximum speed of 45kt on the power of three 1,500hp (1,118kW) Isotta-Fraschini 184C petrol engines. These craft were deleted in the early 1970s, but had already been supplemented and effectively supplanted by the fifteen slightly larger MTBs of the 'T 42' class built between 1955 and 1957 with a 40-ton standard displacement but basically the same armament and performance as the preceding boats. By the late 1940s, however, the Swedish navy had come to appreciate that such boats were useful only for inshore defence. For true coastal defence, a larger type was necessary and here the navy turned to the acknowledged leader in this field, Lürssen of Vegesack, the Second World War designer of Germany's Schnellboote. A prototype was built in 1950 as the *Perseus*, with a CODAG propulsion arrangement of one gas turbine and two diesels, and this paved the way for the 'Plejad' class of diesel-powered FAC(T)s that eventually totalled twelve, built in two batches of six in 1954–55 and 1956–58. Eight of the craft were deleted in July 1977 and the last three in July 1981.

The 'Plejad' type may be regarded as the Western starting point for the design of modern FACs. The hull had an overall length of 48m (157ft 6in) and a beam of 5.8m (19ft) for a full-load displacement of 170 tons. The propulsion arrangement comprised three 2,250kW (3,020hp) MTU 20V 672 diesel engines powering three propellers for a maximum speed of 37.5kt. The bridge structure was located just forward of amidships and the armament comprised two guns and six 533mm tubes for heavyweight torpedoes. The barrelled weapons were remotely controlled 40mm Bofors guns in mountings on the forecastle and on the after deck midway between the bridge and the stern, and the torpedo tubes were located three on each side of the deck to fire wire-guided torpedoes. The forward pair of tubes was located outboard of the forward 40mm gun mounting and aligned almost directly ahead, while the two after pairs were located as side-by-side installations outboard of the after 40mm gun mounting and designed to fire more obliquely outboard, so that the torpedoes would clear the turbulent water of the wake streaming back from the bow. The torpedoes were exceptional weapons by the standards of the day, offering considerable speed and range as well as great targeting accuracy with a large high-explosive warhead. Extra operational flexibility was provided by the fact that the torpedo tubes could be unshipped, allowing the craft to operate as mine-layers.

Operational experience convinced the Swedes that in such a FAC(T) they had a highly capable type that was fast, handy and effective in virtually all coastal conditions. The torpedoes provided considerable offensive striking power, and the Bofors guns were a powerful primary anti-aircraft defence weapon as well as a secondary surface-to-surface weapon for use against smaller vessels such as enemy FACs and landing craft.

In the circumstances, it was inevitable that the Swedish navy should capitalize on the advantages provided by this pioneering FAC and develop a series of improved types. The first step was the commissioning, between 1966 and 1968, of the six 'Spica' (later 'Spica I') class FAC(T)s. The design of these craft was not merely an upgraded version of the 'Plejad' design, but rather a considerable reworking of the original FAC(T) concept to take full advantage of technical developments of the late 1950s and early 1960s in fields such as propulsion, weapons and sensors. The 'Spica I' class therefore switched to gas turbine propulsion, using three 4,240hp (5,685kW) Rolls-Royce Proteus 1274 gas turbines powering three shafts for a maximum speed of 40kt. The more compact nature of the gas turbine powerplant allowed a slight reduction in overall length of 42.5m (140ft 1in) but an increase in beam to 7.1m (23ft 4in) for a full-load displacement of 235 tons. Sensor developments allowed the incorporation of Skanter 009 surface search and navigation radar and also the Hollandse Signaal-apparaten WM-22 fire-control system with co-mounted search and tracking radar antennae in the single spherical glass-fibre radome carried above the bridge. This was located farther aft than in the 'Plejad' class to allow the installation on the forecastle of a significantly improved gun, the 57mm Bofors SAK 57 automatic weapon. Its siting gave this weapon excellent fields of fire, and the Swedes reckoned that, in combination with an advanced fire-control system, its calibre, accuracy, lethal projectile, high rates of traverse and elevation, and high rate of fire (200 rounds per minute) made it a more effective anti-aircraft weapon than current surface-to-air missile systems; the gun also possessed a most useful surface-to-surface capability, which enhanced its overall tactical utility. The torpedo armament was basically similar to that of the 'Plejad' class, with two tubes flanking the gun (in a location where they have to be swung out through several degrees before torpedoes can be launched) and the other four in side-by-side pairs flanking the rear part of the superstructure; as in the 'Plejad' class, the tubes could be unshipped to allow the craft to serve as minelayers. The Swedes prepared plans for two or all four of the after torpedo tubes to be replaced by four or eight container-launchers for anti-ship missiles, but this plan was never implemented and all twelve 'Spica I'-class craft were deleted in the later 1980s.

Further evolution of the same basic design resulted in the twelve units of the 'Spica II' class which were commissioned between 1973 and 1976. These each have a full-load displacement of 230 tons on a modified hull, and the same propulsion arrangement as in the 'Spica I' class, resulting in a maximum speed of 41kt. The electronics are improved by a more advanced fire-control system, the PEAB (now Bofors) 9LV 200 unit using separate air/surface search and target designation radars; and the original weapons fit included the same arrangement of six torpedo tubes matched with the significantly enhanced Mk 2 version of the SAK 57 Mk 1 gun used in the 'Spica I' class. From 1985 the craft were rebuilt with one Ericsson Sea Giraffe low-level air search radar (reflecting the increased threat from Soviet attack aircraft in this period) and provision for the four after torpedo tubes to be replaced by up to eight container-launchers for RBS 15M anti-ship missiles.

The success of the type was attested by the development of two export variants, the Malaysian 'Spica-M' class and the Danish 'Willemoes' class. The four 'Spica-M' class craft have a diesel power-plant and two twin container-launchers for the MM.38 original version of the Aérospatiale Exocet anti-ship missile, while the ten Danish craft retain the gas turbine powerplant but feature a varied but powerful armament of two or four 533mm (21in) tubes for wire-guided torpedoes, two single or twin container-launchers for two or four McDonnell Douglas RGM-84 Harpoon anti-ship missiles, and one 76mm (3in) OTO Melara Compact gun.

To increase the overall capabilities of their FAC forces, the Swedes decided to add a moderately substantial FAC(M) type, this smaller but missile-armed class being seen as a complement to the larger craft with a mixed torpedo and missile armament. The result was the 'Hugin' class, whose sixteen units were commissioned between 1978 and 1982. The design was evaluated in a prototype, *Jagaren*, completed in 1972 as a Swedish derivative of the Norwegian 'Snogg' class. *Jagaren* underwent considerable evaluation and development before the 'Hugin' class was ordered from two Norwegian yards in May 1975; guns and electronic equipment were supplied by Sweden together with the machinery, which comprised the engines removed from the 'Plejad'-class craft and returned to West Germany for overhaul and uprating by MTU before redelivery to Norway.

To keep cost to the minimum, the design was completed with a two- rather than three-engined propulsion arrangement, and this results in a maximum speed of 35kt at a full-load displacement of 150 tons. The electronic suite includes search radar and the Mk 2 digital version of the 9LV 200 Mk 1 analogue fire-control system used in the 'Spica II' class; while the weapons include the SAK 57 Mk 1 57mm dual-purpose gun on the forecastle forward of the bridge, and six container-launchers for the RB 12 anti-ship missile. This latter is a Swedish-Norwegian development of an important Norwegian weapon, the Kongsberg Penguin Mk II, which uses an inertial navigation system for the cruise phase of its flight and a passive infra-red seeker package for the terminal phase of the attack.

The line-up of Swedish fast combat craft is completed by two units of the remarkable 'Spica III' class, which were redesignated 'Stockholm' class before the craft were commissioned in 1985. This type may be taken as a current highpoint in FAC design, for many advanced features are combined in a most compact fashion on a hull that is large but only modestly so. The type was designed as a flotilla leader with weapons and sensors giving it equal capabilities against surface vessels and submarines and only a slightly lesser capability against close-range attack aircraft.

The sensor suite includes the impressive Sea Giraffe combined air/surface search radar with the updated Mk 3 version of the 9LV 200 fire-control system for effective use of the missile armament, which comprises four twin container-launchers for the powerful and long-ranged RBS 15M anti-ship missile. As shorter-range backing for these missiles, each craft carries two wire-guided heavyweight torpedoes. Further capability against ships, and also against aircraft, is provided by two Bofors guns, one of them the potent SAK 57 Mk 2 57mm weapon and the other a modern development of the legendary 40mm L/70 weapon, with fire-control provided by a 9LV 300 system using an optronic director. Detection of submarines is entrusted to an active sonar, the Salmon variable-depth equipment, and attack is co-ordinated by a separate attack sonar using four wire-guided lightweight torpedoes, the ahead-throwing Elma rocket system (which creates a pattern of high-explosive grenades sinking through volume of water believed to contain the target) and depth-charges released from two racks. Paralleling this offensive capability is a useful defensive capability centred on an electronic support measures system whose warning element detects enemy radar emissions and controls the operation of two launchers that fire 'chaff' and flare packages into the air to confuse enemy radar and infra-red seeker units. Despite this mass of equipment and weaponry, the two craft have sufficient internal volume for a small co-ordinating centre that allows the embarked senior officer to control his flotilla.

The Bofors 40 L/70, Bofors SAK 57 and OTO Melara Compact are the heavier guns used by most FACs of Western origin, so it is worth looking in slightly greater detail at these important weapons. The Bofors 40mm gun has its origins in 1928, when its designers began work on a powerful anti-aircraft weapon to bridge the gap between the light cannon and the medium-calibre gun, and as such firing a considerably heavier projectile than the cannon at a considerably higher rate of fire than the medium-calibre gun. The first weapon was fired in 1931, and the type entered service in 1936 as an L/60 gun – i.e., with a barrel whose length was 60 times the calibre of the projectile. In this initial form the Bofors gun was the single most important anti-aircraft weapon of its type in the Second World War. Using experience gained in this conflict, Bofors in 1948 produced an upgraded and updated L/70 weapon. This has been extensively developed for land and naval use on powered and unpowered mountings which can be open or enclosed and fitted with a control system that ranges from the unsophisticated manual type with optical sights to the sophisticated remote type with a radar and/or optronic fire-control system. In typical modern form as built by Bofors or under licence in Italy by Breda, the Bofors 40mm L/70 naval gun can be traversed through 360° at 85° per second and elevated through an arc of 100° (−20° to +80° or −10° to +90°) at 45° per second. A simple locally controlled mounting weighs some 2,800kg (6,173lb), while a remotely controlled mounting designed for completely automatic use turns the scales at some 3,300kg (7,275lb). Although designed primarily for anti-aircraft use, the Bofors 40mm gun is a genuinely effective dual-purpose type with a maximum horizontal range of 12,000m (13,125 yards) and an effective slant range of 4,000m (4,375 yards), and with a cyclic rate of fire of between 300 and 330 rounds per minute. The gun can fire several types of ammunition, but the most important anti-aircraft type is the PFHE (Pre-Fragmented High-Explosive). This weighs 2.4kg (5.29lb) and fires its 0.96kg (2.12lb) projectile with a muzzle velocity of 1,025m (3,363ft) per second. The projectile is fitted with a pulse-Doppler proximity fuse that ensures detonation at a distance of between 5 and 7m (16.4 and 23ft) from the target, whereupon the pre-fragmented casing shatters into 2,400 or more jagged fragments and 650 lower-drag tungsten-carbide pellets that have better armour-penetration capabilities. The PFHE Mk 2 round is optimized for use against sea-skimming anti-ship missiles, and with a detonation trigger distance of 1m (3.3ft) can be used against targets as low as 5m (16.4ft).

The concept embodied in the 40mm weapon is taken a step further in the Bofors SAK 57, a 57mm gun designed specifically to provide fast combat craft with a powerful anti-ship and anti-aircraft weapon in a single lightweight mounting protected by a weatherproof plastic turret. The mounting can be used in gyro-stabilized local control, but was designed for electro-hydraulically powered remote control using a Hollandse Signaalapparaten or Philips Elektronikindustrie (later Bofors) radar and/

or optronic fire-control system. The complete mounting can be traversed through 360° at 55° per second, and the gun can be elevated in an arc between −10° and +75° at 40° per second. The mounting accommodates 40 ready-use rounds, and another 128 rounds are stowed in an under-deck mounting and lifted by two fixed hoists. The weapon itself is water-cooled, and fires its projectile types to a maximum horizontal range of 17,000m (18,590 yards) and an effective slant range of about 6,000m (6,560 yards). The weapon has a cyclic rate of fire of some 200 rounds per minute, and the two ammunition types are PFHE and He, the former being a proximity-fused type for use against aerial targets and the later an impact-fused type for use against surface targets. Each type of ammunition weighs 6.1kg (13.45lb) and fires its 2.4kg (5.29lb) projectile with a muzzle velocity of 1,025m (3,363ft) per second. The Mk 1 version of the weapon weighs 6,000kg (13,228lb) without ammunition and has provision for emergency manual control, while the more advanced Mk 2 weighs 6,500kg (14,330lb) and has no provision for anything but remote control. The Mk 2 has 120 rounds of ready-use ammunition and, with resupply from an under-deck magazine, has a cyclic rate of 220 rounds per minute.

One of the most important features of the SAK 57 Mk 2 is the precise control of the mounting in traverse and of the weapon in elevation, which is carried out by microprocessor-controlled electro-hydraulic servo systems slaved to the computerized fire-control system. This allows exceptional pointing accuracy despite the movement of the platform craft, which can be lively in any type of sea. The result is a very high level of firing accuracy. The same is also true of the OTO Melara Compact mounting, the unmanned type that made it feasible to introduce a medium-calibre gun on fast combat craft.

The OTO Melara 76/62 Compact is a 76mm (3in) dual-purpose mounting, and is now one of the most widely used and important equipments of its type in service anywhere in the world. This type was designed as a highly effective lightweight gun mounting requiring minimum installation volume and offering operation as a fully automated system. The origin of the gun lies with the OTO Melara 76/62 MMI 76mm (3in) dual-purpose mounting produced for the Italian navy: this was designed to use standard US Navy 3in (76mm) ammunition, then considered the smallest that could be fitted with a proximity fuse. The type was planned as the main

armament of corvettes and frigates, and as the secondary armament of destroyers and cruisers. The mounting weighs 12,000kg (26,455lb) complete with ammunition and associated systems, and is powered by an electro-hydraulic system; this provides traverse through 360° at 70° per second (with an acceleration of 70° per second^2) and elevation in an arc between −15° and +85° at the rate of 40° per second (with an acceleration of 70° per second^2). The magazine accommodates 59 rounds and is located under the splinter-proof turret; rounds are fed automatically to the loading tray, from which they are power-rammed into the gun, which can fire between 55 and 65 rounds per minute under remote or single-man local control.

The MMI marked the limit of feasibility for its time, but by the early 1960s it was clear that much improvement could be made to the basic design. This led to the OTO Melara 76/62 Compact, which began to enter service in 1969 in response to a NATO requirement for an MMI successor with light weight, compact dimensions, a rate of fire of at least 80 rounds per minute, a large ready-use ammunition capacity (to allow sustained engagements without the need to replenish the system), high rates of traverse and elevation (to permit the system to track high-speed targets under all weather conditions) and rapid reaction time (made possible by an entirely unmanned mounting controlled by a gun captain at a remote monitoring station and an under-deck ammunition replenishment crew).

The 76/62 Compact thus emerged as a single unit with an under-deck trunk accommodating the 80-round rotating drum magazine and ammunition hoist, and an above-deck gunhouse accommodating the elevating mass, the loading system, the loading tray, the feed drum and the two rocking arms that take ammunition from the hoist and insert them in the feed drum. Rounds are hoisted and loaded in a series of short movements that reduce acceleration to the moving parts and ammunition. The rounds are then power-rammed with the ordnance at any angle of elevation and with the mounting at any angle of traverse. The mounting is driven by three identical servo motors (one for traverse and two for elevation), any one of which can drive the mounting at reduced speed. Standard traverse and elevation rates are respectively 60° per second (with an acceleration of 72° per second^2) through 360° and 35° per second (with an acceleration of 72° per second^2) through an arc between −15° and +85°. Given the weapon's high rate of fire, continuous

▶ Typical of large patrol craft is this unit of the Libyan navy's four-strong 'Garian' class built by Brooke Marine.

▶ RSS *Independence* (P69), a Type A fast attack craft of the Singapore navy.

▶ *Isku*, the Finnish navy's experimental missile boat fitted with four SS-N-2 missile-launchers.

cooling is essential and this is undertaken during firing with salt water, followed after the engagement by fresh-water flushing. The gun has a muzzle brake and a bore extractor.

The key to the 76/62 Compact's performance is the loading system. As the magazine turns, each round is drawn into the screw feeder hoist, which lifts it to a point below the left trunnion, where it is seized by the two rocking arms and carried to the loading drum on the cradle. The drum transfers the round to the vertically oscillating loading tray operated by the recoil of the ordnance; as the ordnance recoils, the tray is moved up to accept the spent case and the fresh round; and as the ordnance runs out, the tray drops down to allow the fresh round to be rammed and the spent case to be ejected forward through the gun shield. The standard 12.36kg (27.24lb) round fires its 6.3kg (13.89lb) projectile at a muzzle velocity of 925m (3,035ft) per second. The most important ammunition types are HE with proximity or impact fuses, and Flash Non-Fragmentation. The basic Italian-made mounting weighs 7,350kg (16,204lb) and has effective horizontal and slant ranges of 8,000 and 5,000m (8,750 and 5,470 yards) respectively.

The 76/62 is also built under licence in Spain by Bazan and in the USA by the FMC Corporation. The Spanish mounting is essentially similar to the basic Italian one, and its specification includes a weight of 8,520kg (18,783lb) and a maximum horizontal range of 16,300m (17,825 yards). The mounting can be traversed through 360° at the rate of 70° per second (with an acceleration of 100° per second^2), while the ordnance can be elevated in an arc between $-15°$ and $+85°$ at the rate of 40° per second (with an acceleration of 60° per second^2). The American mounting, known as the Mk 75, is identical in all important respects to the Italian original.

In 1984 the Italian company announced the OTO Melara 76/62 Super Rapid. Essentially this is the 76/62 Compact modified to incorporate mechanical and structural features of the Otomatic land ordnance – such as titanium rather than steel for many components, and strengthening of the rocker arms and buffering system – and fitted with a local stabilization system to secure a higher rate of more accurate fire. In the 76/62 Compact the rate can be varied between 10 and 85 rounds per minute by the gun captain, and in the 76/62 Super Rapid the maximum rate is boosted to 120+ round per minute, giving this medium-calibre gun almost the fire rate

capability of large-calibre cannon – but with considerably more devastating projectiles.

To match the capabilities of the 76/62 Super Rapid, OTO Melara has produced the new MOM (Multi-role OTO Munition) round, a type optimized for the destruction of missiles. The projectile of this round has a body of high-quality steel filled with cubes of tungsten alloy. The projectile is detonated by a proximity fuse and the powerful bursting charge ensures that the tungsten alloy cubes are dispersed in a spherical pattern at the high velocity necessary for maximum penetration of the target. The projectile can also be fired with the proximity fuse paralysed, thus operating with its impact detonation fuse in a fashion similar to that of the SAPOM (Semi-Armour-Piercing OTO Munition) type with a delayed-action fuse. The 76/62 Super Rapid will also be able to fire two new rounds currently under development: the first is a guided projectile designed jointly by OTO Melara and British Aerospace for use against aerial targets (aircraft and missiles); the second is an extended-range projectile for use against surface targets.

In 1989 the Dutch electronics company Hollandse Signaalapparaten announced that, in co-operation with the German ammunition manufacturer Diehl, it was developing the HSA/Diehl CORAS (Correctable Ammunition System) for the 76/62 Compact (and presumably for the 76/62 Super Rapid) gun. The object of the programme, which parallels that between British Aerospace and OTO Melara (see later), is to produce a course-correctable projectile as the means of dealing with the PHP (Predicted Hitting Point) problem. A conventional projectile is wasted if, after it has left the muzzle, there is any change in the ballistic parameters on which its fire-control solution was based; the most obvious reason for such a change is any modification of the target's course and/or speed. CORAS is designed to provide a simple radio data-uplink to the projectile so that any modifications to the fire-control solution can be transmitted in real time by a controller unit in the form of steering orders. It is thought that the Diehl projectile contains pressurized gas that is allowed to escape through lateral holes to change the projectile's vector and so ensure a continued high-hit probability at the target's altered position. HSA claims that the system will be effective at between 800 and 3,000m (875 and 3,280 yards), and that its cost will be not more than 25 per cent of that for a comparable missile system.

In addition to its local stabilization for improved accuracy, the 76/62 Super Rapid mounting is also fitted with a secondary feed system that permits swift change from automatic fire against aerial targets to semi-automatic fire against surface targets and vice versa. Reliability has also been upgraded through the addition of BITE (Built-In Test Equipment) using small computers, and extra safety has been provided by features such as a pointing accuracy check and provision of safety firing arcs.

Features of the 76/62 Super Rapid can be retrofitted to the 76/62 Compact to boost the rate of fire to about 100 rounds per minute. The 76/62 Super Rapid has provision for the incorporation of a stabilized line-of-sight local fire-control system (such as the OTO Melara Local Control Unit, a TV-based system with its stabilized tracking head on top of the 76/62's gunshield), but the types are designed for use primarily with the parent vessel's main fire-control system, most notably Dutch and Italian systems; the former are mostly variants of the Hollandse Signaalapparaten WM-20 series, and the latter the series produced by Elsag, Officine Galileo, OTO Melara and Selenia using a variety of radar and optronic sensors.

It can truly be said that the advent of the 76/62 Compact and SAK 57 have revolutionized fast combat craft. These weapons provide an exceptional anti-aircraft capability, with effective ranges beyond the stand-off attack distances of most air-launched weapons (except highly expensive missiles), and also offer a powerful secondary anti-ship capability. The guns are effective against medium-sized vessels and devastating against smaller craft, opening the possibility of gun engagements as an alternative to the use of costly anti-ship missiles. An additional benefit of these medium-calibre gun mountings is that they are light enough to allow larger fast combat craft also to be armed with a smaller-calibre mounting (such as the 40mm single Bofors or the 35mm or 30mm twin Oerlikon-Buhrle cannon), and so create a two-layer air-defence capability.

In addition to financial considerations, it was the particular geographical and tactical conditions of the Baltic Sea that persuaded Sweden to make fast combat craft a major component of her naval defences against possible Soviet aggression. These factors applied with equal cogency to others of the Scandinavian states, notably Finland and Denmark. Like Sweden, Finland is now a neutral state, although in this instance as a result not only of natural inclination but also of international mandate in the form of the February 1947 Treaty of Paris. This was a consequence of Finland's role as a German ally in the Second World War, and among the treaty's provisions were a navy of not more than 10,000 tons and 4,500 men. Submarines and torpedoes were specifically forbidden to the Finnish navy at the demand of the Soviets, who feared that such weapons could effectively deny them the use of Leningrad as a base, this major city lying at the head of the Gulf of Finland. Finland thus had to dispose of her five submarines and remove the torpedo tubes from her MTBs. Since that time the Finnish navy has received relatively little in the way of funding, and had concentrated its efforts on two conventional corvettes and larger forces of mine warfare vessels, patrol vessels and fast combat craft.

The patrol vessels form a flotilla based at Helsinki, and comprise three 'Ruissalo'-class and two 'Rihtniemi'-class large patrol craft. Armed with a 40mm Bofors gun but capable of only 15kt, these vessels, which were launched between 1956 and 1959, are of little real operational value. In the 1960s they were joined by thirteen units of the 'Nuoli' class of gun-armed FACs. Although fast, these craft were indifferently armed with only a 40mm Bofors gun and therefore of only limited combat value. By the late 1960s the Finnish navy had become fully aware of the importance of the anti-ship missile, and in December 1969 launched *Isku* as an experimental FAC(M). With a full-load displacement of 140 tons, this single unit was based on the hull of a landing craft (and thus capable of only 15kt) and was commissioned in 1970 as a trials and training type. The armament comprises two 30mm cannon in a twin mounting above the after part of the superstructure, and four container-launchers for the MTO/68 anti-ship missile, as the Finns designate the SS-N-2A 'Styx'.

Experience with *Isku* made its sensible for the Finns to order four 'Osa'-class craft in the early 1970s, and these were delivered in 1974 and 1975 for completion with Finnish electronics and Western radar under the designation 'Tuima' class. By 1980 the Finns had sufficient experience with these four vessels to consider a locally designed type, and this matured as the aluminium-hulled 'Helsinki' class designed for a 30-year operational life. The design was proved in *Helsinki*, which was commissioned in 1981 as a true FAC(M/G) with Swedish and Soviet guns as well as a powerful combination of Swedish anti-ship missiles and Swedish radar. The Finns then ordered another three 'Helsinki'-class units, and in 1987 followed with an order for the first four of a planned eight 'Helsinki 2'-class FAC(M/G)s with a slightly larger hull and waterjet propulsion.

On the south-western side of the Baltic lies Denmark, a member of the NATO alliance. Although small, Denmark is of crucial importance to the Western alliance as she dominates the Kattegat, the eastern half of the exit from the Baltic into the North Sea. The Danish navy is therefore ideally placed to prevent an enemy fleet – until recently the threat was the Soviet Baltic Fleet – from moving out of the Baltic. The Danish navy also possesses a wider-ranging role, but for operations in the shallow western part of the Baltic relies on a force of small submarines and fast combat craft.

In the late 1950s, the Danish navy ordered a new class of FAC(T)s based on the Second World War German Schnellboot. These four craft were the 'Falken' class, commissioned in 1962 and 1963. With a displacement of 119 tons and a length of 35.9m (117ft 9in), each of these boats was powered by three 2,250kW (3,020hp) Mercedes-Benz diesels and carried as primary armament four 533mm (21in) torpedoes in two tubes on each side of the deck. The rest of the armament comprised one 40mm Bofors gun over the stern and one 20mm cannon in a well on the forecastle.

This four-craft class was essentially a stopgap and considerably greater capability was provided by the six FAC(T)s of the 'Søløven' class, a derivative of the British 'Brave' class. The first two units were built by Vosper at Portsmouth, and the other four by the Royal Dockyard in Copenhagen. The armament is an improved version of that carried by the 'Falken' class, with four torpedo tubes and two 40mm Bofors guns. The forward gun is located on the forecastle in an open mounting, while the after gun is located over the stern and can be enclosed in a weatherproof turret, although in this case the two after torpedo tubes have to be unshipped. However, the real advantage of the 'Søløven' class over the 'Falken' class lies in its CODAG propulsion arrangement, with two diesels powering the wing propellers for a quiet cruising speed of 10kt but shut down in favour of three 4,250hp (3,170kW) Rolls-Royce Proteus gas turbines for the highly impressive maximum speed of 54kt.

Libya ordered three slightly different craft as the 'Susa' class. These boats have the same propulsion arrangement and a similar performance on a slightly modified hull, but with the decidedly indifferent missile armament of eight container-launchers for the SS.12M short-range missile, a navalized version of the AS.12 wire-guided missile designed for helicopter launch against targets such as bunkers and other fixed defences.

By the early 1970s, the Danish navy had appreciated that the days of the small FAC(T) were numbered, and that continued viability of its fast combat craft force depended on the adoption of a more advanced type. The service selected as the core of its new 'Willemoes' class the hull of the Swedish 'Spica II' with a CODOG propulsion arrangement for a long-range cruising speed of 12kt and a combat speed of 38kt. The class was commissioned between 1976 and 1978, the early units in FAC(G/T) form with one 76mm (3in) OTO Melara Compact gun on the forecastle and four 533mm (21in) tubes for Swedish wire-guided heavyweight anti-ship torpedoes. The aim was to create a FAC(M/G/T) type, however, with the RGM-84 Harpoon anti-ship missile that became available only in the late 1970s. Although it was possible to replace the complete torpedo armament with missiles, the standard fit includes both torpedoes and missiles, with the two after torpedo tubes replaced by two single or twin container-launchers for this important missile.

The Harpoon can also be installed in Denmark's latest type of FAC, the Standard Flex 300 design being produced as the 'Flyvefisken' class. This was conceived as a very economical type with a straightforward hull and a CODAG propulsion arrangement in which the two wing shafts are powered by diesels and the central shaft is powered by either one electric motor or one gas turbine. Use of just the two wing shafts produces an economical cruising speed of 20kt, while the central shaft can be used on its own in the electrically powered mode for a virtually silent creeping speed of 6kt, or in concert with the other two shafts in the gas turbine-powered mode for the respectable maximum speed of 30kt.

The 'Flyvefisken' design is made particularly cost-effective by its use of the modern concept of modular or 'plug-in' weapons and electronics. Thus the sixteen craft are being delivered in FAC(G) form with one 76mm (3in) OTO Melara Super

Rapid gun and a basic electronic suite including a relatively simple surface search radar together with the advanced 9LV 200 Mk 3 Sea Viking fire-control system, which has optronic and infra-red sights as well as a laser rangefinder. In this form the type will replace the nine 'Daphne'-class seaward defence vessels, but can then be retrofitted with specialized electronics and weapons to replace the eight 'Sund'-class coastal minesweepers and/or the six 'Søløven'-class FAC(T)s. In its maximum-capability form, the 'Flyvevisken' class is a FAC(M/G/T) with the 76mm gun complemented by four anti-ship missiles, one surface-to-air missile system and two 533mm (21in) wire-guided heavy-weight torpedoes.

The fourth member of the Scandinavian community to make extensive use of fast combat craft is Norway, whose comparatively short southern coastline dominates the Skaggerak, the western half of the exit from the Baltic into the North Sea. Far longer, however, are Norway's western and northern coastlines, which stretch from the North Sea through the Norwegian Sea right up into the Arctic Ocean. Open-sea conditions in these areas can be rough in the extreme, and indeed far too dangerous for sustained operations by fast combat craft, but the Norwegian navy is faced with the difficult tactical problem of defending one of the world's longest coastlines while receiving only modest funding as the country has a small population. A significant submarine force is maintained, together with a small but now obsolescent force of deep-water warships, but the main strength of the Norwegian navy rests with its force of fast combat craft. These are ideally suited to coastal operations along Norway's littoral, which is scattered with the islands and fjords that make excellent lurking and hunting grounds for torpedo- and missile-armed fast combat craft.

At the end of the Second World War, the Norwegian navy was re-established in its own country with ex-British destroyers and escorts, ex-German submarines, and light forces that comprised ex-British MTBs and ex-German Schnellboote. Between 1951 and 1956 the Norwegian builder Westermoens Boatbyggeri delivered from its Mandal yard six MTBs of the 'Rapp' class as Norway's first indigenously produced fast combat craft. They proved well suited to operational conditions in Norwegian waters, but had Packard engines using dangerously inflammable petrol as fuel.

This was a primary reason for the development of the 'Nasty' class, no fewer than 42 of which were built between 1959 and 1967. The design was of fairly standard MTB design with a full-load displacement of 77 tons on a hull measuring 24.5m (80ft 5in) in length and 7.5m (24ft 7in) beam. The hull was of unusual construction for the period, however, for it was a sandwich of fibre-glass between two layers of mahogany to create a light and resilient structure. The petrol engines of the 'Rapp' class were abandoned in favour of a diesel-engined arrangement with two lightweight Napier Deltic T 18–37 diesels delivering 6,200hp (4,620kW) to two shafts for a maximum speed of 43kt. The boats were completed with provision for two basic armament fits to create MTBs or MGBs. The MTB fit was centred on four 21in (533mm) tubes for heavyweight anti-ship torpedoes, and included one 40mm Bofors gun and one 20mm cannon, while the MGB sacrificed two of the tubes so that the 20mm cannon could be replaced by a second 40mm Bofors. The boats could also be used as minelayers by unshipping all the tubes. The Norwegian navy received 20 such boats as the 'Tjeld' class, and these are gradually fading from service.

The other 22 boats were built for export. Two were delivered to the West German navy in 1962, but this service found the comparatively wide-beamed design of the 'Nasty' class less suited to operations in the southern waters of the Baltic than its narrower-beam craft of Lürssen design. The two boats were loaned to Turkey in 1964, were later transferred and finally deleted in the mid-1970s. Greece received six boats, one of which was deleted in 1972, but the other five survived to be placed in reserve during the early 1980s. Oddly enough, four of these obsolete craft were refurbished and recommissioned in 1988. The other fourteen boats were delivered to the USA, where they were classified as PTFs (fast patrol boats) and fitted with a variety of armaments, before gradual deletion in the later 1960s and early 1970s.

Like the Soviets and other major operators of fast combat craft in the early 1960s, Norway decided that the best tactical effect could be gained from the use of mixed FAC(T) and FAC(M) forces. Although the anti-ship missile was still in its infancy as a weapon type, Norway decided to produce her own weapon to ensure that it would be fully optimized for the operational requirements imposed by the country's geographical situation. The result was the West's first dedicated anti-ship missile, the

Kongsberg Penguin, which was based on an infra-red seeker (the first completely passive seeker fitted on any surface-to-surface missile) and the warhead of the ASM-N-7/AGM-12 Bullpup air-to-surface missile. The missile is delivered as a maintenance-free round in a container which is installed on the deck of the FAC to serve as a launcher after the necessary umbilical electrical connection has been made.

The Norwegian navy decided that as the missions planned for craft with this missile would be of short range and minimal endurance, habitability could be partially sacrificed to a larger number of missiles on the type of small hull that was best suited to operations in Norwegian coastal waters. The result was the 'Storm' class of FAC(M)s, comprising 20 units commissioned between 1965 and 1968. This type has a full-load displacement of only 135 tons on a hull with a maximum length of 36.5m (119ft 9in) and beam of 6.1m (20ft 0in). Power as well as habitability had to be sacrificed, however, and each of the 'Storm'-class craft has only two 2,700kW (3,620hp) Maybach MD 872A (later redesignated MTU 16V 538) diesels for a maximum speed of just 32kt, which is perhaps adequate for the type of 'hide and seek' operations planned by the Norwegians. The armament is impressive, for in addition to six Penguin Mk I anti-ship missiles (introduced in 1972 and now supplemented by the longer-range Penguin Mk II with an improved seeker), each of these craft carries two Bofors guns in the form of one forecastle-mounted 76mm (3in) automatic weapon for the surface-to-surface role and one stern-mounted 40mm weapon for the anti-aircraft role. The electronic fit was adequate, but is being upgraded in the late 1980s and early 1990s with a modern fire-control system that includes an optronic tracker and a laser rangefinder.

In 1970 and 1971 Norway supplemented the 'Storm'-class craft with six vessels of the 'Snogg' class, which are based on a hull that is in essence a steel version of the wooden hull used in the 'Storm' class. The performance of the 'Snogg' class is roughly comparable to that of the 'Storm' class for obvious operational reasons, but the weapon fit was modified to turn these craft into FAC(M/T)s. Thus the 76mm (3in) gun was removed and its place taken by the 40mm weapon in an open mounting, leaving the after part of the deck clear for a quartet of container-launchers for Penguin missiles. The armament is completed by four deck-edge 533mm

(21in) tubes for Swedish wire-guided heavyweight anti-ship torpedoes. Like the 'Storm' class, the 'Snogg' class initially possessed only moderately advanced electronics, but in recent years these have been upgraded with an improved torpedo fire-control system as well as the same surface-weapon fire-control system as the updated 'Storm'-class craft. Even so, it must be conceded that both 'Storm' and 'Snogg' classes are now obsolescent.

By the mid-1970s the Norwegian navy had appreciated this slide into obsolescence and started the process of developing a successor type on the basis of *Jagaren*, the Norwegian-built prototype for the Swedish 'Hugin' class. This resulted in the fourteen units of the 'Hauk' class which were commissioned between 1977 and 1980. This type has a full-load displacement of 148 tons and the standard Norwegian propulsion arrangement of two diesels delivering 5,400kW (7,240hp) to two shafts for a maximum speed of 34kt. The gun armament comprises the typical 40mm Bofors weapon as well as a 20mm cannon; the missile fit is six container-launchers for Penguin missiles, and additional capability is provided by two 533mm (21in) tubes for Swedish wire-guided heavyweight torpedoes. The electronics are of the upgraded standard retro-fitted in the 'Storm' and 'Snogg' classes, but an unusual feature is the provision for active search sonar even though the craft carry no dedicated anti-submarine armament.

On the southern side of the Baltic, Denmark was allied with West Germany (now the western part of a Germany that has been unified since 1990) within NATO, while potential Warsaw Pact opponents were East Germany and Poland.

East Germany became a member of the Warsaw Pact in 1955, and her navy began to develop a fast combat craft capability in 1957 with the receipt of the first of an eventual 23 'P 6'-class MTBs. These were deleted between 1968 and 1978, when the boats were scrapped, turned into targets or converted into inshore patrol craft. Further capability was added between 1954 and 1968 when the USSR transferred twelve 'Osa I'-class FAC(M)s, and these were followed in 1976 by three more units. The USSR also transferred eighteen 'Shershen' class FAC(T)s between 1968 and 1976. The combination of the 'Osa' and 'Shershen'-class craft provided East Germany with a missile and torpedo punch for coastal operations, while inshore capability was generated by two classes of small MTBs, the 'Iltis' and 'Libelle' classes.

About 45 units of the 'Iltis' class were built between 1962 and 1965, each displacing 30 tons, reaching 45kt on the 2,250kW (3,020hp) delivered by two diesels, and being armed with two or three 533mm (21in) aft-firing tubes for heavyweight anti-ship torpedoes, although these could be unshipped to allow the carriage of mines or small landing parties. All had been deleted by the early 1980s. The 'Libelle' class was an improved version of which some 30 or more were built between 1973 and 1980 with greater displacement and a longer hull. The two aft-firing torpedo tubes are located under a built-up hull that allows the installation of a twin machine-gun mounting for light anti-aircraft defence.

Shortly before the collapse of communism in Eastern Europe and the unification of the two Germanies, East Germany had decided to replace her obsolete 'Osa I'-class FAC(M)s with a class of perhaps twelve larger FAC(M)s, and the first of these was commissioned in 1989. Given the temporary NATO designation 'Balcom 10' class, this appears to be an East German derivative of the 'Tarantul' class with a new anti-ship missile system. It is unlikely that this programme has continued since the reunification of Germany.

The USSR ordered a major rearmament of Poland from 1950, and after a basic programme had produced the core of a modern navy, a thorough modernization was started in 1957. With a longer coastline and a greater commitment to the Baltic Sea region, the Polish navy was developed with a greater offshore capability than that of the East German navy, but was also given a considerable coastal role. Although the Polish navy created in the immediate aftermath of the Second World War had been provided with two ex-German Schnellboote, its first modern fast combat craft were 20 'P 6'-class MTBs transferred by the USSR between 1956 and 1958. These were later complemented by thirteen 'Osa I'-class FAC(M)s transferred between 1963 and 1965. The 'P 6'-class boats were deleted between 1973 and the mid-1980s, but twelve of the 'Osa I' class remained operational at the time of Poland's departure from the communist bloc in 1990. It is likely that these units will be deleted in the early 1990s.

The one fast combat craft developed and built in Poland was the 'Wisla' class of FAC(T)s. Design of this type began in the early 1960s and production began in the early 1970s. The type was notable amongst communist-bloc fast combat craft for its high level of automation and its advanced structure in light alloy. Its CODAG propulsion provided for the impressive maximum speed of 50kt, but the armament of Soviet guns and torpedoes was no better than adequate.

In 1956 West Germany was permitted to start rearming as a key component of the Western alliance. Her first surface ships were ex-Allied types, but it was clear from the beginning that Germany's expertise in the Second World War in the design and construction of advanced submarines and Schnellboote (including six built after the war as the 'Silbermowe' class) would soon result in the indigenous production of coastal submarines and fast combat craft. A head-start with the latter had been provided by Lürssen's design of the Swedish *Perseus* and the company's part in the construction of the resulting 'Plejad' FAC(T) class. This was reflected in Lürssen's 'TNC-42' design for the 'Jaguar' FAC(T) type which entered service as the 'Type 140' and 'Type 141' classes that differed only in their use of Mercedes-Benz or Maybach diesels, and had great similarities to the Swedish 'Spica I' class.

Such coastal warfare types were needed for the protection of West Germany's maritime frontiers on the Baltic and North Seas, east and west respectively of the Schleswig-Holstein isthmus connecting northern Germany with Denmark. The 40 'Jaguar'-class units were delivered in the late 1950s and early 1960s as orthodox but effective craft with a full-load displacement of 220 tons on a typical Lürssen non-magnetic hull that has an overall length of 42.6m (139ft 9in) and a beam of 7.0m (23ft 0in) under an aluminium alloy superstructure. The hull is of wooden construction, and reveals its Schnellboot ancestry in the raised turtledeck forecastle with a semi-well for the forward gun. The propulsion arrangement was also typical of its time, with four MTU diesels delivering 8,940kW (11,990hp) to four shafts for a maximum speed of 35kt or more, and the armament was a mix of the standard and slightly unusual. The standard part is the gun armament, which comprises a pair of 40mm Bofors guns located forward and aft in open mountings, while the more unusual part is the torpedo armament, which comprises two aft-facing tubes to launch Seal wire-guided torpedoes over the stern. Fire-control is entrusted to the WM-20 system, which has the antennae for the search and tracking radars in a spherical glass-fibre radome above and behind the bridge.

The 'Jaguar' class has all but disappeared from German service, which now designates the upgraded survivors as the 'Type 142' or 'Zobel' class. The type's relegation was made possible by the advent of more capable craft, but coincided with the need of some of Germany's NATO allies for improved coastal forces. Thus Greece and Turkey each received seven operational craft as well as three units to be cannibalized for spares. Another three craft were later transferred to Saudi Arabia.

Additional construction resulted in eight craft for Indonesia and nine revised craft for Turkey. The Indonesian vessels were completed as FAC(T)s, four of them with steel hulls and the other four with wooden hulls. The wooden-hulled type proved to have the greater survivability in tropical waters, and the two surviving craft are of this type. The craft built for Turkey comprised the 'Kartal' class of FAC(M/T)s, and these in fact preceded the transfer of ex-West German 'Jaguar'-class FAC(T)s. There are a few detail differences from the baseline 'Jaguar' class in the hull, but the propulsion arrangement and performance are broadly similar. Where the 'Kartal' class is a distinct improvement over the 'Jaguar' class, however, is in the impressive armament. This retains the two 40mm Bofors guns and two 533mm (21in) tubes of the 'Jaguar' class, and makes additional provision either for two more tubes for a total of four heavyweight torpedoes in the FAC(T) mode, or for four container-launchers for Penguin Mk II anti-ship missiles in the FAC(M/T) mode. In line with its FAC(M) capability, the 'Kartal' class also possesses a more sophisticated electronic suite than the 'Jaguar' class, its main element being the WM-28 radar fire-control system.

The 'TNC-42' design was the first of a family of Lürssen designs that have dominated the market for fast combat craft since the mid-1960s. These craft have been produced with aluminium-alloy superstructures on hulls of different construction (steel for the export market and wood over steel frames for the domestic market), and are characterized by a high length/beam ratio, a flush deck without the turtledeck forecastle of the 'TNC-42' design, and the bridge structure located just forward of the amidships position with a deckhouse generally located farther aft on the units of the larger classes. This layout allows the installation of guns forward and aft, with room for torpedo tubes on each side of the deck and/or missiles between the bridge and after deckhouse. The machinery space and after

portion of the hull are arranged in such a fashion that different propulsion arrangements are possible, with different numbers of diesel engines powering two, three or four shafts as demanded by the purchaser's operational needs and financial resources.

The smallest of Lürssen's FAC designs is the 'FPB-36' type dating from the early 1960s. Some nineteen of the type have been delivered to five customers in various forms as comparatively simple FACs with two or three shafts and gun, torpedo and missile armaments. Typical of them is the Spanish 'Barcelo' class, whose lead unit was built by Lürssen and the other four under licence in Spain by Bazan, which also licence-produced the MTU diesels. These five craft were delivered, and are currently used, as straightforward FAC(G)s with an armament of one 40mm Bofors gun, two 20mm Oerlikon-Bührle cannon in single mountings and two 0.5in (12.7mm) machine-guns also in single mountings. The Spanish Navy recognized, however, that the basic combination of hull and propulsion arrangement offered the possibility of greater combat capability, and therefore made provision for this in case it was required at a later date. The craft are thus fitted for, but not with, two 533mm (21in) tubes for heavyweight torpedoes in the FAC(T) role, while the omission of tubes and the removal of the 20mm cannon allow the installation of four container-launchers for anti-ship missiles in the FAC(M) role.

The 'FPB-38' class may be regarded as the larger half-brother of the 'FPB-36', with slightly greater size and displacement allowing the installation of heavier armament. Four such craft are in service as FAC(G)s with the navies of two Persian Gulf states, their most notable feature being a main armament of two 40mm Bofors guns built under licence in Italy by Breda and installed in a Breda twin mounting. Malaysia requires eighteen of the type, but these are to be used mainly in the high-speed patrol role with armament limited to two 20mm Oerlikon-Bührle cannon and two 7.62mm (0.3in) machine-guns.

Next up in size from the 'FPB-38' class is the 'TNC-42' design with which this important family of fast combat craft started. A general modernization and slight enlargement of the design, to a length of some 45.0m (147ft 8in) for a full-load displacement of about 260 tons, resulted in the remarkably successful 'FPB/TNC-45' type with provision for a two-, three- or four-shaft propulsion arrangement.

▶USS *Gallup* (PG-85), a patrol gunboat of the 'Asheville' class, seen during the Vietnam War. *Gallup* accelerated from 0–40 knots in 60 seconds thanks to a 13,500hp gas turbine engine. [*USN*]

▶Below decks engine room, typical of any number of modern FACs.

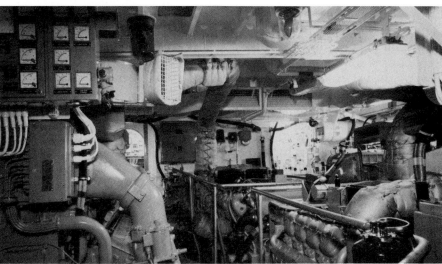

▶P677 is the *Pertuisane*, one of the French navy's four 'Patra' class patrol craft.

The country responsible for the design was Israel, which had already turned to the concept of large fast combat craft after a reappraisal of the balance of naval power in the eastern Mediterranean during the first half of the 1960s. The correctness of this change of emphasis from medium-sized surface warships, such as destroyers and frigates, to a mix of small submarines and smaller surface combatants, such as the larger types of fast combat craft, was then confirmed by the shock loss during the October 1967 'Six-Day War' of the Israeli navy's flagship, the admittedly elderly destroyer *Eilat*, together with 47 men killed and another 99 wounded from a complement of 199. The loss was attributed to hits by SS-N-2A 'Styx' missiles fired by 'Komar'-class FAC(M)s of the Egyptian navy, whose most modern equipment had been supplied by the USSR. Israel now decided to press ahead with all speed towards the creation of a navy based primarily on gun- and missile-armed fast combat craft for both offensive and defensive purposes.

In the late 1940s Israel had bought at least three and possibly as many as nine Vosper 70ft (21.3m) MTBs from the UK, complementing these between 1951 and 1952 with six French-built 'Ayah'-class MTBs. These latter were delivered with four 850kW (1,140hp) Arsenal-Marine Otto petrol engines powering two shafts for a maximum speed of 42kt, and were armed with two 457mm (18in) tubes for medium-weight torpedoes as well as light guns. These 62-ton craft were generally operated as MGBs with the torpedo tubes removed, but in the early 1960s they were revised as MTBs with the two tubes and a new propulsion arrangement of two 2,500hp (1,865kW) Napier Deltic lightweight diesels. In 1967 the Vosper MTBs were reported to be unserviceable, but it is estimated that Israel could call on eight MTBs during the 1967 'Six-Day War' against her Arab neighbours. At the naval level, the war showed conclusively that such boats were too small to be effective, and that missile-armed fast combat craft offered considerable advantages over torpedo-armed boats.

The tactical importance of the anti-ship missile had been appreciated by Israel as early as the late 1950s, and the development of an all-Israeli missile of this type was put in hand during the early 1960s by MBT, a subsidiary of Israel Aircraft Industries and later known as Israel Military Industries. The resulting weapon is the Gabriel, which proved itself temperamental during its development testing in the late 1960s but soon matured into a highly capable tactical missile by the early 1970s. The weapon is based on a cylindrical body containing the electronics, the 100kg (220lb) high-explosive warhead, and the solid-propellant booster and sustainer rockets, and is supported in flight by a cruciform of rectangular wings which are located on the missile's mid-body section and trailed by a cruciform of smaller tail surfaces indexed in line with the wings.

The missile is mounted on a launch rail inside a container-launcher that can be located on a turntable on the launch craft's deck. This allows the missile to be fired on the target's bearing, launch data being provided by the launch craft's fire-control system using data provided by search radar. After the boosted launch, the missile cruises on its sustainer motor at about 800km/h (497mph) at a height of 10m (33ft) above the sea under the control of an inertial system, though course corrections can be made by radio commands or by slaving the missile to an optical director. For the terminal phase of the attack, the missile's semi-active radar seeker is activated and guides the weapon onto the energy of the launch craft's radar reflected by the target; alternatively, the slaved optical guidance can be continued right up to missile impact. The Gabriel I missile has a range of only 21km (13 miles), but the Gabriel II introduced wider-span wings and a longer body for a larger sustainer rocket, and can reach a speed of 850km/h (528mph) and a range of 36km (22.4 miles). Further development yielded the Gabriel III with a larger 150kg (331lb) warhead, a longer body for a larger motor producing a range of more than 60km (37.3 miles), and another seeker option in the form of active radar. The Gabriel III cruises at 100m (330ft) and then descends 20m (66ft) for the approach to the target before making the final attack at a pre-set height of 4, 2.5 or 1.5m (13.1, 8.25 or 4.9ft) according to the sea state. A much improved Gabriel IV is currently under consideration with a turbojet sustainer for a range of 200km (124 miles) or more. The possibility of using the various marks of the Gabriel missile in three differing models (fire-and-forget, fire-and-update, and fire-and-control) allowed the Israelis to develop the concept of a 'cocktail' attack by several missiles operating in different modes to confuse the enemy and his electronic counter-measures.

This was still in the future, however, as Israel embarked on a large-scale programme to develop her navy along new lines after the 1967 War. For technical and tactical reasons, it made sense for the Israelis to turn to the Western world's leading designer and producer of fast combat craft, namely Lürssen. For emotional and political reasons, however, it was impossible for Israel to procure weapons openly from Germany, so the order was handled through an intermediary, Constructions Méchaniques de Normandie of Cherbourg in France.

The resulting design was that now known as the 'FPB/TNC-45' type, and in 1965 and 1966 Israel ordered two batches of six such craft as the 'Saar' class. The early history of these vessels was chequered in the extreme. An initial four had been delivered without armament in 1967 before the outbreak of the 'Six-Day War', and were therefore not operational in this conflict. A fifth unit was delivered shortly after this, but then France embargoed the delivery of the remaining craft under pressure from the Arab nations. Israel nonetheless managed to extricate another five craft from Cherbourg in December 1969, under the Panamanian flag and in the guise of Norwegian oilfield supply craft, and these five vessels then gave the basic design a classic reputation for seaworthiness and range by reaching Israel in January 1970. The last two craft were delivered later by France.

The first six craft were completed in Israel with three 40mm Bofors gun as FAC(G)s but also possessed a useful anti-submarine capability through the installation of four 12.75in (324mm) tubes for lightweight anti-submarine torpedoes launched on the basis of data provided by ELAC search and attack sonar. The second six craft were completed to a more powerful FAC(G) standard with a 76mm (3in) OTO Melara Compact gun mounting in place of the single 40mm weapon located forward of the bridge; for reasons of weight, this installation meant that anti-submarine capability had to be omitted.

Useful though it was, this FAC(G) standard was only an interim step on the way to the creation of a FAC(M) using the Gabriel missile. The first and last six craft were thus developed respectively to 'Saar 2' and 'Saar 3' missile-armed standards. In the 'Saar 2' this involved the installation of two single container-launchers for Gabriel missiles near the edges of the deck between the bridge and the forecastle-mounted 40mm gun, and the replacement of the two after 40mm guns with trainable triple container-launchers for the same missile type. It was possible to omit the triple container-launchers and instead fit over the stern two twin 12.75in (324mm) tubes for lightweight anti-submarine torpedoes used in conjunction with EDO 780 variable-depth sonar. The 'Saar 3' standard is comparable but limited to six rather than eight Gabriel missiles in two triple container-launchers replacing the two 40mm guns.

The obvious capabilities of the 'Saar 2' and 'Saar 3'-class FAC(M)s were confirmed in Israel's 1973 'Yom Kippur' War with Egypt and Syria, when thirteen Israeli fast combat craft with 63 Gabriel missile-launchers were pitted against 27 Arab 'Komar' and 'Osa'-class fast combat craft with 84 launchers for the longer-ranged 'Styx'. On the first night of the war, five Israeli craft operating off the Syrian port of Latakia, some 200 miles (320km) from their home base, encountered three Syrian 'Osas' in history's first missile-versus-missile surface action. The Israeli craft defeated twelve 'Styx' missiles fired in two six-missile salvoes, shooting one of them down with 76mm (3in) gunfire and evading the rest by using electronic counter-measures. The Israelis then closed the range during the next eighteen minutes to fire a salvo of Gabriel missiles that struck all three Syrian craft. Two of these sank immediately, and the Israelis used 40mm gunfire to finish off the crippled third unit.

Two nights later, six Israeli craft were operating off the Egyptian port of Dumyat when they encountered a force of four Egyptian navy 'Osa'-class craft. The Israeli vessels evaded twelve 'Styx' missiles fired in four salvoes, and then destroyed three of the Egyptian craft, two of them with Gabriel missiles and the third with gunfire. During actions later in this short war, Arab craft fired another 28 'Styx' missiles at Israeli vessels, again without scoring a single hit, for a 0 per cent hit record during the war. The success rate of the Gabriel, on the other hand, was 85 per cent. The Israelis were able to roam far and wide: typical operations saw patrols off the Syrian coast, where a complete armoured brigade was retained in case these harassments presaged an Israeli landing, and an incursion into the Egyptian anchorage of Ras Ghareb, where nineteen armed fishing boats were sunk. In the course of the entire war, the Israeli navy suffered the loss of only three men killed and 24 wounded in the course of operations that resulted in the sinking of nineteen warships of the Arabs' regular navies.

The naval operations of the 'Yom Kippur' War

saw the fast combat craft come of age in coastal warfare. For the first time the emphasis was placed on operations by FACs rather than larger surface vessels for tasks as diverse as gunfire support of army units operating in coastal regions, and attacks on the enemy's naval bases. This latter was particularly important, for it denied the enemy the tactical advantages of manoeuvrability while operating on the open sea. In these operations, the Israelis also made extensive use of helicopters for the mid-course guidance of missiles launched from their own FACs, and for decoying missiles launched by the enemy's FACs.

Even before the 'Yom Kippur' War, the manifest capabilities of the Israeli 'Saar'-class craft had attracted an order for similar 'FPB/TNC-45'-type craft from Argentina, which was at loggerheads with the neighbouring South American country of Chile over a disputed frontier in the Beagle Channel region at the extreme south of the continent, where there may be considerable oil and natural gas deposits. Despite its often extreme weather conditions, the region is an ideal operational area for fast combat craft as it comprises a maze of confined channels and islands. In 1970 Argentina ordered two West German-built 'FPB/TNC-45'-class craft, and these were commissioned during 1974 in the FAC(G/T) role. Although there was no open warfare in the region, Argentina's possession of these two craft gave her a decided superiority that was only counterbalanced, and indeed reversed, in 1988 when Chile bought from Israel two of her 'Saar 3'-class FAC(M)s.

The next order came from South-East Asia, where the small nation of Singapore attests its strategic importance and wealth by maintaining moderately large and very well equipped armed forces for the preservation of peace in this potentially volatile region. Singapore comprises one larger island and some 54 smaller islands, and this archipelago is an ideal operational area for fast combat craft. In 1970, therefore, Singapore ordered six 'FPB/TNC-45'-class FAC(M/G)s as two initial craft from West Germany to be followed by four indigenously built craft. The armament of these vessels is a powerful and interesting combination of Swedish and Israeli weapons. The gun armament is Swedish, and comprises one Bofors SAK 57 57mm gun on the forecastle and one Bofors 40mm weapon aft. The missile armament initially comprised the first export installation of the Israeli Gabriel, and consisted of five Gabriels in two fixed single

container-launchers and one trainable triple container-launcher, although the latter can now be replaced by two twin container-launchers for an American weapon, the RGM-84 Harpoon.

The Singapore order was followed by two other contracts from the same region. Here national volatilities combine with a great density of commercial maritime traffic, resurgent piracy, and island-studded confined waters to produce waters admirably suited to fast combat craft operations. The first order was placed by Malaysia for six licence-built craft. These were completed to a less formidable FAC(G) standard with the same gun armament as the Singapore craft but less capable electronics and reduced performance based on a three- rather than four-shaft propulsion arrangement. Thailand followed with a contract for three licence-built units essentially similar to the Singapore craft.

Other orders were received from Ecuador for three FAC(M/G)s with a notably useful armament that includes the 76mm (3in) OTO Melara Compact gun as well as the MM.38 early version of the French Exocet anti-ship missile; from three Persian Gulf states for a total of seventeen FAC(M/G)s, all carrying the OTO Melara Compact gun and the later MM.40 version of the Exocet missile; and from Ghana for two FAC(G)s with the OTO Melara Compact gun but only a modest two-shaft propulsion arrangement. The 'FPB/TNC-45' is still available, and further orders may yet be placed for this enduring design whose versatility means continued viability through the installation of modern weapons and sensors.

Despite the proved seaworthiness and endurance of the original 'Saar' class, Israel came to feel in the late 1960s that a new type of FAC(M) was required for longer-range operations in the Mediterranean and, to a lesser extent, the Red Sea. A major factor in this decision was the emergence as a major power in the Mediterranean theatre of Libya, a fervently Moslem state. A strong believer in pan-Arab power, Libya was using a large percentage of her considerable oil revenues to create large and offensively orientated armed forces. These included a navy with a considerable missile capability in vessels ranging in size up to corvettes.

The result of these Israeli concerns was the 'Saar 4' class of FAC(M)s derived by the Israelis from 1968 on the basis of their experience with the earlier 'Saars'. At a length of 58.0m (190ft 3in) and a full-load displacement of 450 tons, the type is somewhat larger than the 'Saar 2' and 'Saar 3' classes, but as range rather than speed was the prime performance requisite, the four-shaft propulsion arrangement remained essentially unaltered to yield a speed of 32kt but a range of 7,400km (4,600 miles) instead of a speed of 40kt or more and a range of 4,650km (2,890 miles). The 'Saar 4' proved its exceptional seaworthiness and range when four of the class made the passage from Israel's Mediterranean coast to the port of Eilat on Israel's Red Sea coast by sailing right round Africa via the Strait of Gibraltar and the Cape of Good Hope, and relying exclusively on refuelling at sea.

Apart from additional fuel bunkerage, the greater volume and deck area of the 'Saar 4'-class units are used for greater habitability (aided by full air-conditioning), improved electronics (including an operations centre for an altogether improved combat control capability), a superior weapons layout, and significantly upgraded sensor and counter-measures capabilities. In their original form, the 'Saar 4'-class craft each carried two 76mm (3in) OTO Melara Compact guns, two 20mm Oerlikon-Bührle cannon in single mountings and/or a maximum of six 0.5in (12.7mm) machine-guns in twin mountings, and six container-launchers for Gabriel missiles. The after gun mounting was later replaced by a 20mm six-barrel cannon in an American-supplied Phalanx close-in weapon system mounting for improved last-ditch defence against sea-skimming anti-ship missiles. From 1978 the missile armament was revised after Israel began to receive the RGM-84 Harpoon anti-ship missile, which can be installed in one or two twin or quadruple container-launchers, replacing a similar number of Gabriel container-launchers for further enhancement of the 'cocktail' attack concept. In addition to the operations centre, the electronics of the 'Saar 4' class include a capable French search radar, an Italian fire-control system with associated radar, a French active search sonar (despite the type's lack of anti-submarine armament), electronic support measures incorporating Israeli and Italian elements, and an impressive Israeli electronic counter-measures system that includes one 45-barrel, four or six 24-barrel, and four single-barrel 'chaff'-launchers. One unit has been fitted with an aft-mounted helicopter platform for trials with a helicopter and mid-course targeting update of the Harpoon missile, but the hull is really too small for such an installation, which has not therefore been adopted for other units of the class.

Israel built ten 'Saar 4'-class craft for her own use, but subsequently sold two of them to Chile. Another three units of the original configuration were built in the same Israeli yard for South Africa, where another nine have been built under licence.

The commissioning of 'Saar 4'-class units gave the Israeli Navy an impressive force of modern and sophisticated fast combat craft. Early experience in the 1967 war, confirmed by operations in the 1973 war, indicated that these forces could be deployed more effectively in flotillas led by a still more sophisticated flotilla leader with specialized equipment and accommodation for the flotilla commander and his staff. This resulted in the 'Saar 4.5' class which was based on the hull, propulsion arrangement, armament (in upgraded form) and electronics of the 'Saar 4' class. The hull was lengthened to allow the incorporation in two units (at the expense of part of the missile armament) of a hangar and deck pad for a single light helicopter used in the surveillance and missile targeting update roles. The Israelis later decided that despite its longer hull, the 'Saar 4.5' class was not ideally suited to helicopter operations, and this was one of the primary reasons for the design of the 'Saar 5' class of guided-missile corvettes.

These large fast combat craft classes have given Israel exceptional capabilities in coastal operations, but her navy also felt the need for smaller fast combat craft optimized for the inshore role, where high performance and manoeuvrability are more important than exceptional firepower and electronic sophistication. This resulted in the 'Dvora' class, currently the world's smallest FAC(M) type. These craft are small and light enough for easy land transport, and indeed storage on land to ease maintenance. Despite their tiny size, however, the 'Dvora'-class units pack a considerable punch with their two Gabriel missiles. The combination of offensive power and low cost, which is about 15 per cent of the price of a large FAC(M), has made the type attractive to other countries such as Sri Lanka and Taiwan.

To fill the operational gap between the 'Dvora' and 'Saar' classes, Israel opted for an American-designed FAH(M) type, the 'Flagstaff 2' design. With very high performance and exceptionally powerful missile armament (two Gabriel IIIs and four RGM-84 Harpoons) for a type of only limited size, the 'Flagstaff 2' design has great potential. There have been considerable production difficulties and operational teething problems, however, and Israel decided to curtail her order at three craft rather than press ahead with the full requirement for twelve.

The proved success of the 'Saar 2' and 'Saar 3' classes in Israeli service was a very useful advertisement for the quality of Lürssen fast combat craft designs, and resulted in a steady stream of orders for vessels based on the 'FPB/TNC-45' design. Lürssen also took a further step up the size ladder, for the company recognized that the type of weapon and electronic fit demanded by its customers was on the verge of swamping the capabilities of the 'FPB/TNC-45' design. Lürssen thus appreciated that greater size would not only facilitate the installation of current weapons and sensors as well as a new generation of these items, but also fit in with the procurement plans of many of the world's smaller navies. Having gained a measure of operational, if not combat, experience with fast combat craft, these navies were now beginning to feel themselves capable of expansion into a larger type of warship. Many of these navies belonged to third-world countries which had emerged relatively recently from colonial rule into independence and therefore felt that, for cost as well as technical reasons, their expansion should not be into major warships optimized for a single role. Instead, they generally felt that they should adopt a type one step up from the medium-sized FAC, namely a large fast combat craft offering multi-role capability through the adoption of a combination of hull and propulsion arrangement that would support later upgrading with more and/or better weapons and sensors.

The result was the versatile 'FPB/PB-57' design with a full-load displacement of some 400 tons on a hull 58.1m (190ft 7in) long and capable of accepting two-, three- and four-shaft propulsion arrangements. The lead customer was not a third-world country but Spain, whose navy was in the throes of a major modernization, including the local construction of fast combat craft initially fitted with limited armament for the patrol role but capable of rapid development into powerful FAC(M)s in times of crisis. The first of Spain's six 'Lazaga'-class twin-shaft craft was commissioned from Lürssen, but the other five were produced under licence by Bazan. In their present form, these vessels are simple FAC(G)s with capable electronics but useful mainly for patrol and training. However, provision was made in the design for the retrofit of potent anti-ship and anti-submarine armament, so that the present 76mm (3in) OTO Melara Compact and 40mm Bofors guns would be supplemented by two twin container-launchers for RGM-84 Harpoon anti-ship missiles and/or two 12.75in (324mm) triple tubes for lightweight anti-submarine torpedoes.

Bazan also produced for Morocco four units of a FAC(M/G) variant with the same comparatively low-powered propulsion arrangement. In addition, the Spanish firm developed its own 'Cormoran' class as an export derivative and this has been supplied to Morocco as a two-shaft FAC(G) of low performance and indifferent armament, and to Venezuela as a three-shaft FAC(M/G) with higher performance and a combined missile and gun armament.

Lürssen itself has, and is, building craft for Ghana, Indonesia and Kuwait, and also supplied the lead craft of the 'Dogan' class to Turkey, where another seven of this very powerful FAC(M/G) class were built under licence.

The largest operator of the type, however, is Germany with 20 craft in service. These were ordered in two batches each of ten units. The first batch was the 'Type 143' class with the type of composite hull construction favoured by the West German navy, and these highly impressive FAC(M/G/T)s were ordered in 1972 to replace the earliest of the 'Type 141' FAC(T)s. The new craft were commissioned in 1976 and 1977 with a four-shaft propulsion arrangement for a maximum speed of 40kt and a 30kt cruising range of 2,400km (1,490 miles) on 116 tons (118 tonnes) of fuel. The electronics are particularly impressive, for the West German navy was faced with the prospect of operations against sophisticated opponents in the form of the Soviet navy and its allies. Thus the conventional fit of a surface search and tracking radar used in conjunction with the WM-27 fire-control system is boosted by the provision of a combat engagement centre with an AGIS action information system, and defensive capability is enhanced by an electronic support measures system that uses data from an intercept and warning element to control a Hot Dog/Silver Dog flare and 'chaff'-launcher.

As delivered, the craft each fitted nicely balanced and highly effective armament in the form of two 76mm (3in) OTO Melara Compact gun mountings located on the forecastle and over the stern, two twin container-launchers for the MM.38 version of the Exocet missile, and two 533mm (21in) tubes for Seal wire-guided torpedoes. The increasing threat of Soviet tactical air power demanded that steps be taken to improve air-defence capability, and this resulted in the modification of the 'Type 143' class craft to 'Type 143B' standard by the replacement of the after 76mm (3in) gun by the RAM (Rolling Airframe Missile) surface-to-air-missile system using the EX-31 launcher for 24 RIM-116 missiles.

The intermediate designation applies to ten craft that were ordered in 1978 as replacements for the 'Type 142' FAC(T)s, upgraded 'Zobel'-class survivors of the obsolete 'Type 141' or 'Jaguar' class. These craft were commissioned between 1982 and 1984, and each carried a single 76mm (3in) gun mounting removed from the craft of the 'Type 143' class as they were prepared for improvement to 'Type 143B' standard. In other respects the craft are similar to the 'Type 143B'-class units, and like them were only later retrofitted with the RAM surface-to-air missile system. The major differences between the two current 'Type 143'-class standards is the propulsion arrangement, for the 'Type 143A'-class units have less power than their 'Type 143B'-class near-sisters. This does not reduce maximum speed, but helps to increase cruising range.

The rationale for producing the larger and heavier 'FPB/PB-57' design as a successor to the 'FPB/TNC-45' continued into the 1980s, and the result was Lürssen's largest type to date, namely the 'FPB/MGB-62' which verges on corvette size as it has a full-load displacement of over 600 tons and a length of 62.95m (206ft 6in). The first customer for the type was Bahrain, which ordered two craft to an impressive FAC(M/G) standard with powerful armament and a comprehensive electronic system that includes full electronic support measures and counter-measures capabilities. Particularly notable in this variant is the provision for an embarked helicopter carrying anti-ship missiles, for this considerably enhances the vessels' ability to strike at remoter targets.

The variants for the other two current operators lack the helicopter of the Bahraini model, but possess exceptional armament. That of the Singapore vessels includes powerful guns and missiles as well as a state-of-the-art anti-submarine capability, while that of the Abu Dhabi vessels is notable for the two layers of air defence provided by different surface-to-air missile systems backed by a potent dual-purpose gun.

Both 'FPB/MGB-62' variants for Arab countries carry the MM.40 version of the Exocet anti-ship missile. This is the later version of a missile that has been one of the most important Western naval weapons since its service debut in 1974. The missile was developed by Aérospatiale to meet a French navy requirement for a fire-and-forget weapon capable of defeating targets such as major warships. The initial missiles were used for manufacturer's trials in mid-1972, and from October of the same year service evaluation was undertaken by the French navy in association with the British and West German navies, which were to become major operators of the type. As a result of the service evaluation, an important improvement programme was undertaken in 1973, and the first production rounds were fired in the following year, achieving a success rate of 91 per cent in 30 firings. The missile is based on a cylindrical body containing the 165kg (364lb) high-explosive warhead, the electronics and the solid-propellant booster and sustainer rockets. The body also supports the flying surfaces, which comprise a cruciform of swept and tapered wings well behind the missile's mid-point and, at the tail, a cruciform of smaller and trapedoizal control fins mounted in line with the wings.

The missile is accommodated in a boxlike container-launcher, and before launch its onboard guidance package is primed with data about the target's bearing and range from the launch vessel's fire-control system. The missile is then launched with the aid of its booster rocket, and then flies on the power of its long-burning sustainer rocket under the control of its inertial navigation system. The cruise phase of the flight is undertaken at low level, and at a point some 10km (6.2 miles) from the target's anticipated position the missile's active radar seeker is switched on. Once the seeker has locked on to the target, the missile descends to sea-skimming height (one of three heights being set before launch on the basis of sea state and the nature of the target) and impacts with the target, where considerable damage is caused by the missile's kinetic energy, the explosion of its warhead, and the burning of any unused rocket propellant.

The initial MM.38 version of the Exocet weighs 750kg (1,653lb) and possesses a maximum range of 45km (28 miles). Operational experience with this type revealed it to be an excellent weapon of considerable power and good reliability. Experience also showed that greater range was desirable. This resulted in the MM.40 version, which has a longer body containing much improved booster and sustainer rockets for a range of 70km (43.5 miles).

◀ *Daphne* was commissioned in 1960 as the lead unit of the Danish navy's eight-strong class of seaward defence craft.

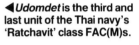

◀ *Udomdet* is the third and last unit of the Thai navy's 'Ratchavit' class FAC(M)s.

◀ *L'Audacieuse* (right) and *La Capricieuse* of the French navy's 'P400' class at sea.

The MM.40 is also fitted with the improved seeker introduced on late-production MM.38s to provide greater resistance to electronic counter-measures. The MM.40 missile weighs 850kg (1,874lb), but this 100kg (220lb) increase in mass is more than offset in real operational terms by the adoption of a new lightweight container-launcher, which is also considerably more compact than that of the MM.38. This means that smaller craft can be fitted with the type; alternatively larger craft can carry larger numbers of Exocets. This has also been produced in an air-launched version, and an encapsulated variant for submarine launch is also in service.

The only Western missile to rival the Exocet in terms of numbers produced and operational flexibility has been the American Harpoon, which was produced by McDonnell Douglas in response to a rapidly emerging US Navy interest in such weapons after the 1967 sinking of *Eilat*. The programme began in 1968 with the intention of producing an AGM-84 air-launched weapon with a range of 57.5 miles (92.5km), but a ship-launched RGM-84 version was added from 1970, while an encapsulated UGM-84 version for submarine launch was produced in 1972. The Harpoon was planned as a low-risk development, so no completely novel technology was incorporated in a type intended as a capable yet comparatively cheap weapon that emphasized reliability rather than outright performance in everything except electronic performance and range. The last was provided by the propulsion arrangement of one solid-propellant booster rocket and one liquid-propellant sustainer turbojet deriving its oxygen from aspirated air rather than stored oxidant.

In configuration the Harpoon is similar to the Exocet in its cylindrical body, cruciform of swept and tapered wings located aft of the mid-body point, and cruciform of swept control surfaces at the tail. The body of the Harpoon is also used in much the same way as that of the Exocet. In the nose is the active radar seeker with the guidance electronics behind it, the 500lb (227kg) warhead is between the electronics and the wings, and the rest of the body is occupied by the sustainer engine; for the Harpoon this is a 680lb (308kg) thrust turbojet aspirated via a flush inlet between the two lower wings and supplied with fuel from tankage between the warhead and the engine, itself located at the rear of the weapon to exhaust straight to the rear after the finned section containing the booster rocket has been jettisoned.

Some 34 of the initial 40 missiles were fired for development purposes in 1974 and 1975, fifteen of these being of the RGM-84A ship-launched model. Production started in 1976 and since that time the Harpoon has been a great technical and commercial success in the American and export markets. The Harpoon's basic range-and-bearing mode of operation is identical to that of the Exocet, with cruise course and height controlled respectively by an inertial navigation system and radar altimeter, and the active radar seeker activated only at the last moment to provide accurate homing without giving the target much opportunity to implement any counter-measures. The Harpoon is a more versatile weapon than the Exocet, however, and another operating system is the bearing-only mode, in which the active radar is switched on comparatively early to locate a target whose exact position was uncertain at the moment of launch. If it finds no target, the missile undertakes a pre-programmed search pattern and, after locking on to the target, performs the standard attack. In Block I missiles with a 60-mile (97km) maximum range, this is a pop-up climb followed by a steep and rapidly accelerating dive onto the target's more vulnerable upper surfaces. The Block IB missile has a range of 68 miles (110km), and the Block IC missile adds a sea-skimming attack profile to reduce the target's reaction time still further. The RGM-84B model has a 570lb (259kg) warhead, improved electronics including enhanced capability against electronic counter-measures, and a more flexible flight profile, including the ability to fly a dogleg approach via three pre-programmed waypoints. The RGM-84C model combines the capabilities of the earlier models with further improvements, including a range of 120 miles (193km).

It is claimed that the Harpoon's capabilities include the ability to destroy any Soviet fast combat craft up to the size of a 'Nanuchka'-class unit with a single round, to disable a frigate or destroyer with two rounds, to cripple a cruiser with four rounds, and to knock out a battlecruiser or aircraft-carrier with five rounds.

The Harpoon can be launched in a number of ways, but for fast combat craft the standard method is from a sealed container-launcher. The missile is delivered in this container as a sealed round, and this needs only to be installed on the launcher frame (twin or quadruple Mk 141 launcher) and to have its electrical connections completed before the missile is ready for firing. Soviet anti-ship missiles are disposed in launchers aligned along the parent craft's deck, requiring blast deflectors to deflect the exhaust plume outboard and so prevent damage to the parent craft's deck and superstructure. The launchers for Western missiles such as Exocet and Harpoon are usually installed on the outer sides of the deck at an oblique angle: the launched missile therefore flies across the deck, but its exhaust plume is directed outward and downward well clear of the deck and superstructure.

These two missile types arm most of the fast combat craft operated by the navies of Western-aligned countries. Oddly enough, though, the Exocet has not found a place in any of France's comparatively small number of fast combat craft. There is no place for such craft in French tactical thinking so far as European waters are concerned, so the country's few fast combat craft are used for patrol and training rather than any real operational role. Many of the French fast combat craft are deployed overseas in French dependencies and colonies.

Nevertheless, France has developed two important types of fast combat craft, the 'La Combattante' and 'PR 72' classes. The more important of these types in commercial as well as operational terms is the 'La Combattante' class, itself derived from a West German design by Lürssen. As it was producing the 'Type 141' FAC(T)s for the West German navy on the basis of its 'TNC-42' design, Lürssen was also developing a general-purpose hull that could be fitted with different numbers and types of engines and weapons according to the requirements and purse of the purchaser. For political reasons this design was transferred to France, where Constructions Méchaniques de Normandie lengthened and modified it for construction as *La Combattante*, the sole unit of the 'La Combattante I' class, a twin-shaft type that was used mainly as a trials vessel, although provision was made for the type to carry up to 80 commandos for a short passage.

The hull was of the laminated wood plastic favoured by the Germans for its anti-magnetic properties, and the armament comprised two 40mm Bofors guns located forward and aft as well as a quadruple launcher for the SS.12 missile, a wire-guided type of too little range and striking power for worthwhile use by a FAC. What soon became clear, however, was the fact that the hull lines were excellent, and an important factor in the unit's good seakeeping qualities, although performance was limited by the two-shaft propulsion arrangement. With the support of Lürssen, CMN refined the hull in a steel-built form and lengthened it slightly to produce the multi-role 'La Combattante II' design with considerably higher performance provided by a four-shaft propulsion arrangement using West German rather than French diesels. The type was offered with a host of electronic and weapon options, although the French exercised considerable pressure on potential customers to adopt French electronics and the Exocet missile.

The largest single order was placed by the West German navy, which contracted for 20 'Type 148' class craft. CMN and Lürssen built twelve and eight hulls respectively, and these were then delivered to the Lorient Naval Dockyard for completion with a basically French electronics suite, French missiles, and Italian and Swedish guns. An interesting feature of the electronics suite is the inclusion of a Link 11 data-link, which allows real-time electronic communication between the craft and a shore establishment. In effect, this gives the craft a high-quality combat centre, and among the data-link's provisions is capability for the Exocets to be primed with launch data and fired by the shore establishment.

Other customers for the 'La Combattante II' class have been Greece, Iran, Libya and Malaysia. The four Greek craft are FAC(M/T)s with a French electronics suite, comparatively light but effective gun armament in the form of four powerful 35mm Oerlikon-Bührle cannon in two twin mountings, four Exocet missiles, and two 533mm (21in) tubes for West German SST-4 heavyweight torpedoes. This last is a wire-guided anti-ship weapon with an active/passive acoustic homing system, and can deliver its 260kg (573lb) high-explosive warhead to a range of some 20km (12.4 miles).

The twelve Iranian craft were ordered in 1974 with a Dutch fire-control system and provision for a moderately powerful armament in the form of a 76mm (3in) OTO Melara Compact gun backed by a 40mm Bofors, and two twin container-launchers for RGM-84 Harpoon missiles. The first nine units were delivered before the fall of the Shah in 1979, but Iran received only twelve missiles before this crucial event, which saw the immediate ending of American support and deliveries of American weapons. The efficiency of the Harpoon was indicated during the Iraq-Iran War when the missiles were used to sink one 'Polnochny'-class landing ship and several 'P 6'-class MTBs. The other three of Iran's 'La Combattante II'-class FACs were delivered in 1981, and at least two were later lost in combat.

The Libyan order was placed in 1977 and covered ten craft with French electronics and Italian weapons. The gun armament was one 76mm (3in) OTO Melara Compact weapon and two 40mm Bofors built by Breda and installed in a Breda twin mounting, while the missile armament comprised four Otomat Mk 1s in single container-launchers. In March 1986 one such unit was sunk by American attack, and another was severely damaged a few days later.

The Malaysian craft were ordered in 1970 to a standard similar to that of the Greek units but with a more powerful gun armament, including one 57mm Bofors in a SAK 57 Mk 1 mounting located on the forecastle and one 40mm Bofors in an open mounting over the stern.

The 'La Combattante II' class proved most successful in service, but several potential customers expressed the desire for a slightly larger derivative providing better seakeeping qualities and the ability to support heavier armament, as well as offering greater endurance (through increased fuel bunkerage and improved habitability) and a much enhanced command facility (through the additional volume that allowed a flotilla commander and his small staff to be embarked). The resulting 'La Combattante III' type is 9.2m (30ft 2in) longer than the 'La Combattante II' design, which results in a full-load displacement of some 430 tons compared with the earlier design's 275 tons. Much the same absolute performance can be provided by a more powerful four-shaft propulsion arrangement, and range is either maintained or improved by the provision of additional fuel bunkerage.

The major operator of the type is the Greek navy, which ordered four craft from CMN and then built another six under licence. The main difference between the French- and Greek-built craft is the latter's less powerful propulsion arrangement, a sacrifice that the Greeks had to make for economic reasons. As in the earlier class, the electronics suite is largely of French origin, but the armament combines French missiles with Italian and Swiss guns, and in some craft German torpedoes. All the craft have two 76mm (3in) OTO Melara Compact guns located forward and aft, and four 30mm Oerlikon-Bührle cannon in two twin anti-aircraft mountings located on each side of the superstructure's rear portion. The French-built craft have

Exocet missiles in two twin container-launchers, but the Greek-built vessels have Penguin Mk II missiles in six single container-launchers. The French-built craft also possess two 533mm (21in) aft-firing tubes for SST-4 wire-guided torpedoes.

Smaller numbers of the 'La Combattante III' class have been procured by the Nigerian, Qatari and Tunisian navies. The Qatari and Tunisian units are similar to the Greek craft, while the Nigerian craft have a relatively light missile and main-calibre gun armament, but feature two-layer anti-aircraft defence with 40mm and 30mm weapons.

In purely commercial terms, the 'PR 72' class has not proved as successful as the two 'La Combattante' classes, but is large enough to serve as a flotilla leader. The lead customer was Morocco, which took two units in FAC(G) configuration that has provision for upgrading to FAC(M/G) standard. Thus the Moroccan craft are each armed with the fairly standard large fast combat craft combination of one 76mm (3in) OTO Melara Compact gun on the forecastle and one 40mm Bofors at the stern, but have provision for the retrofit of two twin container-launchers for MM.38 Exocet missiles. Peru placed a more significant order for six FAC(M/G)s with a more powerful propulsion arrangement of the same four-shaft type for higher performance and with an armament that includes two twin container-launchers for MM.38 Exocet missiles, one 76mm (3in) OTO Melara Compact gun on the forecastle, two 40mm Bofors in a twin mounting over the stern, and two 20mm cannon in single mountings. The least effective of the 'PR 72' variants is represented by the single unit for Senegambia, which has no provision for upgrading to FAC(M) standard but by local standards is an effective FAC(G) with two 76mm (3in) OTO Melara Compact guns located forward and aft.

Other French fast combat classes, which are not as powerful as the 'La Combattante' or 'PR 72', include the 'P 48S', 'P 400' and 'Patra' classes.

The two main British designers of fast combat craft are Brooke Marine and Vosper Thornycroft. In general terms, Brooke Marine specializes in robust craft well suited to the demands of third-world navies with difficulties in finding adequate numbers of trained personnel, while Vosper Thornycroft specializes in the more sophisticated end of the market where an advanced hull and propulsion are combined with an integrated suite of modern weapons and capable electronics.

Within the spectrum of fast craft, the smallest of Brooke Marine's standard hull types are the 24.5m and 29m (80ft and 95ft) designs, and these have proved successful in securing considerable export orders. They are mostly patrol craft of limited performance and light armament, however, and thus fall outside the fast combat craft category. Next up in size is the 32.6m (107ft) design that has formed the basis for two types of fast combat craft, both delivered to African nations and featuring a two-shaft propulsion arrangement for low purchase cost but also low performance. The three units for Kenya were delivered as patrol craft, but as the Kenyan navy became better trained and more experienced it recognized the latent capabilities of the design, and contracted for the craft to be upgraded to limited FAC(M) standard. The original gun armament of two 40mm Bofors in single mountings was replaced by the considerably more modern fit of two 30mm Oerlikon-Bührle cannon in a twin mounting under the control of an optronic director, and this core armament was supplemented by four container-launchers for Gabriel II anti-ship missiles used in conjunction with an Italian fire-control system. As delivered, the four Nigerian craft were similar to the Kenyan craft in armament but had lower-powered engines and, as a result, a reduced maximum speed that really takes them out of the FAC category. In 1981 the craft were upgraded to a semi-FAC(G) standard with four 30mm Oerlikon-Bührle cannon in two twin mountings, but they are still used mainly for the patrol and training roles.

Next up in size among Brooke Marine's core designs is the 37.5m (123ft) type. This retains a low-powered two-shaft propulsion arrangement similar in concept to that of the 'Brooke Marine 32.6m' design, although with engines of somewhat higher power for better performance. The greater size of the hull provides better sea-keeping qualities, and also offers the right combination of larger area and great volume needed for a more effective armament layout. Placed by Oman, the first order covered three examples of the 'Al Bushra' class of FAC(G)s armed with two 40mm Bofors guns in single mountings forward and aft. These were commissioned in 1973, and were revised between 1977 and 1978 as FAC(M/G)s with two container-launchers for MM.38 Exocet missiles and the Sea Archer fire-control system. Another four units were delivered in 1977 as FAC(G)s with a 76mm (3in) OTO Melara Compact gun on the forecastle under the control of

an optical director, this useful main gun being supplemented by one 20mm cannon and two medium machine-guns. The 'Al Bushra' class was reduced by the loss of the name vessel (swept overboard from a transport ship during a hurricane as it was being returned to Oman in November 1978 after upgrading), and the two units of what now became the 'Al Mansur' class have since been deleted. The 'Al Wafi' class, comprising the four later units, is now useful more for patrol and training than for any real operational role in the waters of the Persian Gulf and the Arabian Sea, which are both the operational areas of highly sophisticated FAC(M)s and advanced tactical warplanes.

The other main operator of the 'Brooke Marine 37.5m' design is Algeria, which has two British- and seven Algerian-built craft of the 'Kebir' class. This is a FAC(G) of modest performance, and the armament comprises one 76mm (3in) OTO Melara Compact on the forecastle as well as two 23mm Soviet cannon in a twin mounting aft, where they replace a single 20mm Oerlikon-Bührle cannon. As in the 'Al Wafi' class, the electronics are comparatively simple.

Barbados and Kenya each ordered single units for the patrol role, but the Kenyan vessel has been transformed into a modestly powerful FAC(M) with the original pair of 40mm Bofors guns in single mountings replaced by four Gabriel II missiles and two 30mm Oerlikon-Bührle cannon in a twin mounting.

The largest of Brooke Marine's designs currently in service is the 41.8m (137.1ft) type, which is used by Australia in the form of the 'Fremantle' class. This comprises fifteen simple FAC(G)s with limited armament and used mainly for patrol. The company also offers a 53.5m (175.5ft) type displacing some 350 tons at full load and capable of 38kt on a three-shaft propulsion arrangement powered by three 4,570hp (3,395kW) Paxman 18CM diesels. Various armament and sensor options are available, but a typical anti-ship weapon fit would be two twin or quadruple container-launchers just aft of the superstructure for four or eight MM.40 Exocet missiles, one 76mm (3in) OTO Melara Compact gun on the forecastle, and two 40mm Bofors in a Breda Compact twin mounting over the stern.

The United Kingdom had done little but toy with the concept of fast combat craft since the end of the Second World War. In the second half of the 1960s,

▲ *Assad el Tadjer* was
originally named *Wadi
M'Ragh*, and is one of four
Libyan navy 'Assad' class
corvettes that may be
regarded as large
FAC(M/G)s.

▶ P24 *Herrera* is a 'PR72P'-
class boat serving with the
Peruvian navy.

however, the Royal Navy became sufficiently concerned with the threat posed by fast combat craft to order a class of three FACs to train the crews of its major warships in the tactics to counter their attacks. The 'Scimitar' class was designed and built by Vosper Thornycroft and the three craft were delivered in 1969 and 1970. With a full-load displacement of 102 tons on a laminated wooden hull measuring 100ft 0in (30.5m) in length and 26ft 8in (8.1m) beam, the 'Scimitar'-class craft were each fitted with a CODOG propulsion arrangement whose two shafts were powered by two 90hp (67kW) Foden diesels for cruising or two 4,500hp (3,355kW) Rolls-Royce Proteus gas turbines for a maximum speed of 40kt.

At much the same time, Vosper Thornycroft evolved its 'Tenacity' class and built a single craft as a private venture. This had a full-load displacement of 220 tons on a hull measuring 144ft 8in (44.1m) in length and 26ft 8in (8.1m) beam. The propulsion arrangement was of the CODOG type with the three shafts powered by two 600hp (445kW) Paxman diesels for cruising or three 4,250hp (3,170kW) Rolls-Royce Proteus gas turbines for a maximum speed of 39kt. The Royal Navy bought the single craft in 1972, subsequently using it for fishery protection and anti-smuggling patrol as well as for training.

This experience is reflected in a number of types which Vosper Thornycroft evolved for the export market during the 1960s and early 1970s. Typical of these are the 'Vosper Thornycroft 103ft', 'Vosper Thornycroft 110ft' and 'Vosper Thornycroft 121ft' classes. The first was built as the 24-strong 'Kris' FAC(G) class for Malaysia, the second was produced in three related FAC(G) forms for Abu Dhabi and Singapore, and the third appeared in three forms including a dedicated FAC(M) type for Brunei and related FAC(G) and FAC(M) variants for Venezuela.

The different conceptual approaches of Vosper Thornycroft and Brooke Marine to the design of fast combat craft is highlighted by the altogether superior combat potential of the former company's 'Tenacity' design, compared with Brooke Marine's less powerful types. This superiority received concrete expression in 1977 when Egypt ordered six FAC(M)s to a design which Vosper Thornycroft extrapolated from that of the 'Tenacity' type. The design of the 'Ramadan' class is a good example of the way in which careful design thinking can pack maximum offensive capability into a comparatively

small hull, in this instance possessing a full-load displacement of 310 tons on a length of 170ft 7in (52.0m). The type has a singular appearance, with its superstructure located well forward and surmounted by a large spherical radome at the top of an enclosed mast structure, together with a deck house located well aft and also surmounted by a spherical radome, although in this instance a smaller unit on an enclosed mast structure of more slender proportions. These radomes give a clue to the sophisticated electronics of the 'Ramadan' class, which include one air/surface search and two tracking radars used in conjunction with a Marconi Sapphire fire-control system and two optronic directors (backed by two optical directors), all co-ordinated through the CAAIS action information system. Each of the craft also possesses a modern electronic support measures system with warning and jamming elements in addition to 'chaff' and flare-launchers for last-ditch defence against incoming missiles. The Italian armament is also impressive, with two twin container-launchers for Otomat Mk 1 missiles between the superstructure and the deck house, one 76mm (3in) OTO Melara Compact gun on the forecastle, and two 40mm Bofors guns in a Breda Compact twin mounting over the stern. The propulsion arrangement is based on West German diesels powering four shafts for a maximum speed of 40kt. The 'Ramadan' class craft were in service by 1982, and provided the Egyptian navy with a qualitative if not quantitive equality with the fast combat craft operated by the Israeli navy.

The 'Ramadan' class contract capitalized on Vosper Thornycroft's existing relationship with the Egyptian navy, which operated a considerable quantity of Soviet equipment but had been without technical support since 1972, when the Egyptian government expelled the 20,000 or so Soviet advisers in the country. In an effort to maintain a viable force of fast combat craft, the Egyptians had launched six 'October'-class craft in 1976 and 1977. These were based on the wooden hull of the 'Komar'-class FAC(M) but were fitted with Italian engines. The craft were completed by Vosper Thornycroft, which installed the weapons and electronics. The weapons comprise two container-launchers for Otomat Mk 1 missiles and four 30mm Oerlikon-Bührle cannon in two twin mountings; the width of the missile installation demanded the addition of wedge-shaped sponsons outboard of the superstructure. The electronics are particularly advanced for so small a FAC(M), and include an air/surface search radar, a tracking radar tied into the Sapphire fire-control system together with an optronic director, and an electronic support measures system controlling 'chaff' and flare-launchers. This capability was not fitted without difficulty, however, and resulted in various cramped features that must hinder operational capabilities; access to the engine room hatches, for example, is via the operations room, which is a removable glass-fibre-reinforced plastics unit.

From the design of the 'Ramadan' class, Vosper Thornycroft developed the 'Province' FAC(M/G) design for Oman, which ordered three craft in the early 1980s and followed with a contract for a fourth in 1986. The design of the 'Province' class provides slightly greater dimensions for a hull of proportionately finer lines and, despite the greater displacement, this ensures high performance with a four-shaft propulsion arrangement with basically the same power as that in the 'Ramadan' class. The craft were delivered in two slightly differing standards, for while all have the same barrelled armament of one 76mm (3in) OTO Melara Compact gun and two 40mm Bofors guns in a Breda Compact twin mounting, the first and last three units have, respectively, two triple and quadruple container-launchers for the MM.40 variant of the Exocet. This difference in standard also extends to the electronics, the first unit having a different search radar and fire-control system from those in the later units.

The same basic type was ordered by Kenya, which thus received two craft with an advanced electronics system (including the CAAIS 450 action information system) and a nicely balanced weapon fit with lighter missile armament than the Omani units. Vosper Thornycroft sees a good future for the basic design despite a current lack of orders, and has proposed a powerful multi-role attack variant as the 'Vita' class with the basic hull and propulsion arrangement of the 'Province' class revised to accommodate any of several combinations of weapons and electronics.

The only other European country that operates a significant force of fast combat craft and also builds such craft is Italy. In the period immediately after the Second World War, the Italian navy made do with a small number of ex-wartime craft such as *MS 474* and *MS 481*, each having a full-load displacement of 72 tons, a speed of 27kt on three 1,150hp (860kW) Isotta-Fraschini petrol engines, and an armament of one or two 40mm Bofors guns

plus two 450m (17.7in) torpedoes. In 1951 Italy received ex-American PT boats in the form of eleven Higgins 78ft (23.8m) craft, and these bridged the operational gap until the advent of Italy's first modern fast combat craft.

The first of these was a prototype, the single 'Folgore'-class unit with a full-load displacement of 190 tons, a length of 39.4m (129ft 3in), a speed of 38kt on four 1,865kW (2,500hp) diesels, and an armament of two 40mm Bofors guns in single mountings, located forward and aft, plus two torpedoes. This vessel was commissioned in 1955 and paved the way for the two 'Lampo'-class craft that entered service in the first half of the 1960s. These each had a full-load displacement of 210 tons, a length of 43.0m (141ft 1in), and a speed of 39kt on the CODOG propulsion arrangement of two 2,700kW (3,620hp) Fiat diesels and one 8,725kW (11,700hp) Nuove Reggiane-built Metrovick gas turbine. The craft could be configured as FAC(T)s or FAC(M)s, each carrying one 40mm Bofors gun and two 533mm (21in) tubes in the former role, and two or three 40mm Bofors plus one missile launcher in the latter role. Further evolution produced the two units of the 'Freccia' class which entered service in 1965 with an upgraded version of the same propulsion arrangement. This comprised two 3,175kW (4,260hp) Fiat diesels and one 8,850kW (11,870hp) Nuove Reggiane-built Metrovick gas turbine for a speed of 40kt on a hull 46.1m (151ft 3in) long and having a full-load displacement of 205 tons. The armament was basically similar to that of the 'Lampo' class in FAC(T) and FAC(M) options, although the torpedo fit was strengthened to four 533m (21in) tubes.

Two more units of the 'Freccia' class were to have been built, but in the Italian concept of fast combat craft the displacement or planing hull was then overtaken by the notion of hydrofoils. In the early 1960s both the USA and Italy became interested in the possibilities of the hydrofoil for high-speed combat craft, and in 1964 the Italian Government joined an Italian builder of commercial hydrofoils, Carlo Rodriguez of Messina in Sicily, and the American company Boeing to establish Alinavi. Through the rest of the 1960s, this organization examined the potential of the Boeing-designed 'Tucumcari' design and finalized details of the all-aluminium *Sparviero* which was built between 1971 and 1974. This prototype was based on the Boeing jetfoil system with three retractable foils (one unit forward and two aft). The CODOG propulsion arrangement comprised one diesel delivering 180hp (134kW) to one propeller for hull-borne operation and one Rolls-Royce Proteus gas turbine delivering 4,500hp (3,360kW) to a waterjet system for foil-borne operation up to a maximum speed of 42kt in heavy seas or 50kt in calm water. *Sparviero* was commissioned in 1974 and proved to have a good overall performance, although hull-borne and foil-borne ranges were limited respectively to 1,950km (1,210 miles) at 8kt and 600km (375 miles) at 42kt. The Italian navy appreciated that the range was decidedly low, but felt that this was acceptable for short-range operations, especially in the island-studded Adriatic Sea. Given the type's full-load displacement of just 63 tons, the armament was notably heavy. The weapons were one 76mm (3in) OTO Melara Compact gun located just forward of the superstructure, close to the boat's centre of gravity, and two container-launchers for Otomat Mk 1 missiles at the stern, flanking the rear of the superstructure.

Sparviero was evaluated exhaustively before the Italian navy ordered six examples of the 'Sparviero'-class production model with superior radar and longer-range Otomat Mk 2 missiles. This is the current limit of the Italian navy's interest in fast combat craft, but Italian industry has been a successful exporter of such craft in the form of medium-sized craft to the Thai navy and larger craft to the navies of Ecuador, Iraq and Libya.

The smaller and earlier of the two types for Thailand is the 'Ratcharit' FAC(M/G) class, whose three units offer a modest but locally useful combination of typical armament, with four MM.38 Exocet missiles backed by a 76mm (3in) OTO Melara Compact gun and a 40mm Bofors gun. The same yard, Fincantieri, was responsible for the larger 'MV 400' class, again of three units. This is a FAC(G) type with two 76mm (3in) OTO Melara Compact guns and two 40mm Bofors in a Breda Compact twin mounting, but has the deck area and electronic sophistication for comparatively straightforward retrofit to FAC(M/G) standard should the Thai navy decide that this would provide additional capability in time of crisis.

The country that paved the way for Fincantieri's type of large fast combat craft was Libya, which made strenuous efforts from the early 1970s to create more substantial armed forces, including not just greater numbers of men but also more advanced weapons with a capability that included offensive operations. So far as the Libyan navy was concerned, this effort meant a considerable development programme that centred largely on fast combat craft. Initially these were comparatively simple vessels suited to the service's current lack of technical sophistication, but longer-term plans called for developing technical expertise to be matched by more advanced craft offering a multi-role capability in extended-range operations.

Libya had already begun to develop an offshore capability with a simple gun-armed corvette delivered by Vosper in 1966, and by 1974 the Libyan navy felt itself capable of handling superior types. The result was an order for four fast combat craft of the 'Wadi' class, renamed the 'Assad' class in 1981. In this type, the Italian design team produced a multi-capable vessel that was in effect a light corvette capable of accepting a number of weapon and sensor options. The variant ordered by the Libyans has little more than FAC(M/G) armament, but the larger hull offers better habitability together with an attractive combination of greater range and improved sea-keeping, even though speed is reduced by comparison with FACs using a comparable four-shaft propulsion arrangement. Notable features of the basic design are thus a fifteen-day endurance, full NBC protection, and a multi-role armament that includes four single container-launchers for Otomat Mk 1 missiles, one 76mm (3in) OTO Melara Compact gun, two 35mm Oerlikon-Bührle cannon in a twin mounting, two triple 324mm (12.75in) tubes for lightweight anti-submarine torpedoes, and provision for sixteen mines. Libya was well pleased with the craft, which could double as a multi-role combat type in its own right or serve as a fast combat craft flotilla leader, and in May 1980 ordered four more of the class. Before work could begin, however, Libya had fallen under an international cloud for its sponsorship of international terrorism and the order was embargoed.

In the early 1980s the Iraqi navy ordered six of a similar type in two sub-variants. The first two units to be delivered comprise one of these distinct sub-variants and have an armament comparable with that of the Libyan vessels, although the secondary gun armament is two 40mm Bofors in a Breda Compact twin mounting. The main difference between the Libyan craft and these two Iraqi units, however, is the helicopter capability of the latter, in the form of a telescopic hangar accommodating an Agusta (Bell) AB.212ASV/ASW helicopter. This is a sophisticated machine that can be used in the anti-ship and anti-submarine roles, and its operating platform is revealed by the forward retraction of the hangar. The four other units lack the helicopter capability, and were thus completed with heavier armament in the form of two additional container-launchers for Otomat anti-ship missiles (giving a total of six) and an Albatros quadruple launcher for Aspide surface-to-air missiles.

Between these two types for Arab customers, the Italian team had produced an upgraded version for Ecuador, which needed a small but powerful fast combat craft type as the spearhead of its surface warfare capability. The resulting 'Esmeraldas' class, of which six were delivered, can be regarded as a derivative of the Libyan design with features of the Iraqi class and a more powerful version of the same four-shaft propulsion arrangement. Each of the Ecuadorean craft therefore has one 76mm (3in) OTO Melara Compact gun and two 40mm Bofors guns in a Breda Compact twin mounting (the latter controlled by the radar-directed Dardo system), two triple container-launchers for six long-range MM.40 Exocet missiles, one Albatros launcher for Aspide surface-to-air missiles, two triple 324mm (12.75in) tubes for lightweight anti-submarine torpedoes, and a platform allowing a Bell Model 206B helicopter to be embarked. These weapons are used with an advanced electronics system to turn each member of the class into what is in effect a multi-role corvette or perhaps even a light frigate.

The latest type from an Italian yard is *Saettia*, the prototype for a versatile FAC that could secure very useful orders.

As noted previously, Italy went into the concept of hydrofoil-fitted fast combat craft with the USA, which has only toyed with the concept of fast combat craft since the end of the Second World War. In the period immediately after this war, most of the wartime PT boats disappeared from American service. Most were scrapped, but some were transferred to America's allies. In the early 1950s the US Navy again turned slight interest towards the type, commissioning *PT 809* to *PT 812* as a four-strong class of 105ft (32m) experimental craft, each powered by four petrol engines and armed with two 40mm Bofors guns as well as four 20mm cannon. By 1962 two of the type had been deleted, and the two survivors had been reclassified in the fast patrol boat (PTF) category. The US Navy classified fourteen Norwegian-delivered 'Nasty'-class craft in the same category, but half of these had been

deleted by 1975. By this time Trumpy of Annapolis had delivered six examples of an improved 'Nasty' design, and Sewart had produced four examples of the 'Osprey' class of 112-ton fast patrol boats. These latter were each capable of 40kt on a two-shaft propulsion arrangment based on two 3,100hp (2,310kW) Napier Deltic diesels, and their armament was one 40mm Bofors gun, one 81mm (3.2in) mortar and one 0.5in (12.7mm) machine-gun on a combined mounting, and two 20mm cannon in single mountings. There were also a few survivors from the large inshore and riverine patrol craft which the US Navy had ordered for service in the Vietnam War.

In the fifteen years after the Second World War the USA had produced or funded for overseas construction a considerable number of motor gunboats (*PGM 33-83*, *PGM 91* and *PGM 102-124*), but these were for Allied rather than American use. In the early 1960s, however, the Cuban missile crisis highlighted the US Navy's lack of fast combat craft for use in confined waters such as the Gulf of Mexico. It was therefore decided to build a 22-strong class of motor gunboats, though the classification was altered to patrol combatant during 1967. The resulting 'Asheville' class was developed for coastal patrol and blockade, but in the event only seventeen of the class were completed between 1966 and 1971 by Tacoma Boatbuilding and Peterson Builders. The type has a CODOG propulsion arrangement for long range at a modest cruising speed and high speed for combat, and the armament is based on a 3in (76mm) gun in an enclosed mounting forward of the bridge and a 40mm Bofors in an open mounting over the stern.

Most of these craft saw extensive patrol service in the Vietnam War, and in the mid-1970s four of them were adapted as FAC(M)s with an armament of four Standard missiles (in its anti-radar form) for service in the Mediterranean as counters to Soviet 'tattletale' vessels. The craft had a very good reputation for seaworthiness, but were decidedly uncomfortable in any sort of sea and suffered propeller cavitation problems which prevented them from attaining their theoretical maximum speed of 40kt or more.

In the late 1950s the US Navy also began to acquire an interest in hydrofoil craft for very high speeds. The first concrete expression of this interest was *High Point*, a three-foil unit commissioned in 1963 as a test-bed for the possible anti-submarine application of hydrofoil concepts. The type has one diesel and two gas turbines powering one and two shafts respectively for hull-borne and foil-borne operation, and is still in service for trials work.

During the mid-1960s the US Navy's emphasis shifted to the FAH(G) application, and this resulted in the design and construction of another two experimental platforms, *Flagstaff* and *Tucumcari*, which were both commissioned in 1968 as competitive prototypes for the US Navy's PHM (missile-armed patrol hydrofoil) requirement. This had been schemed by the US Navy as a replacement for the 'Asheville' class in the latter's anti-'tattletale' role in the Mediterranean. A large-scale programme was established with Italy and Germany, but as costs rose the two European partners dropped out. The US Navy initially remained true to the initial concept, and planned a class of 30 units with a CODOG propulsion arrangement with waterjets for hull-borne and foil-borne operation. Changing requirements then caused the reduction of the total to a mere six, and then the last five were cancelled in 1977, just three months before the commissioning of *Pegasus*. A month late Congress ordered that the other five units be reinstated, and these 'Pegasus'-class FAH(M/G)s were commissioned between 1981 and 1983.

The six craft are each armed with a single 76mm (3in) Mk 75 gun forward of the bridge structure and two quadruple container-launchers for eight RGM-84 Harpoon missiles above the stern. As such, the craft are the US Navy's most potent combatants on the basis of firepower per displacement ton. These vessels can be highly effective in the right conditions, but they lack the range, endurance and versatility of larger warships. The 'Pegasus'-class FAH(M/G)s thus fall outside the main tactical organization of their operating service, which is concerned primarily with deep-water operations. The 'Pegasus' class therefore form a special squadron based on an island off the coast of Florida, where they can undertake surveillance missions in the Caribbean Sea and Gulf of Mexico when not continuing work on the development of fast combat craft tactics and how such tactics may be countered.

Even though the 'Asheville' class failed to find any real favour with the US Navy, Tacoma Boat-building was confident that the basic type had an export potential, especially among East and South-East Asian nations. The company therefore used the 'Asheville' design as the basis of its Patrol Ship Multi-Mission Mk 5 (PSMM Mk 5) type with a two-shaft COGOG propulsion arrangement using no fewer than six gas turbines.

The first customer for the type was South Korea, which operates a large force of fast combat craft against the constant threat of North Korean aggression. The parent company built the first four of the eight craft, the initial three of them reflecting the type's ancestry in a missile armament of four Standard missiles (each carrying a seeker designed to home on the target vessel's radar emissions) and an American 3in (76mm) gun. The last American-built unit switched to the definitive armament of two twin container-launchers for the RGM-84 Harpoon missile and the 76mm (3in) OTO Melara Compact gun, together with a modified electronics suite optimized for the revised armament. Construction of the last four units was undertaken by a South Korean subsidiary, and this has also built four somewhat different 'Dagger'-class FAC(M)s for Indonesia with a CODOG propulsion arrangement and the revised armament of two twin container-launchers for four MM.38 Exocet missiles, one 57mm Bofors gun in a SAK 57 Mk 1 mounting, one 40mm Bofors gun and two 20mm cannon.

Lying between Malaysia and Singapore to the north and Australia to the south, Indonesia faces no real threat of military aggression, but nonetheless maintains moderately strong armed forces. The navy has a nicely balanced mix of warship types and numbers, and includes many fast combat craft that have proved themselves invaluable for patrol among the many thousands of islands that constitute the Indonesian archipelago.

Another customer for the 'PSMM Mk 5' class was Taiwan, the island nation that until recently regarded itself as being at war with the communist regime on the Chinese mainland. Clearly the main Chinese threat to Taiwan's continued independence was a seaborne invasion, and against this threat Taiwan maintains powerful naval defences. For a country of its size, Taiwan maintains a large number of major warships of the destroyer and frigate types. Although these are generally old vessels, many of them dating from or shortly after the Second World War, they have all been kept viable against the Chinese threat by constant updating of their weapons and sensors. These larger warships provide the capability for intercepting an invading force at some distance from Taiwan's shores, but the nation also feels a powerful force of fast combat craft to be essential for the destruction of any elements of the invading force that break though the main offshore defences.

Tacoma Boatbuilding thus produced the first unit of the Taiwanese 'Lung Chiang' class, a type similar to the South Korean vessels with a two-shaft CODOG propulsion arrangement and a barrelled armament of one 76mm (3in) OTO Melara Compact

gun backed by two 30mm Oerlikon-Bührle cannon in an Emerson Electric twin mounting. The missile armament comprises four container-launchers for

▼ The French SFCN PR72 fast patrol boat under construction. P25 serves in the Peruvian navy and the combination of 34kt speed, 76mm and twin 40mm guns and four Exocet missile-launchers makes it a potent weapon for those waters.

the Hsiung Feng I (licence-built version of the Israeli Gabriel) missiles, which are used with an Italian fire-control system. The second unit was licence-built in Taiwan, which planned a large class with the RGM-84 Harpoon missile and an American fire-control system. Under Chinese pressure, the Americans refused to export the Harpoon to Taiwan, which then dropped its plan for a major 'Lung Chiang' class.

The only other operator of the 'PSMM Mk 5' type is Thailand, which has six 'Sattahip'-class craft. These are FAC(G)s, useful mainly for patrol and training with their low-powered propulsion arrangement and comparatively light gun armament.

Peterson Builders also have construction capability for a range of ship types and sizes, and this is reflected in the company's main export success in the field of fast combat craft, the nine units of the 'Al Siddiq' class of FAC(M/G)s for Saudi Arabia. In size these craft are near the upper end of the fast combat craft scale, but have a two-shaft CODOG propulsion arrangement for high gas turbine-engined speed and good diesel-engined range. They were designed specifically for the anti-ship role, and the armament of each unit is thus centred on one 76mm (3in) OTO Melara Compact gun, located on the forecastle forward of the superstructure, and the modest anti-ship missile fit of two twin container-launchers for RGM-84 Harpoons, located near the stern. Aft of the missile installation is the Phalanx close-in weapon system mounting, whose 20mm six-barrel rotary cannon has excellent fields of fire for its primary task of destroying incoming anti-ship missiles.

By far the world's largest operator of fast combat craft is China, whose navy has been confined almost exclusively to the coast defence role until very recent times, when deeper strategic thinking and the possibility of natural resources in the South China Sea combined to persuade the Chinese to begin development of a technologically more advanced navy possessing offshore capability.

China has a long coastline whose many good harbours are supplemented by even larger numbers of well positioned smaller harbours. With no real naval threat but the posturing and nuisance raids of Taiwan to fear, China rightly decided that the best way to ensure coastal security, and at the same time build the nucleus of a strong navy, lay in the creation of a large force of fast combat craft that could become technologically more sophisticated as Chinese industry and service personnel evolved the necessary skills. The core of this operational philosophy evolved in the very early 1950s, when the Chinese navy used armed examples of local craft.

On this basis, and with considerable technical and material assistance from the USSR, the Chinese began to develop a more advanced fast combat craft capability towards the middle of the 1950s. Precise details are still lacking, but it seems that from 1952 more than 70 'P 4'-class MTBs were transferred from the USSR to China. It is probable that a comparatively small number of improved 'P 6'-class MTBs were transferred at a slightly later date, and that these were used as pattern craft for Chinese construction of about 80 boats. This experience allowed the Chinese to begin development of their own types, starting with the 'Huchuan' FAH(T), which entered production in 1966 as the world's first foil-equipped naval vessel. Despite the fact that the type was only of the semi-foil variety, with the forward part of the hull lifted by the foil and the rear part planing, the design was clearly successful in meeting Chinese expectations, and production totalled just under 200 units.

Like the Soviets, however, the Chinese had by now seen the virtue of combining torpedo- and missile-armed FACs for the type of two-handed punch that could knock an enemy force off balance and inflict severe losses. In the early 1960s the Chinese navy had received from the USSR some seven or eight 'Komar'-class FAC(M)s, and from this simple type the Chinese evolved the 'Hegu' design with a steel rather than wooden hull of slightly modified form and the position of the missile container-launchers moved slightly inboard, compared with the Soviet original. In their time these were limited but effective FAC(M)s, but the Chinese have maintained the type in service long past the date when simple electronic counter-measures have made it easy for any modestly sophisticated navy to defeat the missile carried by the 'Hegu'-class craft.

As in the pattern established earlier with the MTBs, the Soviets followed deliveries of the 'Komar'-class craft with some four examples for China of the two improved 'Osa I'-class (in this instance with four 30mm rather than 25mm cannon in two twin mountings), as well as the technical information that allowed the Chinese to build this type as the 'Huangfen' class. The Chinese-built craft differ in detail from the Soviet original, and for an unexplained reason the class is credited with a maximum speed of 41kt compared with the Soviet type's 35kt. The 'Huangfen' class is still the backbone of the Chinese fast combat craft force but, as with the 'Hegu' class operating the same missile, its combat capability has been virtually removed in recent years by the widespread adoption of electronic counter-measures in potentially hostile navies. This fact has been recognized by China, which is now retrofitting a more modern type of anti-ship missile, which has the additional advantages of smaller size and reduced weight so that a greater number of missiles can be installed.

In recent years the Chinese have made considerable but largely unsuccessful attempts to upgrade their fast combat craft capability, often with the aid of Western companies. Older missiles have been supplemented and largely replaced by more modern weapons, but the Chinese government's suppression of the emergent democracy movement led to the effective halt on all programmes of Western technical support for types such as the 'H3' class. China's torpedo- and missile-armed fast combat craft classes are backed by large numbers of FAC(G)s, such as the units of the 'Hainan' and 'Shanghai' classes. These are generally of elderly concept, and as such are better suited to the coastal patrol task than to a more aggressive offensive or defensive role.

Aligned with China on the same side of the political fence is North Korea, a sternly orthodox communist state that remains implacably opposed to the separate existence of a non-communist South Korea. North Korea maintains a large army and a substantial air force, both of them well equipped in overall terms. The navy is not as large even in relative terms, and is certainly not as well equipped. The main task of the North Korean Navy is coastal defence against the assumed threat of South Korean invasion, and for this task the service numbers a few warships and conventional submarines, but more importantly a sizeable number of fast combat craft. These are mostly ex-Soviet and ex-Chinese types, but North Korea has also produced a few indigenous classes of indifferent quality.

It is evident, therefore, that in many parts of the world the concept of fast combat craft is alive and flourishing. Many emerging countries find such craft an ideal way to begin development of their navies, with larger and more sophisticated vessels being bought to match their developing skills and increased operational ambitions. Many less affluent countries have discovered that such craft are a cost-effective means of maintaining a national presence in territorial waters and offshore zones of potentially great commercial importance. But in general the countries that make the greatest and potentially most effective use of fast combat craft are those with confined coastal waters or chokepoints where major maritime routes are constricted by geographical factors. It is therefore no accident that areas where concentrations of fast combat craft are to be found include the Baltic Sea and its exit into the North Sea; the Mediterranean (especially at its western end near the Strait of Gibraltar, its centre near the Sicilian Narrows, its north offshoot in the Adriatic Sea, its north-eastern corner in the Aegean Sea, and its eastern end where Israel and several Arab nations vie with each other); the Persian Gulf; South-East Asia, where there are several chokepoints such as the Malacca Strait; the eastern coast of Asia; and various parts of South America where limited finance and confined waters combine with nationalistic and economic rivalries.

At the technical level, fast combat craft have grown considerably in size since the end of the Second World War, with MTBs of about 100 tons giving way gradually to larger FACs with displacements now approaching 500 tons in 'ordinary' craft and reaching 600 tons in the largest FACs which have virtual corvette capability. This increase in size and displacement has been parelleled and indeed driven by the desire of operator navies for heavier and more versatile armament, matched by more comprehensive electronics. The armament has developed from a simple fit optimized for anti-ship operations with two or four torpedoes, backed by a 40mm gun, 20mm cannon and machine-guns for secondary offensive and primary defensive purposes, to a genuinely multi-role fit that can now include two or even three calibres of gun for offensive and defensive use, offensive anti-ship missiles and in some cases defensive lightweight surface-to-air missiles, and torpedoes of the heavyweight type for anti-ship use or of the lightweight type for anti-submarine use. The electronics have burgeoned along similar lines, with simple surface search radar and optical sights giving way to a steadily more impressive suite that can now include: air/surface search radar, separate fire-control systems for each weapon type and based on their own radar, optronic, optical and/or acoustic sensors, an action information system to integrate the offensive and defensive capabilities of the vessel, a data-link for the real-time transmission and/or receipt of data to and/or from other vessels and shore stations, together with defensive electronics that include an intercept element to warn of enemy radars and control electronic jammers or physical counter-measures such as 'chaff' and flares.

The future continues to look good for fast combat craft. There are currently a number of experimental types of the surface-effect type, but it remains to be seen whether these will pave the way for a whole new type of fast combat craft or supplement the hydrofoil type for particular applications. The standard type remains the surest bet, for developments in various hydrodynamic, propulsion, weapon, sensor and data-processing technologies continue to offer new possibilities and capabilities.

The immediate future is perhaps epitomized by the 'La Combattante IV' class proposed by Constructions Méchaniques de Normandie as a successor to its older types. This is planned as a steel-hulled vessel with a full-load displacement of 565 tons on a hull that measures 62.0m (203ft 5in) in length and 9.1m (29ft 10in) beam. The propulsion arrangement will be of the four-shaft type powered by four 3,950kW (5,300hp) diesels for a maximum speed of 37kt and a range of 2,800km (1,740 miles) at 25kt. The type is being planned in alternative anti-ship and anti-submarine models with role-optimized sensors and electronics. The anti-ship model will have two quadruple container-launchers for eight MM.40 Exocet anti-ship missiles as its primary armament, and other weapons will include a 57mm Bofors gun in a SAK 57 Mk 2 mounting on the forecastle, a Crotale Naval surface-to-air missile system over the stern with an eight-round RAPAC launcher for VT-1 missiles and an associated multi-sensor director, and a Mistral point-defence system amidships with a six-round Tarantale turret for short-range surface-to-air missiles. The anti-submarine model will have towed-array sonar, and its weapons will include one 57mm Bofors gun in a SAK 57 Mk 2 mounting, one 40mm Bofors gun, two six-round SADRAL launchers for Mistral short-range surface-to-air missiles, and two triple 324mm (12.75in) tubes for lightweight anti-submarine torpedoes such as the Murene, a new and very advanced French weapon.

▼In smaller navies, FACs can be supported or commanded by frigates such as the *Almirante*

Padilla, one of the Colombian navy's four 'Type FS 1500' class vessels.

PART TWO

Technical Directory of Fast Combat Craft

'AB' class   Turkey

Type: fast attack craft (gun)
Displacement: ? tons standard; 170 tons full load
Dimensions: length 40.2m (132.0ft); beam 6.4m (21.0ft);
    draught 1.7m (5.5ft)
Gun armament: 1 or 2 × 40mm Bofors L/70 AA in single
    mountings; 1 × 20mm Oerlikon L/75 AA in an A41A
    single mounting (in craft with 1 × 40mm gun); 2 × 0.5in
    (12.7mm) machine-guns in single mountings
Missile armament: none
Torpedo armament: none
Anti-submarine armament: 1 × Mk 20 Mousetrap four-
    tube rocket-launcher; 1 × depth-charge rack for ? ×
    depth-charges
Electronics: 1 × surface search and navigation radar; 1 ×
    hull-mounted search and attack sonar
Propulsion: 4 × SACM-AGO V16 CSHR diesels
    delivering 3,600kW (4,830hp) and 2 × cruising diesels
    delivering 220kW (295hp), in each case to two shafts
Performance: maximum speed 22kt; range ? km (? miles)
    at ? kt
Complement: ?

1. Turkey

Name	Pennant No	Builder	Commissioned
AB 25	P1225	Taskizak Naval Yard	
AB 26	P1226	Taskizak Naval Yard	
AB 27	P1227	Taskizak Naval Yard	
AB 28	P1228	Taskizak Naval Yard	
AB 29	P1229	Taskizak Naval Yard	
AB 30	P1230	Taskizak Naval Yard	
AB 31	P1231	Taskizak Naval Yard	
AB 32	P1232	Taskizak Naval Yard	
AB 33	P1233	Taskizak Naval Yard	
AB 34	P1234	Taskizak Naval Yard	
AB 35	P1135	Taskizak Naval Yard	
AB 36	P1236	Taskizak Naval Yard	

Commissioned between 1967 and 1970, these are simple
FAC(G)s optimized for the patrol and coastal anti-
submarine roles. The craft are now obsolete.

'Aliya': see 'Saar 4.5' class

'Al Siddiq' class   USA/Saudi Arabia

Type: fast attack craft (missile and gun)
Displacement: 425 tons standard; 480 tons full load
Dimensions: length 190.5ft (58.1m); beam 26.5ft (8.1m);
    draught 11.0ft (3.4m)
Gun armament: 1 × 76mm (3in) L/62 DP in a Mk 75
    (OTO Melara Compact) single mounting; 1 × 20mm
    six-barrel rotary cannon in a Phalanx Mk 15 CIWS
    mounting; 2 × 20mm Oerlikon L/80 AA in A41A single
    mountings; 2 × 81mm (3.2in) mortars; 2 × 40mm Mk 19
    grenade-launchers
Missile armament: 2 × twin Mk 141 container-launchers
    for 4 × RGM-84 Harpoon anti-ship missiles
Torpedo armament: none
Anti-submarine armament: none
Electronics: 1 × SPS-55 surface search radar; 1 ×
    tracking radar used in conjunction with; 1 × Mk 92/94
    (WM-25/28) gun and SSM fire-control system; 1 × Mk
    24 optical director; 1 × SLQ-32(V)1 ESM system with
    warning element; 2 × Mk 36 Super RBOC six-barrel
    'chaff'/flare-launchers
Propulsion: CODOG arrangement of 1 × General
    Electric LM2500 gas turbine delivering 23,000shp
    (17,150kW) and 2 × MTU 12V 652 TB91 diesels
    delivering 3,000kW (4,025hp) to two shafts
Performance: maximum speed 38kt on gas turbine or
    15.5kt on diesels; range 3,350 miles (5,390km) at 14kt
Complement: 5+33

1. Saudi Arabia

Name	No	Builder	Commissioned
Al Siddiq	511	Peterson Builders	Dec 1980
Al Farouq	513	Peterson Builders	Jun 1981

Name	Pennant No	Builder	Commis- sioned
Abdul Aziz	515	Peterson Builders	Aug 1981
Faisal	517	Peterson Builders	Nov 1981
Kahlid	519	Peterson Builders	Jan 1982
Amyr	521	Peterson Builders	Jun 1982
Tariq	523	Peterson Builders	Aug 1982
Oqbah	525	Peterson Builders	Oct 1982
Abu Obaidah	527	Peterson Builders	Dec 1982

Although comparatively large, these craft are confined in offensive terms to anti-ship operations with a powerful missile and gun armament. The CIWS mounting provides a useful defensive capability against anti-ship missiles. The nine craft of this class were ordered in February 1977 to the American PGG-type design, and they are essentially scaled-down versions of the 'Badr'-class corvettes (American PCG type) with the same machinery and a reduced complement of the same basic armament fit but without anti-submarine armament. The craft are named after members of the Saudi royal family.

'Al Wafi' class: *see* 'Brooke Marine 37.5m' class

'Assad' class
Italy/Libya

Type: fast attack craft (missile, gun and torpedo)
Displacement: 630 tons standard; 670 tons full load
Dimensions: length 61.7m (202.4ft); beam 9.3m (30.5ft); draught 2.2m (7.6ft)
Gun armament: 1 × 76mm (3in) L/62 DP in an OTO Melara Compact single mounting; 2 × 35mm Oerlikon L/90 AA in an OE/OTO twin mounting
Missile armament: 4 × container-launchers for 4 × Otomat anti-ship missiles
Torpedo armament: none
Anti-submarine armament: 2 × ILAS 3 triple 324mm (12.75in) mountings for ? × A 244 torpedoes
Mines: up to 16
Electronics: 1 × RAN 11L/X air/surface search radar; 1 × TM1226C navigation radar; 1 × RTN 10X radar used in conjunction with; 1 × Argo NA10/2 gun fire-control system; 1 × Elsag Nettuno optronic director; 1 × Diodon active search and attack hull sonar; 1 × IPN 10 action information system; 1 × Selenia INS 1 ESM system with warning element
Propulsion: 4 × MTU 16V 956 TB91 diesels delivering 13,400kW (17,970hp) to four shafts
Performance: maximum speed 34kt; range 8,150km (5,065 miles) at 14kt
Complement: 8+50

1. Iraq

Name	No	Builder	Commis- sioned
Mussa Ben Hussair*	F210	CNR, Muggiano	Sep 1986
Tariq Ibn Zyiad*	F212	CNR, Muggiano	Oct 1986
Abdullah Ben Abi Sarh	F214	CNR, Breda, Mestre	1987
Khalid Ibn al Walid	F216	CNR, Breda, Mestre	1987
Saad Ibn Abi Waccade	F218	CNR, Breda, Marghera	1988
Salah al Din al Ayuri	F215	CNR, Breda, Marghera	1988

*Equipped to carry a helicopter

The Iraqi vessels are similar to the Libyan units, but have a full-load displacement of 675 tons, an overall length of 62.3m (204.4ft), a secondary armament of 2 × 40mm Bofors L/70 guns in a Breda twin mounting (not in the helicopter-carrying units), and a missile armament of 6 × Teseo 2 container-launchers for 6 × Otomat Mk 2 anti-ship missiles (only two in each of the helicopter-carrying units) and 1 × Albatros Mk 2 quadruple launcher for 16 × Aspide SAMs. Two of the ships are fitted to carry an Agusta (Bell) AB.212ASW helicopter in a telescopic hangar aft. The electronic fit includes 1 × RAN 12L/X air/surface search radar, 1 × 3RM 20 navigation radar, 1 × Elsag NA18 optronic director, 1 × Gamma ESM system and 2 × SCLAR 'chaff'/flare-launchers. A propulsion arrangement of 4 × MTU 20V 956 TB92 diesels provides 18,000kW (24,140hp) for a speed of 38kt. The basic complement is 8+41.

2. Libya

Name	No	Builder	Commis- sioned
Assad el Tadjer	412	CNR, Muggiano	Sep 1979
Assad el Touggour	413	CNR, Muggiano	Feb 1980
Assad al Khali	414	CNR, Muggiano	Mar 1981
Assad al Hudud	415	CNR, Muggiano	Mar 1981

These are highly capable light combat craft with potent anti-ship and useful anti-submarine capability.

'Azteca' class
UK/Mexico

Type: fast attack craft (gun)
Displacement: 130 tons standard; 165 tons full load
Dimensions: length 111.8ft (34.1m); beam 28.1ft (8.6m); draught 6.8ft (2.0m)
Gun armament: 1 × 40mm Bofors L/70 AA in a single mounting; 1 × 20mm Oerlikon L/75 AA in an A41A single mounting
Missile armament: none
Torpedo armament: none
Anti-submarine armament: none
Electronics: 1 × surface search and navigation radar

Propulsion: 2 × Ruston-Paxman Ventura diesels
delivering 7,200hp (5,370kW) to two shafts
Performance: maximum speed 24kt; range 2,875 miles
(4,625km) at 12kt
Complement: 2+22

1. Mexico

Name	No	Builder	Commis-sioned
Andres Qintanao Roo	P01	Ailsa Shipbuilding	Nov 1974
Matias de Cordova	P02	Scott & Sons	Oct 1974
Miguel Ramos Arizpe	P03	Ailsa Shipbuilding	Dec 1974
Jose Maria Izazaga	P04	Ailsa Shipbuilding	Dec 1974
Juan Bautista Morales	P05	Scott & Sons	Dec 1974
Ignacio Lopez Rayon	P06	Ailsa Shipbuilding	Dec 1974
Manuel Crescencio Rejon	P07	Ailsa Shipbuilding	Jul 1975
Juan Antonio de la Fuente	P08	Ailsa Shipbuilding	Jul 1975
Leon Gusman	P09	Scott & Sons	Apr 1975
Ignacio Ramirez	P10	Ailsa Shipbuilding	Jul 1975
Ignacio Mariscal	P11	Ailsa Shipbuilding	Sep 1975
Heriberto Jara Corona	P12	Ailsa Shipbuilding	Nov 1975

Name	Pennant No	Builder	Commis-sioned
Jose Maria Mata	P13	J. Lamont & Co	Oct 1975
Felix Romero	P14	Scott & Sons	Jun 1975
Fernando M. Lizardi	P15	Ailsa Shipbuilding	Dec 1975
Francisco J. Mujica	P16	Ailsa Shipbuilding	Nov 1975
Pastor Rouaix	P17	Scott & Sons	Nov 1975
Jose Maria del Castillo Velasco	P18	J. Lamont & Co	Jan 1975
Luis Manuel Rojas	P19	J. Lamont & Co	Apr 1976
Jose Natividad Macias	P20	J. Lamont & Co	Sep 1976
Esteban Baca Calderon	P21	J. Lamont & Co	Jun 1976
General Ignacio Zaragoza	P22	Veracruz	Jun 1976
Tamaulipas	P23	Veracruz	1979
Yucatan	P24	Veracruz	1979
Tabasco	P25	Salinacruz	Jan 1979
Veracruz	P26	Veracruz	Jan 1979
Campeche	P27	Veracruz	1980
Puebla	P28	Salinacruz	1982

▼P-04, *Jose Maria Izazgu*, an 'Azteca'-class large patrol craft of the Mexican navy.

Name	Pennant No	Builder	Commissioned
Margarita Maza de Juarez	P29	Veracruz	1980
Leona Vicario	P30	Veracruz	1980
Josefa Ortiz de Dominguez	P31	Salinacruz	1980

Ordered in March 1973 from Associated British Machine Tool Makers, this type was designed by T.T. Boat Designs. The craft are simple FAC(G)s used for the patrol role, and the first 21 were modernized from 1987 with refurbished engines and an air-conditioning system.

'Balcom 10' class   Germany

Type: fast attack craft (missile and gun)
Displacement: ? tons standard; about 500 tons full load
Dimensions: length 52.0m (170.6ft); beam 9.5m (31.2ft); draught 2.2m (7.2ft)
Gun armament: 1 × 76mm (3in) L/60 DP in a single mounting; 1 × 30mm six-barrel rotary cannon in an ADGM-630 CIWS mounting
Missile armament: 2 × quadruple container-launchers for 8 × SS-N-X anti-ship missiles
Torpedo armament: none
Anti-submarine armament: none
Electronics: 1 × 'Plank Shave' air/surface search radar; 1 × navigation radar; 1 × 'Bass Tilt' gun fire-control radar; 1 × ESM system with warning element; 2 × 'chaff'-launchers; 1 × 'Square Head-A' IFF system; 1 × 'Salt Pot' IFF system
Propulsion: 4 × diesels delivering ? kW (? hp) to four shafts
Performance: maximum speed 38kt; range ? km (? miles) at ? kt
Complement: 45

1. Germany (East)

Name	No	Builder	Commissioned
	91		1989

This new class of FAC(M) is being produced as a replacement for the 'Osa I'-class craft operated by Germany (East), and a total of at least twelve are expected. The type appears to be a development of the 'Tarantul'-class hull with diesel propulsion. The missile is a new type as yet undesignated in the West, and resembles the French Exocet to judge by the external appearance of the container-launchers.

'Barcelo' class: *see* 'Lürssen FPB-36'

'BES-50' class   Spain

Type: fast attack surface-effect craft (missile)
Displacement: ? tons standard; 350 tons full load
Dimensions: length 55.0m (180.4ft); beam 14.5m (47.6ft); draught ? m (? ft)
Gun armament: 2 × 40mm Bofors L/70 AA in a Breda Compact twin mounting
Missile armament: 2 × quadruple Mk 141 container-launchers for 8 × RGM-84 Harpoon anti-ship missiles
Torpedo armament: none
Anti-submarine armament: helicopter-launched weapons (see below)
Aircraft: 1 × Sikorsky S-70L Seahawk helicopter
Electronics: 1 × surface search and navigation radar; 2 × 'chaff'/flare-launchers; other systems
Propulsion: 2 × diesels delivering ? kW (? hp) to two waterjets for propulsion and 2 × diesels delivering ? kW (? hp) to ? fans for lift
Peformance: maximum speed 35kt+; range ? km (? miles) at ?kt
Complement: ?

1. Spain

Name	No	Builder	Commissioned
		Bazan	

Little has been revealed about this interesting type, which should enter service in the mid-1990s and point the possible way for future missile-armed attack craft.

'Bogomol' class   USSR

Type: fast attack craft (gun)
Displacement: ? tons standard; 245 tons full load
Dimensions: length 39.0m (128.0ft); beam 7.8m (25.6ft); draught 1.8m (5.9ft)
Gun armament: 1 × 76mm (3in) L/60 DP in a single mounting; 2 × 30mm L/65 AA in a twin mounting
Missile armament: none
Torpedo armament: none
Anti-submarine armament: none
Electronics: 1 × surface search and navigation radar; 1 × 'Bass Tilt' gun fire-control radar
Propulsion: 3 × M 504 diesels delivering 11,250kW (15,090hp) to three shafts
Performance: maximum speed 37kt; range 925km (575 miles) at 35kt
Complement: 30

1. Guinea-Bissau (1 craft)
This is the first unit of a new Soviet FAC(G) class built in the Pacific region specifically for the export market. The type is based on the hull and propulsion arrangement of the 'Osa' class, and this unit was delivered in 1988.

'Brooke Marine 32.6m' class   UK/Kenya

Type: fast attack craft (missile)
Displacement: 120 tons standard; 145 tons full load
Dimensions: length 107.0ft (32.6m); beam 20.0ft (6.1m);
    draught 5.6ft (1.7m)
Gun armament: 2 × 30mm Oerlikon L/85 AA in a GCM-
    A03 twin mounting
Missile armament: 4 × single container-launchers for 4 ×
    Gabriel II anti-ship missiles
Torpedo armament: none
Anti-submarine armament: none
Electronics: 1 × AC1226 surface search and navigation
    radar; 1 × RTN 10X tracking radar used with; 1 × Argo
    NA10 fire-control system; 1 × optronic director
Propulsion: 2 × Paxman Valenta diesels delivering
    5,400hp (4,025kW) to two shafts
Performance: maximum speed 25.5kt; range 2,875 miles
    (4,625km) at 12kt
Complement: 3+18

1. Kenya

Name	No	Builder	Commis-sioned
Madaraka	P3121	Brooke Marine	Jun 1975
Jamhuri	P3122	Brooke Marine	Jun 1975
Harambe	P3123	Brooke Marine	Aug 1975

Ordered in May 1973 as patrol craft, these vessels were converted to FAC(M)s in 1981, 1983 and 1982 respectively by the addition of Israeli anti-ship missiles and, in a further upgrade of their capabilities, new guns and an optronic director.

2. Nigeria

Name	No	Builder	Commis-sioned
Makurdi	P167	Brooke Marine	Aug 1974
Hadejia	P168	Brooke Marine	Aug 1974
Jebba	P171	Brooke Marine	Apr 1977
Oguta	P172	Brooke Marine	Apr 1977

The first two craft of this FAC(G) class were ordered in 1971 and the second pair followed in 1973. With standard and full-load displacements of 115 and 143 tons respectively, these vessels have a propulsion arrangement of 2 × Paxman Ventura YCJM diesels delivering 3,000hp (2,235kW) to two shafts for a maximum speed of 20.5kt. The armament originally comprised two 40mm Bofors L/60 AA in Mk 9 single mountings, but was revised in 1981 by Brooke Marine (first pair) and in Nigeria (second pair). The armament now comprises 4 × 30mm Oerlikon

▼NSS *Hadejia*, a Brooke Marine '32.6m'-class fast patrol craft serving with the Nigerian navy.

▲ *Mamba* (P3100) is a 'Brooke Marine 37.5m'- class boat of the Kenyan navy.

▼SNV *Al Mansur*, another 'Brooke Marine 37.5m'- class boat, serves with the Oman navy.

L/85 AA in 2 × EMERLEC-30 twin mountings, and the electronic suite includes TM1226 surface search and navigation radar. The complement is 4+17, and the four craft are used in the patrol role.

'Brooke Marine 37.5m' class   UK/Algeria

Type: fast attack craft (gun)
Displacement: 166 tons standard; 200 tons full load
Dimensions: length 123.0ft (37.5m); beam 22.6ft (6.9m); draught 6.0ft (2.2m)
Gun armament: 1 × 76mm (3in) L/62 DP in an OTO Melara Compact single mounting; 2 × 23mm L/87 AA in a twin mounting
Missile armament: none
Torpedo armament: none
Anti-submarine armament: none
Electronics: 1 × TM1226 surface search and navigation radar
Propulsion: 2 × MTU 12V 538 TB92 diesels delivering 4,500kW (6,035hp) to two shafts
Performance: maximum speed 27kt; range 3,800 miles (6,115km) at 12kt
Complement: 3+24

1. Algeria ('Kebir' class)

Name	No	Builder	Commis-sioned
El Yadekh	341	Brooke Marine	1982
El Mourakeb	342	Brooke Marine	1983
	343	ONCN/CNB, Mers-el-Kebir	1988
	344	ONCN/CNB, Mers-el-Kebir	1985
	345	ONCN/CNB, Mers-el-Kebir	1985
	346	ONCN/CNB, Mers-el-Kebir	Nov 1985
	347	ONCN/CNB, Mers-el-Kebir	1988
	348	ONCN/CNB, Mers-el-Kebir	1988
	349	ONCN/CNB, Mers-el-Kebir	1988

The design and the first pair of craft were ordered from the British firm in June 1981. The design is based on the standard 'Brooke 37.5m' hull, but these Algerian craft have been completed as FAC(G)s with a gun armament consisting of 1 × 76mm (3in) L/62 DP forward and 1 × 20mm Oerlikon AA aft, or in some craft 2 × 30mm L/65 AA in a twin mounting forward. The first two units were built in Britain and fitted with their armament in Algeria, while the other units were assembled and/or built at Mers-el-Kebir as the first locally built Algerian warships.

Another three units may have been ordered in the late 1980s.

2. Barbados

Name	No	Builder	Commis-sioned
Trident	P01	Brooke Marine	1982

This FAC(P) is similar to the Omani units but with standard and full-load displacements of 155.5 and 190 tons respectively. The armament comprises 1 × 40mm Bofors L/70 AA gun in a Bofors single mounting and 1 × 20mm Oerlikon L/75 AA gun in an A41A single mounting, and the 6,000hp (4,475kW) provided by 2 × Paxman Valenta 12RP-200 diesels allows a maximum speed of 29kt and a range of 3,500 miles (5,630km) at 12kt. The complement is 27.

3. Kenya

Name	No	Builder	Commis-sioned
Mamba	P3100	Brooke Marine	Feb 1974

Ordered in 1971 as a FAC(G) with a primary armament of 2 × 40mm Bofors L/70 AA in single mountings, this single unit was modernized from 1982 as a FAC(M) with missiles, revised gun armament and sensors that include an optronic director. The current standard is based on standard and full-load displacements of 125 and 160 tons respectively on dimensions of: length 123.0ft (37.5m), beam 22.5ft (6.9m) and draught 5.2ft (1.6m). The missile armament comprises 4 × single container-launchers for 4 × Gabriel II anti-ship missiles, and the other weapons consist of 2 × 30mm Oerlikon L/85 AA in a GCM-A02 twin mounting. The electronics fit includes 1 × AC1226 surface search and navigation radar, 1 × RTN 10X tracking radar used in conjunction with an Argo fire-control system, and 1 × optronic director. The propulsion arrangement comprises Ruston-Paxman Ventura 16YJCM diesels delivering 4,000hp (2,980kW) to two shafts for a maximum speed of 25kt and a range of 3,800 miles (6,115km) at 13kt. The complement is 3+22.

4. Oman ('Al Wafi' class)

Name	No	Builder	Commis-sioned
Al Wafi	B4	Brooke Marine	Mar 1977
Al Fulk	B5	Brooke Marine	Mar 1977
Al Mujahid	B6	Brooke Marine	Jul 1977
Al Jabbar	B7	Brooke Marine	Oct 1977

Ordered in April 1974, the 'Al Wafi' class is a variant of the now-deleted 'Al Mansur' class of three FAC(M)s which had been ordered in January 1971 as FAC(G)s with an armament of two 40mm Bofors L/70 AA in single mountings. The current craft are optimized for the FAC(M/G) role with standard and full-load displacements of 135 and 153 tons and dimensions of: length 123.0ft (37.5m), beam 22.5ft (6.9m) and draught 6.0ft (2.2m). The armament comprises 1 × 76mm (3in) L/62 DP in an OTO Melara Compact single mounting (130 rounds) and 1 × 20mm Oerlikon L/75 AA in an A41A single mounting, the main weapon being used in conjunction with 1 × Decca 1226 surface search radar, 1 × Decca 1229 navigation radar, 1 × Sea Archer fire-control system and 1 × Laurence Scott optical director. Propulsion is provided by 2 × Paxman Ventura 16RP-200 diesels delivering 4,800hp (3,580kW) for a maximum speed of 25kt and a range of 3,800 miles (6,115km) at 15kt. The complement is 3+24.

'Brooke Marine 41.8m' class   UK/Australia

Type: fast attack craft (gun)
Displacement: 211 tons standard; ? tons full load
Dimensions: length 137.1ft (41.8m); beam 23.3ft (7.1m); draught 5.9ft (1.8m)
Gun armament: 1 × 40mm Bofors L/60 AA in an AN 4 single mounting; 1 × 81mm (3.2in) mortar in a single mounting; 2 × 0.5in (12.7mm) machine-guns in single mountings
Missile armament: none
Torpedo armament: none
Anti-submarine armament: none
Electronics: 1 × Kelvin Hughes Type 1006 surface search and navigation radar
Propulsion: 2 × MTU 16V 538 TB91 diesels delivering 4,500kW (6,035hp) to three shafts and 1 × Dorman diesel delivering ? hp (? kW) to the central shaft for cruising
Performance: maximum speed 30kt on main engines; 8kt on cruising diesel; range 5,525 miles (8,890km) at 8kt or 1,670 miles (2,695km) at 30kt
Complement: 3+19

1. Australia ('Fremantle' class)

Name	No	Builder	Commis-sioned
Fremantle	203	Brooke Marine	Mar 1980
Warrnambool	204	North Queensland	Mar 1981
Townsville	205	North Queensland	Jul 1981
Wollongong	206	North Queensland	Nov 1981
Launceston	207	North Queensland	Mar 1982
Whyalla	208	North Queensland	Jul 1982
Ipswich	209	North Queensland	Nov 1982
Cessnock	210	North Queensland	Mar 1983
Bendigo	211	North Queensland	May 1983

Name	Pennant No	Builder	Commis-sioned
Gawler	212	North Queensland	Aug 1983
Geraldton	213	North Queensland	Dec 1983
Dubbo	214	North Queensland	Mar 1984
Geelong	215	North Queensland	Jun 1984
Gladstone	216	North Queensland	Sep 1984
Bunbury	217	North Queensland	Dec 1984

Ordered in September 1977, these are simple craft used almost exclusively for patrol.

'Bulgarian' class   Algeria

Type: fast attack craft (gun)
Displacement: 600 tons standard; ? tons full load
Dimensions: length 59.3m (194.6ft); beam 8.5m (27.9ft); draught 2.6m (8.5ft)
Gun armament: 1 × 76mm (3in) L/62 DP in an OTO Melara Compact single mounting; 2 × 40mm Bofors L/70 AA in a Breda Compact twin mounting
Missile armament: none
Torpedo armament: none
Anti-submarine armament: none
Aircraft: none
Electronics: not revealed
Propulsion: 3 × MTU 20V 538 diesels delivering 11,175kW (14,990hp) to three shafts
Performance: maximum speed 36kt; range not revealed
Complement: not revealed

1. Algeria

Name	No	Builder	Commis-sioned
		Mers-el-Kebir	1988

This simple corvette was built with Bulgarian assistance and the dimensional data suggest that it is a narrow-beam derivative of the 'Nanuchka' class. It is thought that another two units will be built.

'Cacine' class   Portugal

Type: fast attack craft (gun)
Displacement: 292 tons standard; 310 tons full load
Dimensions: length 44.0m (144.35ft); beam 7.7m (26.25ft); draught 2.2m (7.2ft)
Gun armament: 1 or 2 × 40mm Bofors L/70 AA in single mountings; 1 × 20mm Oerlikon L/75 AA in an A41A single mounting; 1 × 37mm rocket-launcher with 32 barrels in a single mounting
Missile armament: none
Torpedo armament: none
Anti-submarine armament: none

Electronics: 1 × Kelvin Hughes Type 975 surface search and navigation radar
Propulsion: 2 × MTU 12V 538 diesels delivering 3,000kW (4,025hp) to two shafts
Performance: maximum speed 20kt; range 8,150km (5,065 miles) at 12kt
Complement: 3+30

1. Portugal

Name	No	Builder	Commissioned
Cacine	P1140	Arsenal do Alfeite	1969
Cunene	P1141	Arsenal do Alfeite	1969
Mandovi	P1142	Arsenal do Alfeite	1969
Rovuma	P1143	Arsenal do Alfeite	1969
Cuanza	P1144	Estaleiros Navais do Mondego	May 1969
Geba	P1145	Estaleiros Navais do Mondego	May 1970
Zaire	P1146	Estaleiros Navais do Mondego	Nov 1970
Zambeze	P1147	Estaleiros Navais do Mondego	Jan 1971
Limpopo	P1160	Arsenal do Alfeite	Apr 1973
Save	P1161	Arsenal do Alfeite	May 1973

This is a simple FAC(G) class now used only for coastal patrol and training. The armament is generally 1 × 40mm gun, the after gun of the same calibre having been removed.

'CG40' class   Sweden/Trinidad and Tobago

Type: fast attack craft (gun)
Displacement: ? tons standard; 210 tons full load
Dimensions: length 40.6m (133.2ft); beam 6.7m (22.0ft); draught 1.6m (5.25ft)
Gun armament: 1 × 40mm Bofors L/70 AA in Bofors single mounting; 1 × 20mm Oerlikon L/75 AA in an A41A single mounting
Missile armament: none
Torpedo armament: none
Electronics: 1 × TM 1226 surface search and navigation radar; 1 × optronic director
Propulsion: 2 × Paxman Valenta 16 RP200 diesels delivering 8,000hp (5,965kW) to two shafts
Performance: maximum speed 30kt; range 5,500km (3,420 miles) at 15kt
Complement: 25 with provision for 9 spare men

1. Trinidad and Tobago

Name	No	Builder	Commissioned
Barracuda	CG5	Karlskrona Varvet	June 1980
Cascadura	CG6	Karlskrona Varvet	June 1980

Ordered in August 1978, these are simple FAC(G)s based on the hull of the Swedish 'Spica'-class FAC. The two craft were refitted from 1988, and in addition to their primary patrol role they are used for oceanographic and hydrodynamic research.

'Cha-ho' class   North Korea

Type: fast attack craft (gun)
Displacement: ? tons standard; 82 tons full load
Dimensions: length 26.0m (85.3ft); beam 5.8m (19.0ft); draught 2.0m (6.6ft)
Gun armament: 1 × 122mm (4.82in) BM-21 Grad 40-barrel rocket-launcher; 4 × 14.5mm (0.57in) machine-guns in 2 × twin mountings
Missile armament: none
Torpedo armament: none
Anti-submarine armament: none
Electronics: 1 × 'Pot Head' surface search and navigation radar
Propulsion: 4 × M 50 diesels delivering 3,600kW (4,830hp) to four shafts
Performance: maximum speed 40kt; range ? km (? miles) at ? kt
Complement: 12

1. Iran (3 craft)
These are standard craft transferred in April 1987.

2. North Korea (66 craft plus 52 of 'Chong-jin' class and 3 of 'Chong-ju' class)
Construction of the 'Cha-ho' class began in North Korean yards during 1974, and the type is based on the hull and propulsion arrangement of the Soviet 'P 6' FAC(T) with the unusual armament of a multi-tube artillery rocket-launcher. The 'Chong-jin' class is a locally developed variant with a full-load displacement of 80 tons on dimensions of: length 27.7m (90.9ft), beam 6.1m (20.0ft) and draught 1.8m (5.9ft). The armament comprises 1 × 85mm (3.35in) L/52 DP gun in a single mounting, and 4 or 8 × 14.5mm (0.57in) machine-guns in 2 or 4 × twin mountings, and the electronics fit includes 1 × 'Skin Head' surface search and navigation radar. Other details are similar to those of the 'Cha-ho'-class craft. Construction of these vessels began in 1975, and it is reported that about one-third of the craft are of a hydrofoil development with a single surface-piercing foil located forward. In 1985 the North Koreans began construction of a third sub-variant as the 'Chong-ju' class with dimensions of: length 42.5m (139.4ft), beam 6.8m (22.3ft) and draught 1.9m (6.2ft), and an armament of 1 × 122mm (4.82in) BM-21 Grad 40-barrel artillery rocket-launcher and 4 × 14.5mm (0.57in) machine-guns in a quadruple mounting.

'Chong-jin' class: *see* 'Cha-ho class
'Choug-ju' class: *see* 'Cha-ho class
'Constitucion' class: *see* 'Vosper Thornycroft 121ft' class

'Cormoran' class

Spain/Morocco

Type: fast attack craft (patrol)
Displacement: ? tons standard; 425 tons full load
Dimensions: length 58.1m (190.6ft); beam 7.6m (24.9ft);
    draught 2.7m (8.9ft)
Gun armament: 1 × 40mm Bofors L/70 AA in a Breda
    single mounting; 2 × 20mm GIAT L/103 AA in DCN
    Type A single mountings
Missile armament: none
Torpedo armament: none
Anti-submarine armament: none
Electronics: 1 × ZW-06 surface search and navigation
    radar
Propulsion: 2 × Bazan/MTU 16V 956 TB82 diesels
    delivering 2,850kW (3,820hp) to two shafts
Performance: maximum speed 22kt; range 11,300km
    (7,020 miles) at 12kt
Complement: 51

1. Morocco

Name	No	Builder	Commis-sioned
L. V. Rabhi	310	Bazan	Sep 1988
Errachiq	311	Bazan	1989
El Akid	312	Bazan	1989
El Maher	313	Bazan	1989
El Majid	314	Bazan	1989
El Bachir	315	Bazan	1989

Retaining the same basic hull as the 'Lazaga' class (itself
a low-powered derivative of the 'Lürssen FPB-57' design)
but using a still lower-powered propulsion arrangement
for reduced speed, these are long-endurance patrol and
fishery protection vessels that clearly possess the potential for later conversion into more heavily armed
FAC(G)s and even FAC(M)s. The first three craft were
ordered from Spain in October 1985, the option for
another three craft being exercised at a later date.

2. Venezuela

Name	No	Builder	Commis-sioned
		Bazan	
		Bazan	
		Bazan	

Ordered in February 1987, these craft are similar to the
Moroccan units in dimensions except for a length of
55.0m (180.4ft), but, with 9,000kW (12,070hp) delivered
by 3 × MTU 16V 956 TB91 diesels to three shafts, are
capable of 35kt and a range of 2,300 miles (3,700km) at
15kt. The craft have been completed as FAC(M/G)s with
an armament of 2 × twin Mk 141 container-launchers for

▼P107, a 'Cormoran'-class
vessel in the Moroccan
navy.

4 × RGM-84 Harpoon anti-ship missiles, 1 × 76mm (3in) L/62 DP in an OTO Melara Compact single mounting and 2 × 40mm Bofors L/70 AA in a Breda twin mounting. The complement is 5+27. A fourth unit may later be built in Venezuela.

'Dagger' class: *see* 'PSMM Mk 5' class
'Dogan' class: *see* 'Lürssen FPB/PB-57' class

'Dvora' class   Israel

Type: fast attack craft (missile)
Displacement: 38 tons standard; 47 tons full load
Dimensions: length 21.6m (70.8ft); beam 5.5m (18.0ft); draught 1.8m (5.91ft)
Gun armament: 2 × 20mm Oerlikon L/75 AA in A41A single mountings; 2 × 0.5in (12.7mm) machine-guns
Missile armament: 2 × single container-launchers for 2 × Gabriel anti-ship missiles
Torpedo armament: none
Anti-submarine armament: none
Electronics: 1 × Decca 926 surface search and navigation radar; 1 × EL/M-2221 tracking radar used in conjunction with; 1 × DG fire-control system
Propulsion: 2 × MTU 12V 331 TC81 diesels delivering 4,050kW (5,430hp) to two shafts
Peformance: maximum speed 36kt; range 1,300km (810 miles) at 32kt
Complement: 10

1. Israel (9 craft including 'Super Dvora' class units)
The 'Dvora' design produced by Israel Aircraft Industries is based on the hull of the 'Dabur'-class patrol craft, of which Israel has 31 units in service. The design for the 'Dvora'-class craft is slightly larger and possesses considerably more power, and the missile armament is notably heavy for so small a hull – in fact the world's smallest with missile armament. In 1987 Israel ordered another five units (perhaps to be supplemented by a further three) as 'Super Dvora'-class FAC(G)s, each 22.4m (73.5ft) long, possessing a full-load displacement of 48 tons, carrying an armament of 2 × 20mm AA in single mountings and 2 × 0.5in (12.7mm) machine-guns but capable of being retrofitted as FAC(M)s with Gabriel missiles, a full-load displacement of 56 tons, and a more powerful propulsion arrangement for a maximum speed of 40kt.

2. Sri Lanka ('Super Dvora' class)

Name	No	Builder	Commissioned
	P453	Israel Aircraft Industries	1984
	P454	Israel Aircraft Industries	1984
	P455	Israel Aircraft Industries	1986
	P456	Israel Aircraft Industries	1986
	P457	Israel Aircraft Industries	1986
	P458	Israel Aircraft Industries	1986

Name	Pennant No	Builder	Commissioned
	P463	Israel Aircraft Industries	1987
	P464	Israel Aircraft Industries	1987
	P465	Israel Aircraft Industries	1988
	P473	Israel Aircraft Industries	1988
	P474	Israel Aircraft Industries	1988
	P475	Israel Aircraft Industries	1988

Possessing a full-load displacement of 47 tons, these are FAC(G)s with an armament of 2 × 20mm Oerlikon L/75 AA in A41A mountings and 2 × 0.5in (12.7mm) machine-guns. The first six vessels have two MTU 12V 331 diesels delivering 2,000kW (2,680hp) to two shafts for a maximum speed of 36kt, and the craft of the second batch of six have greater power for improved speed.

3. Taiwan ('Hai Ou' class – 50 craft)
This is a development of the 'Dvora' class by the Sun Yat-sen Scientific Research Institute, and built by the Tsoying Shipyard of the China Shipbuilding Corporation. The armament comprises 2 × single container-launchers for 2 × Hsiung Feng anti-ship missiles, 1 × 20mm Oerlikon L/75 AA in an A41A single mounting, and 2 × 0.5in (12.7mm) machine-guns. The electronics includes 1 × RCA R76 C5 surface search and fire-control radar, 1 × Kollmorgen Mk 35 optical director and 4 × AV2 'chaff'-launchers. The propulsion arrangement features 2 × MTU 12V 331 TC81 diesels delivering 2,030kW (2,725hp) to two shafts for a maximum speed of 36kt and a range of 1,300km (810 miles) at 32kt. The complement is 10.

'Epitrop' class   Romania

Type: fast attack craft (torpedo)
Displacement: ? tons standard; 215 tons full load
Dimensions: length 36.8m (120.75ft); beam 7.6m (24.9ft); draught 1.8m (5.9ft)
Gun armament: 4 × 30mm L/65 AA in 2 × twin mountings
Missile armament: none
Torpedo armament: 4 × single 533mm (21in) mountings for 4 × Type 53 heavyweight anti-ship torpedoes
Anti-submarine armament: none
Electronics: 1 × 'Pot Drum' surface search and navigation radar; 1 × 'Drum Tilt' fire-control radar; 1 × 'High Pole-A' IFF system
Propulsion: 3 × M 503A diesels delivering 9,000kW (12,070hp) to three shafts
Performance: maximum speed 36kt; range 925km (575 miles) at 35kt
Complement: ?

1.Romania (12 craft (Nos 200 to 211))
These vessels were built at Mangalia from 1980 and entered service from 1981. For their size they are lightly armed, and the Type 53 is also an obsolete weapon.

'Esmeraldas' class   Italy/Ecuador

Type: fast attack craft (missile and gun)
Displacement: 620 tons standard; 685 tons full load
Dimensions: length 62.3m (204.4ft); beam 9.3m (30.5ft);
   draught 2.5m (8.2ft)
Gun armament: 1 × 76mm (3in) L/62 DP in an OTO
   Melara Compact single mounting; 2 × two 40mm
   Bofors L/70 AA in a Dardo twin mounting
Missile armament: 2 × triple container-launchers for six
   MM.40 Exocet anti-ship missiles; 1 × Albatros Mk 2
   quadruple launcher for ? × Aspide SAMs
Torpedo armament: none
Anti-submarine armament: 2 × ILAS 3 triple 324mm
   (12.75in) mountings for ? × A 244/S torpedoes
Aircraft: provision for 1 × Bell 206B JetRanger
   helicopter on a platform amidships
Electronics: 1 × RAN 10S air/surface search radar; 1 ×
   3RM 20 navigation radar; 1 × RTN 10X radar used in
   conjunction with; 1 × Argo NA21 gun fire-control
system and its CO3 directors; 1 × RTN 20X radar used
in conjunction with; 1 × Dardo anti-aircraft fire-control
system; 1 × Diodon active search and attack hull
sonar; 1 × IPN 20 action information system; 1 × ESM
system with Gamma warning and jamming elements; 1
× SCLAR 'chaff'/decoy-launcher
Propulsion: 4 × MTU 20V 956 TB92 diesels delivering
   18,200kW (24,405hp) to four shafts
Performance: maximum speed 37kt; range 7,900km (4,910
   miles) at 14kt
Complement: 51

1. Ecuador

Name	No	Builder	Commissioned
Esmeraldas	CM11	CNR, Muggiano	Aug 1982
Manabi	CM12	CNR, Ancona	Jun 1983
Los Rios	CM13	CNR, Muggiano	Oct 1983

▶ CM15 is *Galapagos*, an
'Esmeraldas'-class corvette
in the Ecuadorean navy.

Name	Pennant No	Builder	Commissioned
El Oro	CM14	CNR, Ancona	Dec 1983
Galapagos	CM15	CNR, Muggiano	May 1984
Loja	CM16	CNR, Ancona	May 1984

Developed from the 'Assad' class with more powerful engines and provision for a helicopter, these vessels offer an exceptional combination of sensors and weapons, and are little short of frigates in their overall capabilities.

'Flagstaff 2'
USA/Israel

Type: fast attack hydrofoil (missile)

Displacement: 91.5 tons standard; 105 tons full load

Dimensions: length 84.0ft (25.6m); beam 24.0ft (7.3m); draught 5.0ft (1.6m)

Gun armament: 4 × 30mm L/85 AA in two TCM-30 twin mountings

Missile armament: 2 × twin container-launchers for 4 × RGM-84 Harpoon anti-ship missiles; 2 × single container-launchers for 2 × Gabriel III anti-ship missiles

Torpedo armament: none

Anti-submarine armament: none

Electronics: 1 × surface search radar; 1 × navigation radar; 1 × EL/M-2221 tracking radar (with data-link system for mid-course update of the Gabriel missiles) used in conjunction with; 1 × DG fire-control system

Propulsion: CODOG arrangement of 2 × General Motors diesels delivering 260hp (194kW) for hull-borne operation and 2 × Allison 501KF gas turbines delivering 5,400shp (4,025kW) to four shafts for foil-borne operation

Performance: maximum speed 48kt; range 3,000 miles (4,830km) at 8kt hull-borne or; 1,150 miles (1,850km) at 42kt foil-borne

Complement: 15

1. Israel

Name	No	Builder	Commissioned
Shimrit	M161	Grumman Lantana	1982
Livnit	M162	Grumman Lantana	1984
Snapirit	M163	Grumman Lantana	1985

An advanced high-performance hydrofoil with two types of anti-ship missiles, the 'Flagstaff 2' class was originally to have numbered twelve units but has been curtailed at just these three, possibly reflecting the severe teething problems encountered with getting the craft into service.

'Flyvevisken' class   Denmark

Type: fast attack craft (gun)
Displacement: ? tons standard; 300 tons full load
Dimensions: length 54.0m (177.2ft); beam 9.0m (29.5ft); draught 2.5m (8.2ft)
Gun armament: 1 × 76mm (3in) L/62 DP in an OTO Melara Super Rapid single mounting; 2 × 0.5in (12.7mm) machine-guns
Missile armament: none
Torpedo armament: none
Anti-submarine armament: none
Electronics: 1 × AWS 6 surface search radar; 1 × Terma Pilot navigation radar; 1 × tracking radar used in conjunction with; 1 × 9LV 200 Mk 3 Sea Viking fire-control system (with TV, FLIR and laser sensors); 1 × ESM system with Sabre warning and Cygnus jamming elements. Other systems as required
Performance: CODAG arrangement of 1 × General Electric LM2500 gas turbine delivering 6,000shp (4,475kW) and two MTU 16V 396 TB94 diesels delivering 5,200kW (6,975hp) to three shafts
Performance: maximum speed 30kt on gas turbine and diesels, and 20kt on diesels; range ? km (? miles)
Complement: 15/18 with a maximum of 28 possible

1. Denmark

Name	No	Builder	Commissioned
Flyvevisken	P550	Karlskrona/Aalborg	Oct 1987
Hajen	P551	Karlskrona/Aalborg	Dec 1989
Havkatten	P552	Karlskrona/Aalborg	1990
Laxen	P553	Karlskrona/Aalborg	1991
Makraelen	P554	Karlskrona/Aalborg	1991
Storen	P555	Karlskrona/Aalborg	1992
Svaerdvisken	P556	Karlskrona/Aalborg	1992

A class of sixteen such craft is planned, this 'Standard Flex 300' type being schemed as replacement for the 'Daphne' class of seaward defence vessels, 'Søløven' class of FAC(T)s, and 'Sund' class of mine counter-measures vessels. The design has thus been optimized for adaptability to several roles with 'plug-in' armament (including 4 × anti-ship missiles, 1 × surface-to-air missile system, 2 × single 533mm/21in tube mountings for heavyweight torpedoes, and mine-counter-measures weapons) and associated electronics. The centre shaft can also be powered by a single electric motor for a speed of 6kt and very quiet operation.

'Franco–Belge' class   France/Ivory Coast

Type: fast attack craft (gun)
Displacement: ? tons standard; 235 tons or (*Le Valeureux* only) 250 tons full load
Dimensions: length 47.5m (155.8ft) or (*Le Valeureux* only) 48.0m (157.5ft); beam 7.0m (23.0ft); draught 2.3m (7.5ft)
Gun armament: 2 × 40mm Bofors L/70 AA in 2 × Breda single mountings; 2 × 0.5in (12.7mm) machine-guns in single mountings
Missile armament: none
Torpedo armament: none
Anti-submarine armament: none
Electronics: 1 × DRBN 32 or (*Le Vigilant* only) Decca surface search and navigation radar
Propulsion: 2 × AGO diesels delivering 3,150kW (4,225hp) or (*Le Vigilant* only) 2 × MGO diesels delivering 1,800kW (2,415hp), in each case to two shafts
Performance: maximum speed 22kt or (*Le Vigilant* only) 18.5kt; range 3,700km (2,300 miles) at 15kt
Complement: 4+30

1. Ivory Coast

Name	No	Builder	Commissioned
Le Vigilant		SFCN, Villeneuve	1968
Le Valeureux		SFCN, Villeneuve	Oct 1976

These craft were ordered in 1966 and 1974 respectively, and are simple FAC(G)s used for the coastal patrol role. The design is similar to that of the 'P 48' class. Unconfirmed reports state that each vessel has been fitted with 2 × twin container-launchers for 4 × MM.40 Exocet anti-ship missiles.

'Freemantle' class: *see* 'Brooke Marine 41.8m' class

'Göteborg' class   Sweden

Type: fast attack craft (missile, gun and torpedo)
Displacement: 300 tons standard; 380 tons full load
Dimensions: length 57.0m (187.0ft); beam 8.0m (26.2ft); draught 2.0m (6.6ft)
Gun armament: 1 × 57mm SAK 57 Mk 2 L/70 DP in a

Bofors single mounting; 1 × 40mm Bofors L/70 AA in a single mounting

Missile armament: 4 × twin container-launchers for 8 × RBS 15M anti-ship missiles

Torpedo armament: 2 × single 533mm (21in) mountings for 2 × Tp 613 wire-guided dual-role torpedoes

Anti-submarine armament: 1 × Elma grenade system with 4 × LLS-920 nine-barrel launchers; 2 × twin 400m (15.75in) mountings for 4 × Tp 431 wire-guided torpedoes (optionally in place of two 533mm torpedo mountings)

Mines: fitted for minelaying

Electronics: 1 × Sea Giraffe 150 HC air/surface search radar; 1 × Terma PN 612 navigation radar; 2 × tracking radars used in conjunction with; 1 × 9LV 400 gun fire-control systems (with TV, FLIR and laser sensors); 1 × RCI-400 missile fire-control system; 2 × 9LV 200 Mk 3 optronic directors; 1 × TSM 2643 Salmon variable-depth active search sonar and 1 × Simrad SS 304 active attack hull sonar used in conjunction with; 1 × 9AU 300 underwater weapons fire-control system; 1 × ESM system with Carol warning and Argo jamming elements; 4 × Philax 'chaff'/flare-launchers

Propulsion: 3 × MTU 16V 396 TB94 diesels delivering 6,450kW (8,650hp) to KaMeWa waterjets

Performance: maximum speed 32kt+; range ? km (? miles)

Complement: 7+29 with a maximum of 40 possible

1. Sweden

Name	No	Builder	Commissioned
Göteborg	K21	Karlskrona	1990
Gävle	K22	Karlskrona	1990
Kalmar	K23	Karlskrona	1991
Sundsvall	K24	Karlskrona	1991

Heavily armed and propelled somewhat unusually among hull-borne FACs by waterjets, these four craft were ordered in December 1985 as replacements for the elderly 'Spica I'-class FAC(T)s. Unlike earlier Swedish FACs, which are armed almost exclusively for the anti-ship role, the 'Göteborg' class has an effective dual capability against surface and underwater vessels, and can also be used for minelaying. The units of the 'Göteborg' class are notable for the weight and diversity of their armament and associated electronics. The torpedo tubes are located on the starboard side to fire eight forward or aft.

'Guacolda' class: see 'Lürssen FPB-36' class

'H3' class   China

Type: fast attack craft (missile and gun)
Displacement: ? tons standard; 239 tons full load

Dimensions: length 47.0m (154.2ft); beam 7.5m (24.6ft); draught 1.9m (6.2ft)

Gun armament: 1 × 76mm (3in) L/62 DP in a single Mk 75 (OTO Melara Compact) mounting; 1 × 20mm six-barrel rotary cannon in a Phalanx Mk 15 CIWS mounting

Missile armament: 8 × single container-launchers for 8 × C-801 anti-ship missiles

Torpedo armament: none

Anti-submarine armament: none

Electronics: 1 × surface search radar; 1 × navigation radar; 1 × tracking radar used in conjunction with; 1 × WM-25 fire-control system; other systems

Propulsion: 3 × Allison 570KF gas turbines delivering 19,000shp (14,165kW) to KaMeWa waterjets

Performance: maximum speed 50kt+; range ? km (? miles)

Complement: not revealed

1. China (1 craft plus others building and more planned)

Planning calls for these boats to be built in the USA by Edward Heinemann and Nickum Spaulding Associates to an eventual total of perhaps fifteen craft. The boats combine Chinese missiles with high-quality Western guns, electronics and engines, but the programme may have been terminated as a result of cooled Sino–American relations after the Tianenmen Square massacre of Chinese students agitating for greater democracy.

'Hainan' class   China

Type: fast attack craft (gun)
Displacement: 375 tons standard; 392 tons full load
Dimensions: length 58.8m (192.8ft); beam 7.2m (23.6ft); draught 4.3m (14.1ft)

Gun armament: 4 × 57mm L/70 DP in 2 × twin mounting; 4 × 25mm L/60 in 2 × 2-M-3 PM110 twin mountings

Missile armament: 4 × single container-launchers for 4 × C-801 anti-ship missiles (provision for)

Torpedo armament: none

Anti-submarine armament: 4 × RBU 1200 five-barrel rocket-launchers; 2 × BMB-2 depth-charge throwers with ? depth-charges; 2 × depth-charge racks with ? depth-charges

Electronics: 1 × 'Pot Head' or 'Skin Head' surface search and navigation radar; 1 × hull-mounted high-frequency active search and attack sonar; 1 × Thomson-Sintra SS 12 variable-depth sonar (only in some craft); 1 × 'High Pole' IFF system

Propulsion: 4 × Type 9D diesels delivering 6,600kW (8,850hp) to four shafts

Performance: maximum speed 30.5kt; range 2,400km (1,490 miles) at 15kt

Complement: 69

1. Bangladesh (8 craft)

These are Durjoy (P811), Nirbhoy (P812) and six others

(P813 to P818) transferred between September 1982 and December 1985. All are similar to the baseline Chinese standard.

2. China (60 craft)
Not all pennant numbers are known, but those that have been ascertained include 267 to 285, 290, 302, 305, 609, 610, 641, 642, 661–670, 677, 678, 680, 686, 687 and 690. The retrofit of anti-ship missiles would create a useful anti-ship capability.

3. Egypt (8 craft)
These are *Al Nour* (430), *Al Hady* (433), *Al Hakim* (436), *Al Wakil* (439), *Al Qatar* (442), *Al Saddam* (445), *Al Salam* (448) and *Al Rafia* (451) transferred between October 1983 and late 1984. The craft are basically similar to their Chinese counterparts, although the secondary gun armament comprises 4 × 23mm L/87 AA in 2 × twin mountings. Two of the vessels are to be fitted with 2 × triple 12.75in (324mm) Mk 32 mountings for 6 × Stingray anti-submarine torpedoes used in conjunction with 1 × Singer Librascope fire-control system, and if this fit proves successful it will be retrofitted to the other six craft. Other elements of the electronics suite include Decca navigation radar.

4. North Korea (6 craft)
These are standard vessels transferred between 1975 and 1978.

5. Pakistan (4 craft)
These craft are *Baluchistan* (P155), *Sind* (P159), *Sarhad*

(P161) and *Punjab* (P163) transferred in pairs during mid-1976 and April 1980. The craft are in all essential respects similar to the Chinese norm.

General note
The design of the 'Hainan' class is basically that of the Soviet 'SO 1' patrol craft, and these Chinese craft are optimized for the patrol and coastal anti-submarine roles. The programme began in 1963 and continues to the present, later units being mainly for export. Later craft are identifiable by their combination of a tripod foremast (in place of a pole foremast) and a short stub mainmast.

'Hai Ou' class: *see* 'Dvora' class

'Hauk' class   Norway

Type: fast attack craft (missile and torpedo)
Displacement: 120 tons standard; 148 tons full load
Dimensions: length 36.5m (119.7ft); beam 6.1m (20.0ft); draught 1.5m (5.0ft)
Gun armament: 1 × 40mm Bofors L/70 AA in a Bofors single mounting; 1 × 20mm Rheinmetall L/92 AA in an S20 single mounting
Missile armament: 6 × single container-launchers for 6 × Penguin Mk II (possibly to be supplanted by Penguin

▼P986, a 'Hauk'-class fast missile attack boat of the Norwegian navy.

Mk III) anti-ship missiles

Torpedo armament: 2 × single 533mm (21in) mountings for 2 × Tp 61 wire-guided torpedoes

Anti-submarine armament: none

Electronics: 2 × TM1226 surface search and navigation radars; 1 × MSI-80S fire-control system (with 1 × TVT-300 optronic tracker and 1 × laser rangefinder); 1 × Simrad SQ-3D/QF active search hull sonar

Propulsion: 2 × MTU 16V 538 TB91 diesels delivering 5,400kW (7,240hp) to two shafts

Performance: maximum speed 34kt; range 815km (505 miles) at 34kt

Complement: 20

1. Norway

Name	No	Builder	Commis-sioned
Hauk	P986	Bergens Mek	Aug 1977
Orn	P987	Bergens Mek	Jan 1979
Terne	P988	Bergens Mek	Mar 1979
Tjeld	P989	Bergens Mek	May 1979
Skarv	P990	Bergens Mek	Jul 1979
Teist	P991	Bergens Mek	Sep 1979
Jo	P992	Bergens Mek	Nov 1979
Lom	P993	Bergens Mek	Jan 1980
Stegg	P994	Bergens Mek	Mar 1980
Falk	P995	Bergens Mek	Apr 1980
Ravn	P996	Westamarin	May 1980
Gribb	P997	Westamarin	Jul 1980
Geir	P998	Westamarin	Sep 1980
Erle	P999	Westamarin	Dec 1980

Ordered in June 1975, these are in essence 'Snogg'-class craft with a more capable fire-control system. They are particularly impressive small FAC(M/T)s with a large missile armament and a capability against closer-range targets with two powerful torpedoes.

'Hegu' class: *see* 'Komar' class

'Helsinki' class   Finland

Type: fast attack craft (missile and gun)

Displacement: 280 tons standard; 300 tons full load

Dimensions: length 45.0m (147.6ft); beam 8.9m (29.2ft); draught 3.0m (9.9ft)

Gun armament: 1 × 57mm SAK 57 Mk 2 L/70 DP in a Bofors single mounting; 4 × 23mm L/60 AA in 2 × twin mountings

Missile armament: 4 × single container-launchers for 4 × RBS 15M anti-ship missiles

Torpedo armament: none

Anti-submarine armament: none

Electronics: 1 × 9LGA 208 surface search radar; 1 × tracking radar used in conjunction with; 1 × 9LV 225 fire-control system; 1 × EOS 40 optronic director; 1 ×

Simrad SS 304 active search hull sonar; 1 × ESM system with Matilda warning element

Propulsion: 3 × MTU 16V 538 TB92 diesels delivering 8,172kW (10,965hp) to three shafts

Performance: maximum speed 30kt; range ? km (? miles)

Complement: 30

1. Finland

Name	No	Builder	Commis-sioned
Helsinki	60	Wartsila	Sep 1981
Turku	61	Wartsila	Jun 1985
Oulu	62	Wartsila	Oct 1985
Kotka	63	Wartsila	Jun 1986

This class has been designed for a 30-year life, with features to make possible the alteration of armament to suit specific roles. *Helsinki* was ordered in 1980 as the prototype for the class, and has only 1 × 23mm twin mounting, while the other three units were ordered three years later to a revised standard.

'Helsinki 2' class   Finland

Type: fast attack craft (missile and gun)

Displacement: 200 tons standard; ? tons full load

Dimensions: length 48.0m (157.5ft); beam 8.0m (26.2ft); draught 2.7m (8.6ft)

Gun armament: 1 × 57mm Bofors SAK 57 Mk 2 L/70 DP in a Bofors single mounting

Missile armament: 4 or 8 × single container-launchers for 4 or 8 × RBS 15M anti-ship missiles

Torpedo armament: none

Anti-submarine armament: 1 × Elma grenade system with 4 × LLS-920 nine-barrel launchers

Electronics: 1 × 9GA 208 surface search radar; 1 × navigation radar; 1 × 9LV 25 tracking radar used in conjunction with; 1 × 9LV 200 Mk 3 Sea Viking fire-control system (with TV, FLIR and laser sensors); 1 × 9LW 300 ESM system with warning element decoy and 'chaff'/flare-launchers

Propulsion: 2 × MTU 16V 538 TB92 diesels delivering 6,000kW (8,045hp) to two waterjets

Performance: maximum speed 30kt+; range ? km (? miles)

Complement: not revealed

1. Finland

Name	No	Builder	Commis-sioned
Luokka	64	Hollming SY	1990
	65	Hollming SY	1991
	66	Hollming SY	1991
	67	Hollming SY	1992

The first four craft were ordered in August 1987 and current plans call for a total of eight units. The craft are being built with only six anti-ship missiles, although there is deck space and electronic capacity for eight missiles to be shipped.

'Huangfeu' class: *see* 'Osa I' and 'Osa II' classes

▼*Helsinki* is a fast patrol boat seen on trials for the Finnish navy.

'Huchuan' class

China

Type: fast attack hydrofoil (torpedo)
Displacement: 39 tons standard; 46 tons full load
Dimensions: length 21.8m (71.5ft); beam 6.3m (20.7ft);

over foils and 5.0m (16.4ft) over hull; draught 1.0m
(3.3ft) foil-borne and 3.6m (11.8ft) hull-borne
Gun armament: 4 × 14.5mm (0.57in) machine-guns in 2 ×
twin mountings
Missile armament: none
Torpedo armament: 2 × single 533mm (21in) mountings
for 2 × Type 53 torpedoes
Anti-submarine armament: depth-charges
Electronics: 1 × 'Skin Head' surface search and
navigation radar
Propulsion: 3 × M 50F diesels delivering 2,700kW
(3,620hp) to three shafts
Performance: maximum speed 55kt foil-borne; range
925km (575 miles) at cruising speed
Complement: 11

1. Albania (32 craft)
These are standard craft and were transferred in 1968
(six), 1969 (fifteen), 1970 (two), 1971 (seven) and 1974
(two).

2. China (120+ craft)
Construction of this large class continues.

3. Pakistan (4 craft)
These are standard craft that were transferred in 1973.

4. Romania (3 craft plus 22 locally built craft)
Three imported Chinese vessels were followed in 1973
onwards by 22 craft built at the Dobreta Shipyard in
Turno at the rate of about two per year. The 23 active
craft are named *VT51* to *VT73*; the other two are *Mars*
and *Jupiter*, which are harbour patrol craft and lack both
the foil and torpedo tubes.

5. Tanzania (4 craft)
Named *JW9841* to *JW9844*, these are standard craft and
were transferred in 1975.

General note
There is nothing exceptional about this useful FAH(T),
which entered production at the Hutong yard in Shanghai
during 1966 as the world's first operational warship with
hydrofoils. Production continues at the rate of about ten
craft per year. Older boats have one gun mounting
amidships and the other aft, while newer boats have one
mounting forward and the other aft of the bridge, which is
moved aft, plus a revised electronics fit.

'Hugin' class

Sweden

Type: fast attack craft (missile and gun)
Displacement: 120 tons standard; 150 tons full load
Dimensions: length 36.6m (120.0ft); beam 6.3m (20.7ft);
draught 1.7m (5.6ft)
Gun armament: 1 × 57mm SAK 57 Mk 1 L/70 DP in a
Bofors single mounting

Missile armament: 6 × single container-launchers for 6 ×
  RB 12 (Penguin Mk II) anti-ship missiles (to be replaced
  by RBS 15M anti-ship missiles)
Torpedo armament: none
Anti-submarine armament: 1 × Elma grenade system
  with 4 × LLS-920 nine-barrel launchers; 2 × depth-
  charge racks
Mines: 24 on two rails (optional replacement for missiles)
Electronics: 1 × Skanter Mk 009 surface search and
  navigation radar; 1 × tracking radar used in
  conjunction with; 1 × 9LV 200 Mk 2 fire-control
  system; 1 × Simrad SQ 3D/SF active search and attack

▲'Hugin'-class craft of the
Swedish navy. Note the
main missile armament of
six Penguin Mk II anti-ship
missiles.

hull sonar; 1 × ESM system with EWS 905 warning
  element
Propulsion: 2 × MTU 20V 672 TY90 diesels delivering
  5,350kW (7,175hp) to two shafts
Performance: maximum speed 36kt; range 1,000km (620
  miles) at 35kt
Complement: 3+19

1. Sweden

Name	No	Builder	Commissioned
Hugin	P151	Bergens Mek	Jul 1978
Munin	P152	Bergens Mek	Jul 1978
Magne	P153	Bergens Mek	Oct 1978
Mode	P154	Westamarin	Jan 1979
Vale	P155	Westamarin	Apr 1979
Vidar	P156	Westamarin	Aug 1979
Mjolner	P157	Westamarin	Oct 1979
Mysing	P158	Westamarin	Feb 1980
Kaparen	P159	Bergens Mek	Aug 1980
Vaktaren	P160	Bergens Mek	Sep 1980
Snapphanen	P161	Bergens Mek	Jan 1980
Spejaren	P162	Bergens Mek	Mar 1980
Styrbjörn	P163	Bergens Mek	Jun 1980
Starkodder	P164	Bergens Mek	Aug 1981
Tordon	P165	Bergens Mek	Oct 1981
Tirfing	P166	Bergens Mek	Jan 1982

This is a capable anti-ship class suited to coastal operations in the Swedish archipelago and in the Baltic. It is reported that some of the class are being retrofitted with variable-depth sonar, reflecting Sweden's increasing fears about Soviet submarine capability. The type is similar to the Norwegian 'Hauk' class and the design was proved in *Jagaren*, a prototype that was commissioned as P151 but is now a gun-armed FAC(P). The success of *Jagaren* led to the May 1975 order for the 'Hugin' class using reconditioned engines from the 'Plejad' FAC(T) class.

'Iwon' class   North Korea

Type: fast attack craft (torpedo)
Displacement: ? tons standard; 25 tons full load
Dimensions: length 19.2m (63.0ft); beam 3.7m (12.1ft); draught 1.5m (4.9ft)
Gun armament: 4 × 25mm L/80 AA in 2 × 2-M-3 110PM twin mountings
Missile armament: none
Torpedo armament: 2 × single 533mm (21in) mountings for 2 × Type 53 heavyweight anti-ship torpedoes
Anti-submarine armament: none
Electronics: 1 × 'Skin Head' surface search radar; 1 × navigation radar; 1 × 'Dead Duck' IFF system
Propulsion: 3 × M 50 diesels delivering 2,700kW (3,620hp) to three shafts
Performance: maximum speed 45kt; range ? km (? miles) at ? kt
Complement: 15

1. North Korea (15 craft)
The design of these FAC(T)s is based on that of the Soviet 'P 2' class, and the craft were built in the late 1950s.

'Jerong' class: *see* 'Lürssen FPB/TNC-45' class
'Kaman' class: *see* 'Combattante II' class
'Kartal' class: *see* 'Lürssen TNC-42' class
'Kebir' class: *see* 'Brooke Marine 37.5m' class

'Komar' class   USSR

Type: fast attack craft (missile)
Displacement: 68 tons standard; 75 tons full load
Dimensions: length 26.8m (87.9ft); beam 6.2m (20.3ft); draught 1.5m (4.9ft)
Gun armament: 2 × 25mm L/80 AA in a 2-M-3 110PM twin mounting
Missile armament: 2 × single container-launchers for 2 × SS-N-2A 'Styx' anti-ship missiles
Torpedo armament: none
Anti-submarine armament: none
Electronics: 1 × 'Square Tie' surface search and navigation radar; 1 × 'Dead Duck' IFF system; 1 × 'High Pole-A' IFF system
Propulsion: 4 × M 50F diesels delivering 3,600kW (4,830hp) to four shafts
Performance: maximum speed 40kt; range 740km (460 miles) at 30kt
Complement: 4+19

1. Bangladesh ('Hegu' class)

Name	No	Builder	Commissioned
Durbar	P8111		Apr 1983
Duranta	P8112		Apr 1983
Durvedya	P8113		Nov 1983
Durdam	P8114		Nov 1983

These are standard ex-Chinese craft with two HY-2 anti-ship missiles.

2. China (110+ 'Hegu' or 'Type 024' class craft)
These are locally built 'Hegu' or 'Type 024'-class developments with 4 × 25mm L/60 AA in two twin mountings and, as a successive retrofit, 4 × C-801 missiles in place of the original 2 × HY-2 (SS-N-2 'Styx') missiles. There is also a single 'Hema'-class FAH(M) with a forward set of foils and an additional 2.0m (6.6ft) of length allowing the installation of a third twin 25mm mounting aft of the missiles.

3. Egypt ('Hegu' class)

Name	No	Builder	Commissioned
	611		Oct 1984
	612		Oct 1984

Name	Pennant No	Builder	Commis- sioned
	613		Oct 1984
	614		Oct 1984
	615		Oct 1984
	616		Oct 1984

These are standard ex-Chinese craft with two HY-2 anti-ship missiles.

4. North Korea (16 craft)
These are eight standard craft and eight locally built 'Sohung'-class developments with another two building.

5. Pakistan ('Hegu' class)

Name	No	Builder	Commis- sioned
Haibat	P0121		May 1981
Jalalat	P1022		May 1981
Jurat	P1023		Oct 1981
Shujaat	P1024		Oct 1981

These are standard ex-Chinese craft with 2 × HY-2 anti-ship missiles.

General note
This elderly Soviet class is disappearing from service, Cuba, Egypt and Syria having disposed of their 'Komars'. However, the Chinese- and North Korean-built versions are still in production and comparatively widespread service. The Soviets designate the craft as torpedo cutters. The type is based on the hull of the 'P 6'-

▲Soviet 'Komar'-class guided missile craft. Although of poor quality, this photograph does illustrate the prominence of the twin SS-N-2 missile-launchers.

class FAC(T), and though it was first seen only in 1960, the design's less sophisticated features (such as open-ended missile container-launchers) clearly indicate that the 'Komar' class pre-dated the 'Osa' class, which was first seen in 1959.

'Kraljevica' class   Yugoslavia/Bangladesh

Type: fast attack craft (gun)
Displacement: 195 tons standard; 245 tons full load
Dimensions: length 43.1m (141.4ft); beam 6.3m (20.7ft); draught 1.8m (5.7ft)
Gun armament: 2 × 40mm Bofors L/60 AA in single mountings; 4 × Oerlikon AA in single mountings
Missile armament: none
Torpedo armament: none
Anti-submarine armament: 2 × RBU 1200 five-barrel rocket-launchers; 2 × depth-charge throwers for ? depth-charges; 2 × depth-charge racks for ? depth-charges
Electronics: 1 × Decca 45 surface search and navigation radar; 1 × QCU 2 hull-mounted high-frequency search and attack sonar
Propulsion: 2 × MAN W8V 30/38 diesels delivering 2,450kW (3,285hp) to two shafts
Performance: maximum speed 19kt; range 2,800km (1,740 miles) at 15kt
Complement: 49

1. Bangladesh

Name	No	Builder	Commissioned
Karnaphili	P314	Tito Shipyard, Kraljevica	1956
Tista	P315	Tito Shipyard, Kraljevica	1956

These are simple patrol craft with limited anti-submarine capability, and resulted from a Yugoslav programme that saw the construction of several units in the period between 1953 and 1959, initially with a primary armament of 1 × 3in (76mm) gun. These two craft were transferred in June 1975.

2. Indonesia

Name	No	Builder	Commissioned
Lajang	819	Tito Shipyard, Kraljevica	1959
Dorang	822	Tito Shipyard, Kraljevica	1959
Todak	823	Tito Shipyard, Kraljevica	1959

These are the survivors of six craft built specifically for Indonesia.

'Kris' class   UK/Malaysia

Type: fast attack craft (gun)
Displacement: 96 tons standard; 109 tons full load
Dimensions: length 103.0ft (31.4m); beam 19.8ft (6.0m); draught 5.5ft (1.7m)
Gun armament: 2 × 40mm Bofors L/60 AA in single mountings
Missile armament: none
Torpedo armament: none
Anti-submarine armament: none
Electronics: 1 × Decca 606 or 707 surface search and navigation radar
Propulsion: 2 × MTU MD 655/18 diesels delivering 2,600kW (3,485hp) to two shafts
Performance: maximum speed 27kt; range 2,600km (1,615 miles) at 14kt
Complement: 3+19

1. Malaysia

Name	No	Builder	Commissioned
Sri Selangor	3139	Vosper, Portsmouth	Mar 1963
Sri Kelantan	3142	Vosper, Portsmouth	Nov 1963
Sri Trengganu	3143	Vosper, Portsmouth	Dec 1963
Sri Sabah	3144	Vosper, Portsmouth	Sep 1964
Sri Sarawak	3145	Vosper, Portsmouth	Sep 1964
Sri Negri Sembilan	3146	Vosper, Portsmouth	Sep 1964
Sri Melaka	3147	Vosper, Portsmouth	Nov 1964
Kris	34	Vosper, Portsmouth	Jan 1966
Sundang	35	Vosper, Portsmouth	Nov 1966
Badek	37	Vosper, Portsmouth	Dec 1966
Renchong	38	Vosper, Portsmouth	Jan 1967
Tombak	39	Vosper, Portsmouth	Mar 1967
Lembing	40*	Vosper, Portsmouth	Apr 1967
Serampang	41	Vosper, Portsmouth	May 1967
Panah	42	Vosper, Portsmouth	Jul 1967
Kerambit	43*	Vosper, Portsmouth	Jul 1967
Beledau	44*	Vosper, Portsmouth	Sep 1967
Kelewang	45	Vosper, Portsmouth	Oct 1967
Rentaka	46	Vosper, Portsmouth	Sep 1967
Sri Perlis	47*	Vosper, Portsmouth	Jan 1968
Sri Johor	49*	Vosper, Portsmouth	Feb 1968

*Training craft

These 21 craft are the survivors of 24 ordered as FAC(G)s for the patrol and training roles in three sub-variants. The original six vessels, of which three remain in service, are of the 'Sri Kehah' class and were ordered in 1961. The following four craft, of which all remain in service, were ordered in 1963. And the other fourteen craft, of which all remain in service, were ordered in 1965. All the craft have air-conditioning and roll stabilization, and the differences between the classes are confined to minor details such as different communication systems.

'Kronshtadt' class   USSR/China

Type: fast attack craft (gun)
Displacement: 303 tons standard; 335 tons full load
Dimensions: length 52.1m (170.9ft); beam 6.5m (21.3ft); draught 2.1m (6.9ft)
Gun armament: 1 × 85mm (3.35in) L/52 DP in a single mounting; 2 × 37mm L/63 AA in single mountings; 6 × 14.5mm (0.57in) L/93 machine-guns in 3 × twin mountings
Missile armament: none
Torpedo armament: none
Anti-submarine armament: 2 × RBU 1200 five-barrel rocket-launchers; 2 × depth-charge racks for ? depth-charges
Mines: 2 × rails for 8 × mines
Electronics: 1 × 'Ball End' or 'Fin Curve' surface search and navigation radar; 1 × Tamir II hull-mounted high-frequency search and attack sonar; 1 × 'Dead Duck' IFF system; 1 × 'Ski Pole' IFF system
Propulsion: 3 × Type 9D diesels delivering 2,475kW (3,320hp) to three shafts
Performance: maximum speed 18kt; range 2,600km (1,615 miles) at 12kt
Complement: 4+47

1. Albania (2 craft)

Four of these FAC(G)s were transferred from the USSR in 1958 but were returned for updating with anti-submarine weapons in 1960 (two craft) and 1961 (two craft). The current two craft are named *350* and *351*, the other two having been deleted. Compared with the Chinese vessels, these two obsolete patrol craft have 2 × depth-charge throwers in addition to the depth-charge racks, and a revised electronics fit that includes 1 × 'Ball Gun' surface search radar, 1 × 'Neptun' navigation radar, and 1 × 'High Pole' IFF system.

2. China (20 craft)

In July 1955 China received from the USSR six 'Kronshtadt'-class FAC(G)s, and subsequently built another fourteen units up to 1957. The craft are now used for patrol and training, with *251* and *258* in service with the North Sea Fleet, *262*, *263*, *630* and *633* to *635* in service with the East Sea Fleet, and *651* to *656* in service with the South Sea Fleet.

3. Romania (3 craft)

Named *V1*, *V2* and *V3*, these Soviet-built craft were transferred in 1956, and in 1981 their armament was revised to the present standard of 2 × 37mm L/63 AA guns and 2 × 14.5mm (0.57in) L/93 machine-guns.

'Ku-song' class   North Korea

Type: fast attack craft (torpedo)
Displacement: ? tons standard; 35 tons full load
Dimensions: length 18.3m (60.0ft); beam 3.4m (11.0ft); draught 1.7m (5.5ft)
Gun armament: 4 × 14.5mm (0.57in) L/93 machine-guns in 2 × twin mountings
Missile armament: none
Torpedo armament: 2 × single 457mm or 533mm (18in or 21in) mountings for 2 × medium- or heavy-weight anti-ship torpedoes
Anti-submarine armament: none
Electronics: 1 × 'Skin Head' surface search and navigation radar; 1 × 'Dead Duck' IFF system
Propulsion: 2 × M 50 diesels delivering 1,800kW (2,415hp) to two shafts
Performance: maximum speed 40kt; range ? km (? miles) at ? kt
Complement: 20

1. North Korea (8 'Ku-song'-class and 'Sin-hung'-class craft; 30 'Sin-hung (Modified)'-class craft)

Based on the Soviet 'D 3' class of FAC(T)s, which were produced in the late 1940s, the basically similar 'Ku-song' and 'Sin-hung'-class craft were built from the mid-1950s to 1970. The 'Sin-hung (Modified)' class is a FAH(T) derivative built between 1981 and 1985.

'La Combattante II' class   France/Greece

Type: fast attack craft (missile and torpedo)
Displacement: 234 tons standard; 275 tons full load
Dimensions: length 47.0m (154.2ft); beam 7.1m (23.3ft); draught 2.5m (8.2ft)
Gun armament: 4 × 35mm Oerlikon L/90 AA in 2 × GDM-A twin mountings
Missile armament: 2 × twin container-launchers for 4 × MM.38 Exocet anti-ship missiles
Torpedo armament: 2 × single 533mm (21in) mountings for 2 × SST-4 wire-guided torpedoes
Anti-submarine armament: none
Electronics: 1 × Triton surface search radar; 1 × Decca 1226C navigation radar; 1 × Pollux tracking radar used in conjunction with; 1 × Vega fire-control system
Propulsion: 4 × MTU 16V 538 diesels delivering 9,000kW (12,070hp) to four shafts
Performance: maximum speed 36.5kt; range 3,700km (2,300 miles) at 15kt or 1,575km (980 miles) at 25kt
Complement: 4+36

1. Germany (West) ('Type 148' class)

Name	No	Builder	Commissioned
Tiger	P6141	CMN, Cherbourg	Oct 1972
Iltis	P6142	CMN, Cherbourg	Jan 1973
Luchs	P6143	CMN, Cherbourg	Apr 1973
Marder	P6144	CMN, Cherbourg	Jun 1973
Leopard	P6145	CMN, Cherbourg	Aug 1973
Fuchs	P6146	Lürssen/CMN	Oct 1973
Jaguar	P6147	CMN, Cherbourg	Nov 1973
Löwe	P6148	Lürssen/CMN	Jan 1974
Wolf	P6149	CMN, Cherbourg	Feb 1974
Panther	P6150	Lürssen/CMN	Mar 1974
Haher	P6151	CMN, Cherbourg	Jun 1974
Storch	P6152	Lürssen/CMN	Jul 1974
Pelikan	P6153	CMN, Cherbourg	Sep 1974
Elster	P6154	Lürssen/CMN	Nov 1974
Alk	P6155	CMN, Cherbourg	Jan 1975
Dommel	P6156	Lürssen/CMN	Feb 1975
Weihe	P6157	CMN, Cherbourg	Apr 1975
Pinguin	P6158	Lürssen/CMN	May 1975
Reiher	P6159	CMN, Cherbourg	Jun 1975
Kranich	P6160	Lürssen/CMN	Aug 1975

These German craft are derivatives of the basic 'La Combattante II' design and were ordered in December 1970 from the French Direction Technique de Constructions Navales, although eight hulls were completed by Lürssen for fitting out in France. The craft are FAC(M/Gs), and have standard and full-load displacements of 234 and 265 tons on dimensions of: length 47.0m (154.2ft), beam 7.6m (24.9ft) and draught 2.5m (8.2ft). The armament consists of 1 × 76mm (3in) L/62 DP in an

▲HS *Ipoploiarhos Konidis* is a 'La Combattante II'-class boat of the Greek navy.

▼This 'La Combattante II'-class Libyan patrol boat is of the type destroyed in the Gulf of Sidra in March 1986 by the US Navy, when approaching the Sixth Fleet.

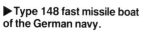

▶Type 148 fast missile boat of the German navy.

OTO Melara Compact single mounting and 1 × 40mm
Bofors L/70 AA in a Bofors single mounting, plus 2 ×
twin container-launchers for 4 × MM.38 Exocet anti-ship
missiles; if the 40mm gun is removed two minelaying rails
can be installed. Sensors include 1 × Triton G air/surface
search radar, 1 × 3RM 20 navigation radar and 1 × Castor
tracking radar used in conjunction with 1 × Vega fire-
control system, and other electronic features are 1 ×
Panda optical director, 1 × Link 11 data-link, 1 × ESM
system with warning element, and 1 × IFF system. The
powerplant comprises 4 × MTU 872 diesels delivering
10,800kW (14,485hp) to four shafts for a maximum speed
of 36kt and a range of 1,125km (700 miles) at 30kt. The
complement is 4+26.

2. Greece

Name	No	Builder	Commis- sioned
Anthipoploiarhos Anninos	P14	CMN, Cherbourg	Jun 1972
Ipoploiarhos Arliotis	P15	CMN, Cherbourg	Apr 1972
Ipoploiarhos Konidis	P16	CMN, Cherbourg	Jul 1972
Ipoploiarhos Batsis	P17	CMN, Cherbourg	Dec 1971

These craft were ordered in 1969 and all four units are to
be modernized by the early 1990s.

3. Iran ('Kaman' class)

Name	No	Builder	Commis- sioned
Kaman	P221	CMN, Cherbourg	Aug 1977
Zoubin	P222	CMN, Cherbourg	Sep 1977
Khadang	P223	CMN, Cherbourg	Mar 1978
Falakhon	P226	CMN, Cherbourg	Mar 1978
Shamshir	P227	CMN, Cherbourg	Mar 1978
Gorz	P228	CMN, Cherbourg	Aug 1978
Gardouneh	P229	CMN, Cherbourg	Sep 1978
Khanjar	P230	CMN, Cherbourg	Aug 1981
Heyzeh	P231	CMN, Cherbourg	Aug 1981
Tabarzin	P232	CMN, Cherbourg	Aug 1981

These Iranian FAC(M/G)s were ordered in two equal
batches during February and October 1974, and are
similar in hull and machinery to the Greek units but with a
different armament and electronics fit. The armament
comprises 1 × 76mm (3in) L/62 DP in an OTO Melara
Compact single mounting, 1 × 40mm Bofors L/70 AA in a
Breda single mounting and 2 × twin container-launchers
for 4 × RGM-84 Harpoon anti-ship missiles used in
conjunction with a WM-28 gun and SSM fire-control
system. The Iranians received only twelve Harpoon

missiles before the imposition of an American embargo
after the fall of the Shah in 1979, and the last three were
not even fitted with Harpoon launchers. The propulsion
comprises four MTU 16V 538 TB91 diesels delivering
10,740kW (14,405hp), but as the full-load displacement is
275 tons the maximum speed is 34.5kt and the range
3,700km (2,300 miles) at 15kt, declining to 1,300km (805
miles) at 33.7kt. A complement of 31 is carried. The
eleventh and twelfth units of the class, Pekyan and
Joshan, were sunk in combat, the former by the Iraqis in
1980 during the Iraq–Iran War, and the latter by the
Americans during April 1988.

4. Libya ('La Combattante IIG' class)

Name	No	Builder	Commis- sioned
Sharara	518	CMN, Cherbourg	Feb 1982
Wahag	522	CMN, Cherbourg	May 1982
Shehab	524	CMN, Cherbourg	Apr 1982
Shouaiai	528	CMN, Cherbourg	Sep 1982
Shoula	532	CMN, Cherbourg	Oct 1982
Shafak	534	CMN, Cherbourg	Dec 1982

▲ *Gorz* is a 'Kaman'-class missile craft serving in the Iranian navy. Note the standard armament layout: 76mm forward, twin missile launchers midships and 40mm aft.

Name	Pennant No	Builder	Commis- sioned
Bark	536	CMN, Cherbourg	Mar 1983
Rad	538	CMN, Cherbourg	May 1983
Laheeb	542	CMN, Cherbourg	Jul 1983

These Libyan FAC(M/G)s were ordered in May 1977 to an enlarged 'La Combattante II' design with standard and full-load displacements of 258 and 311 tons respectively on dimensions of: length 49.4m (162.1ft), beam 7.1m (23.3ft) and draught 2.0m (6.6ft). The missile armament comprises 4 × single container-launchers for 4 × Otomat anti-ship missiles, and the other weapons include 1 × 76mm (3in) L/62 DP in an OTO Melara Compact single mounting and 2 × 40mm Bofors L/70 AA in a Breda twin mounting. The electronics fit is 1 × Triton surface search radar, 1 × Castor I tracking radar used in conjunction with 1 × Vega II fire-control system, and 1 × Panda

optical director. The powerplant of 4 × MTU 20V 538 TB91 diesels delivers 13,400kW (17,970hp) to four shafts for a maximum speed of 39kt and a range of 2,960km (1,840 miles) at 15kt. The complement is 27. A tenth unit, *Waheed* (526), was sunk by US forces in March 1986, and a second 'La Combattante IIG'-class unit was severely damaged two days later.

5. Malaysia ('La Combattante IID' or 'Perdana' class)

Name	No	Builder	Commis- sioned
Perdana	3501	CMN, Cherbourg	Dec 1972
Serang	3502	CMN, Cherbourg	Jan 1973
Ganas	3503	CMN, Cherbourg	Feb 1973
Ganyang	3504	CMN, Cherbourg	Mar 1973

Ordered in 1970, these Malaysian FAC(M/G)s are close to the norm in displacement and dimensions. The missile armament comprises 2 × single container-launchers for 2 × MM.38 Exocet anti-ship missiles, and the other weapons include 1 × 57mm SAK 57 Mk 1 L/70 DP in a Bofors single mounting and 1 × 40mm Bofors L/70 AA in a Bofors single mounting. The electronics suite includes 1 × Triton surface search radar, 1 × Decca 616 navigation radar, 1 × Pollux tracking radar used in conjunction with 1 × Vega fire-control system, 1 × ESM system with warning element, and 4 × 57mm 'chaff'/flare-launchers. The powerplant of 4 × MTU 870 diesels delivers 10,400kW (13,950hp) to four shafts for a maximum speed of 36.5kt and a range of 1,500km (930 miles) at 25kt. The complement is 5+30.

'La Combattante III' class   France/Greece

Type: fast attack craft (missile and gun)
Displacement: 359 tons or (P24/29) 329 tons standard; 425 tons or (P24/29) 429 tons full load
Dimensions: length 56.2m (184.0ft); beam 8.0ft (26.2ft); draught 2.1m (7.0ft)
Gun armament: 2 × 76mm (3in) L/62 DP in OTO Melara Compact single mountings; 4 × 30mm Oerlikon L/85 AA in two EMERLEC-30 twin mountings
Missile armament: 4 × container-launchers for 4 × MM.38 Exocet anti-ship missiles or (in P24/29) 6 × container-launchers for 6 × Penguin Mk II anti-ship missiles
Torpedo armament: 2 × single 533mm (21in) mountings for 2 × SST-4 wire-guided torpedoes (only in P20/23)
Anti-submarine armament: none
Electronics: 1 × Triton surface search radar; 1 × Decca 1226 navigation radar; 1 × Castor II tracking radar and 1 × Pollux tracking radar used in conjunction with; 1 × Vega I or II fire-control system; 2 × two Panda optical directors

Propulsion: 4 × MTU 20V 538 TB92 diesels delivering 15,500kW (20,790hp), or (in P24/29) four MTU 20V 538 TB91 diesels delivering 11,200kW (15,020shp), in each case to four shafts
Performance: maximum speed 35.7kt or (in P24/29) 32.5kt; range 3,700km (2,300 miles) at 15kt or 1,300km (810 miles) at 32.6kt
Complement: 5+37

1. Greece

Name	No	Builder	Commissioned
Antiploiarhos Laskos	P20	CMN, Cherbourg	Apr 1977
Plotarhis Blessas	P21	CMN, Cherbourg	Jul 1977
Ipoploiarhos Mikonios	P22	CMN, Cherbourg	Feb 1978
Ipoploiarhos Troupakis	P23	CMN, Cherbourg	Nov 1977
Simeoforos Kavaloudis	P24	Hellenic Shipyards	Jul 1980
Anthipoploiarhos Kostakos	P25	Hellenic Shipyards	Sep 1980
Ipoploiarhos Deyiannis	P26	Hellenic Shipyards	Dec 1980
Simeoforos Xenos	P27	Hellenic Shipyards	Mar 1981
Simeoforos Simitzopoulos	P28	Hellenic Shipyards	Jun 1981
Simeoforos Starakis	P29	Hellenic Shipyards	Oct 1981

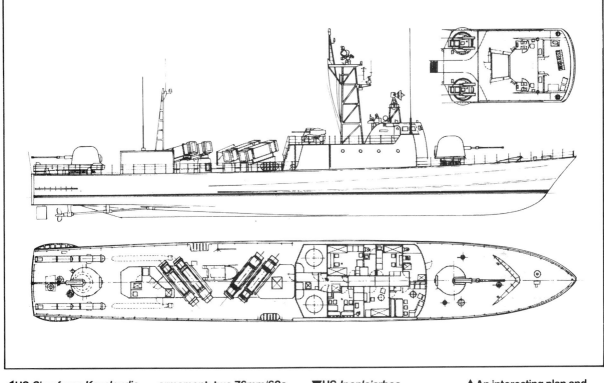

◀HS *Simeforos Kavaloudis* is a 'La Combattante III'-class fast missile craft serving in the Greek Navy. Note the typically heavy

armament: two 76mm/62a guns, twin 30mm EMERLECs amidship and six single Penguin missile-launchers.

▼HS *Ipoploiarhos Troupakis,* another 'La Combattante III'-class vessel in the Greek navy.

▲An interesting plan and side view of the 'Combattante III' type.

These impressive FAC(M/G)s fall into two sub-classes. Ordered in September 1974, the four craft built in France have fewer anti-ship missiles but two anti-ship torpedoes and higher performance, while the six licence-built in Greece after an order placed in 1977 have more anti-ship missiles but no torpedoes and lower performance.

2. Nigeria ('La Combattante IIIB' class)

Name	No	Builder	Commissioned
Siri	P181	CMN, Cherbourg	Feb 1981
Ayam	P182	CMN, Cherbourg	Jun 1981
Ekun	P183	CMN, Cherbourg	Sep 1981

Ordered in November 1977 as potent FAC(M/G)s, these Nigerian craft are named 'Tiger' in the three main Nigerian languages, and have standard and full-load displacements of 385 and 430 tons respectively on dimensions of: length 56.2m (184.4ft), beam 7.6m (24.9ft) and draught 2.1m (7.0ft). The missile armament comprises 2 × twin container-launchers for 4 × MM.38 Exocet anti-ship missiles, and the other weapons consist of 1 × 76mm (3in) L/62 DP in an OTO Melara Compact single mounting (250 rounds), 2 × 40mm Bofors L/70 AA in a Breda twin mounting (1,600 rounds), and 4 × 30mm Oerlikon L/85 AA in 2 × EMERLEC-30 twin mountings (1,970 rounds). The electronics suite includes 1 × Triton surface search radar, 1 × Decca 1226 navigation radar and 1 × Castor II tracking radar used in conjunction with 1 × Vega fire-control system; other features are 2 × Panda optical directors and 1 × ESM system with RDL-2 warning element. The propulsion arrangement comprises 4 × MTU 16V 956 TB92 diesels delivering 15,000kW (20,120hp) to four shafts for a maximum speed of 41kt and a range of 3,700km (2,300 miles) at 15kt. The complement is 42.

3. Qatar ('La Combattante IIIM' class)

Name	No	Builder	Commissioned
Damsah	Q01	CMN, Cherbourg	Nov 1982
Al Ghariyah	Q02	CMN, Cherbourg	Feb 1983
Rbigah	Q03	CMN, Cherbourg	May 1983

Ordered in October 1980, these Qatari craft are similar to the Tunisian units in all essential respects.

4. Tunisia ('La Combattante IIIM' class)

Name	No	Builder	Commissioned
La Galite	501	CMN, Cherbourg	Oct 1984
Tunis	502	CMN, Cherbourg	Nov 1984
Carthage	503	CMN, Cherbourg	Dec 1984

Ordered in August 1981 with French funding and generally similar to the Greek units, these Tunisian FAC(M/G)s have a beam enlarged to 8.2m (26.9ft) for standard and full-load displacements of 345 and 425 tons respectively. The missile armament comprises 2 × quadruple container-launchers for 8 × MM.40 Exocet anti-ship missiles, and the other weapons consist of 1 × 76mm (3in) L/62 DP in an OTO Melara Compact single mounting, 2 × 40mm Bofors L/70 AA in a Breda twin mounting, and 2 × 30mm Oerlikon L/75 AA in a GCM-A03 twin mounting. Among the electronics fit are 1 × Triton surface search radar, 1 × Castor II tracking radar used in conjunction with 1 × Vega II fire-control system, 1 × Sylosat satellite navigation system, 2 × Naja optronic directors, 1 × ESM system with warning element, and 1 × Dagaie 'chaff'/flare-launcher. The propulsion system comprises 4 × MTU 20V 538 TB93 diesels delivering 14,400kW (19,315hp) to four shafts for a maximum speed of 38.5kt and a range of 5,200km (3,230 miles) at 18kt, declining to 1,300km (810 miles) at 33kt. The complement is 35.

'Lazaga' class: *see* 'Lürssen FPB/PB-57' class

'Libelle' class   Germany

Type: fast attack craft (torpedo)
Displacement: ? tons standard; 28 tons full load
Dimensions: length 19.0m (62.3ft); beam 4.5m (14.75ft); draught 2.0m (6.6ft)
Gun armament: 2 × 23mm L/87 AA in a ZU-23-2 twin mounting
Missile armament: none
Torpedo armament: 2 × single 533mm (21in) mountings for 2 × Type 53 heavyweight anti-ship torpedoes
Anti-submarine armament: none
Mines: fitted with mine rails
Electronics: 1 × TSR 333 surface search and navigation radar
Propulsion: 3 × M 50-F3bis diesels delivering 2,700kW (3,620hp) to three shafts
Performance: maximum speed 40kt; range ? km (? miles) at ? kt
Complement: 10

1. Germany (East) – 14 craft (Nos 921–925, 941, 944, 945 and 961–965)

These are the survivors of a 30-strong class of FAC(T)s built by VEB Peenewerft at Wolgast from 1975. The design is obsolete and being phased from service.

'Lung Chiang' class: *see* 'PSMM Mk 5' class

'Lürssen FPB-36' class   Germany/Mauritania

Type: fast attack craft (gun)
Displacement: ? tons standard; 139 tons full load
Dimensions: length 36.2m (118.7ft); beam 5.8m (19.0ft); draught 1.9m (6.2ft)

▲ *Ipoploiarhos Konidis* reveals the Greek navy's 'La Combattante' class gun armament of four 35mm cannon in two twin turrets.

Gun armament: 1 × 40mm Bofors L/70 AA in a single mounting; 1 × 20mm Oerlikon L/75 AA in an A41A single mounting; 2 × 0.5in (12.7mm) machine-guns in single mountings
Missile armament: none
Torpedo armament: none
Anti-submarine armament: none
Electronics: 1 × Raytheon RN 1220/6XB surface search radar; 1 × Panda optical director
Propulsion: 2 × MTU 16V 538 TB90 diesels delivering 4,300kW (5,765hp) to two shafts
Performance: maximum speed 36kt; range 2,225km (1,385 miles) at 17kt
Complement: 3+16

1. Chile ('Guacolda' class)

Name	No	Builder	Commissioned
Guacolda	80	Bazan	Jul 1965
Fresia	81	Bazan	Dec 1965
Quidora	82	Bazan	1966
Tegualda	83	Bazan	1966

Ordered in 1963, these FAC(T)s may be regarded as the precursors of the 'FPB-36' type, with a full-load displacement of 134 tons on dimensions of: length 36.0m (118.1ft), beam 5.6m (18.4ft) and draught 2.2m (7.2ft). The armament is 2 × 40mm Bofors L/60 AA in Bofors single mountings and 4 × single 533mm (21in) British Mk 4 mountings for heavyweight anti-ship torpedoes. The electronics fit is limited to 1 × Decca 505 surface search and navigation radar, and propulsion is provided by 2 × Mercedes-Benz MB 839Bd diesels delivering 3,600kW (4,830hp) to two shafts for a maximum speed of 32kt and a range of 2,800km (1,740 miles) at 15kt. The complement is 20.

2. Congo

Name	No	Builder	Commissioned
Marien N'Gouabi	P601	Bazan	Nov 1982
Les Trois Glorieuses	P602	Bazan	Jan 1983
Les Maloango	P603	Bazan	Mar 1983

Ordered in 1980, these are simple patrol craft derived from the 'Barcelo' class. The displacement, dimensions, propulsion arrangement and performance differ slightly from the Spanish norm, and the armament comprises 1 × 40mm Bofors L/70 AA in a Breda single mounting, 1 × 20mm Oerlikon AA in a single mounting and 2 × 0.5in (12.7mm) machine-guns in single mountings. This armament is used in conjunction with 1 × Decca surface search and navigation radar and 1 × Panda optical director.

▲ Poor-quality but rare photograph of 'Lürssen FPB-36' class FAC(T)s of the Chilean navy's 'Guacolda' class in the Beagle Channel.

▼ Side view of Lürssen 36m type of the Chilean navy.

▲Overhead view of
Guacolda of the Chilean
navy, showing the layout of

the four torpedo tubes, the
rear nearest one of which is
loaded.

▼*Quidora, Tequalda,
Guacolda* and *Fresia* of the
Chilean navy in line astern.

3. Ecuador ('Manta' class)

Name	No	Builder	Commissioned
Manta	LM27	Lürssen	Jun 1971
Tulcan	LM28	Lürssen	Apr 1971
Nuevo Rocafuerte	LM29	Lürssen	Jun 1971

This is a FAC(M) variant of the 'Guacolda' class with upgraded electronics and an additional engine driving a third shaft for higher performance. The standard and full-load displacements are 119 and 134 tons respectively on dimensions of: length 36.4m (119.4ft), beam 5.8m (19.1ft) and draught 1.8m (6.0ft). Each of the three craft was originally armed with 1 × 40mm Bofors L/70 AA in a single mounting and 2 × single 533m (21in) mountings for heavyweight anti-ship torpedoes, but the class was rearmed in 1979 with a smaller-calibre gun and in 1981 with anti-ship missiles. The missile armament comprises 4 × single container-launchers for 4 × Gabriel II anti-ship missiles, and the other component of the weapon system is 4 × 30mm Oerlikon L/85 AA in 2 × EMERLEC-30 twin mountings. The electronics fit comprises 1 × navigation radar and 1 × Pollux tracking radar used in conjunction with 1 × Vega fire-control system. The propulsion arrangement comprises three Mercedes-Benz MB 839Bd diesels delivering 6,750kW (9,055hp) to three shafts for a maximum speed of 42kt and a range of 2,800km (1,740 miles) at 15kt, declining to 1,300km (805 miles) at 30kt. The complement is 19.

4. Mauritania

Name	No	Builder	Commissioned
El Vaiz	P361	Bazan	Oct 1979
El Beig	P362	Bazan	May 1979
El Kinz	P363	Bazan	Aug 1982

These are small and wholly unexceptional FAC(G) limited in practical use to patrol and training. The first two units were ordered in 1976, and the third in 1979. Mauritiana had planned to order another three of this type, which is very similar to the Spanish 'Barcelo' class, but the crisis caused by the independence of the Spanish Sahara led the country to plan more ambitious light forces.

5. Spain ('Barcelo' class)

Name	No	Builder	Commissioned
Barcelo	P11	Lürssen	Mar 1976
Laya	P12	Bazan	Dec 1976
Javier Quiroga	P13	Bazan	Apr 1977
Ordonez	P14	Bazan	Jun 1977
Acevedo	P15	Bazan	Jul 1977
Candido Perez	P16	Bazan	Nov 1977

▼Although poorly focused this is still a valuable photograph of a 'Barcelo'- class fast attack craft in the Spanish navy.

These are simple FAC(G)s that were ordered in December 1973. The type has a full-load displacement of 134 tons on dimensions of: length 36.2m (118.7ft), beam 5.8m (19.0ft) and draught 1.9m (6.2ft). The armament comprises 1 × 40mm Bofors L/70 AA in a Breda single mounting, 2 × 20mm Oerlikon L/85 AA in 2 × GAM-B01 single mountings and 2 × 0.5in (12.7mm) machine-guns in single mountings; the craft are also each fitted for but not with 2 × single 533mm (21in) mountings for heavyweight anti-ship torpedoes, and for but not with 2 or 4 × container-launchers for 2 or 4 × anti-ship missiles in place of the torpedo tubes and 20mm cannon. The electronics fit includes 1 × Raytheon 1220/6XB surface search radar and 1 × Panda optical director. The propulsion arrangement is based on two Bazan-built MTU 16V 538 TB90 diesels delivering 4,300kW (5,765hp) to two shafts for a maximum speed of 36kt and a range of 2,225km (1,385 miles) at 17kt. The complement is 3+16.

'Lürssen FPB-38' class   Germany/Bahrain

Type: fast attack craft (gun)
Displacement: 188 tons standard; 205 tons full load
Dimensions: length 38.5m (126.3ft); beam 7.0m (22.9ft); draught 2.2m (7.2ft)
Gun armament: 2 × 40mm Bofors L/70 AA in a Breda Compact twin mounting; 2 × 20mm Oerlikon L/85 AA in 2 × GAM-B01 single mountings; 2 × 7.62mm (0.3in) machine-guns in single mountings

▼Light patrol craft of the Lürssen FPB-38 type.

Missile armament: none
Torpedo armament: none
Anti-submarine armament: none
Mines: two rails fitted for 14 × mines
Electronics: 1 × 9GR 600 surface search and fire-control radar; 1 × Decca 1226 navigation radar; 1 × Lynx optronic director used in conjunction with; 1 × 9LV 100 fire-control system; 1 × Dagaie 'chaff'-launcher
Propulsion: 2 × MTU 20V 539 TB91 diesels delivering 6,700kW (8,985hp) to two shafts
Performance: maximum speed 33kt; range 2,000km (1,245 miles) at 16kt or 1,100km (685 miles) at 30.5kt
Complement: 3+16 plus provision for 2 spare officers

1. Bahrain

Name	No	Builder	Commissioned
Al Riffa	10	Lürssen	Aug 1981
Hawar	11	Lürssen	Nov 1981

Ordered in 1979, this is a small FAC(G) type with only limited armament and capabilities. The craft were originally to have been fitted with just a single 40mm Bofors L/70 AA in a single mounting.

2. Germany (West)

Name	No	Builder	Commissioned
		Lürssen	

FPB 38

▲FPB-38 in the Bahrain
navy showing twin 40mm
Bofors forward.

▼The Lürssen 'FPB 62'
class has provision for a
single Aérospatiale Dauphin
II helicopter, which together

with 76mm, 40mm and
missile armament makes it
little short of a frigate.

Little has been revealed about Germany's plan for this class of small FAC(G)s, which will probably be used for the coastal patrol role.

3. Malaysia

Name	No	Builder	Commis-sioned
		Lürssen	

This class of light FAC(G)s is eventually to total eighteen and is designed mainly for the patrol role. The type has a full-load displacement of 221 tons on dimensions of: length 38.5m (126.3ft) and beam 7.0m (23.0ft). The armament comprises 2 × 20mm Oerlikon L/85 AA in GAM-B01 single mountings and 2 × 7.62m (0.3in) machine-guns in single mountings. The craft are fitted with surface search radar, and the fire-control system is of the optical type. The propulsion arrangement comprises 2 × MTU diesels delivering 7,360kW (9,870hp) to two shafts for a maximum speed of 34.7kt and a range of 2,225km (1,385 miles) at 24kt, declining to 1,760km (1,095 miles) at 32.5kt. The crew is 7+30 plus provision for one spare officer.

4. United Arab Emirates (Abu Dhabi)

Name	No	Builder	Commis-sioned
		Lürssen	
		Lürssen	

These two craft are in no way exceptions to the general configuration and capabilities of the class.

'Lürssen FPB/MGB-62' class   West Germany/Bahrain

Type: fast attack craft (missile and gun)
Displacement: ? tons standard; 632 tons full load
Dimensions: length 62.95m (206.5ft); beam 9.3m (30.5ft); draught 2.9m (9.5ft)
Gun armament: 1 × 76mm (3in) L/62 DP in an OTO Melara Compact single mounting; 2 × 40mm Bofors L/70 AA in a Breda Compact twin mounting; 2 × 20mm Oerlikon L/93 AA in GAM-B01 single mountings
Missile armament: 2 × twin container-launchers for 4 × MM.40 Exocet anti-ship missiles
Torpedo armament: none
Anti-submarine armament: none
Aircraft: provision for 1 × Aérospatiale SA 365 Dauphin II helicopter on a platform amidships
Electronics: 1 × Sea Giraffe air/surface search radar; 1 × Decca navigation radar; 1 × 9LV 300 radar used in conjunction with; 1 × 9LV 331 fire-control system; 1 × Philips optronic director; 2 × Panda Mk 2 optical directors; 1 × ESM system with Cutlass-E warning and Cygnus jamming elements; 2 × Dagaie 'chaff'/flare-launchers
Propulsion: 4 × MTU 20V 538 TB93 diesels delivering 14,120kW (18,940hp) to four shafts
Performance: maximum speed 34.7kt; range 7,400km (4,600 miles) at 16kt
Complement: 7+36

1. Bahrain ('FPB-62' class)

Name	No	Builder	Commis-sioned
Bans al Manama		Lürssen	Dec 1987
Al Muharraq		Lürssen	Feb 1988

This large FAC(M/G) is little short of a corvette in size and capability, and the light helicopter adds considerably to anti-ship capability as it carries four AS.15TT anti-ship missiles, with four reloads.

2. Singapore ('MGB-62' class)

Name	No	Builder	Commis-sioned
Victory	P88	Lürssen	1989
Valour	P89	Singapore SBEC	1990
Vigilance	P90	Singapore SBEC	
Valiant	P91	Singapore SBEC	
Vigour	P92	Singapore SBEC	
Vengeance	P93	Singapore SBEC	

These small but powerfully armed anti-ship and anti-submarine craft are genuinely of corvette capability, with the lead vessel built by the designer and the others under licence in Singapore. The full-load displacement is 600 tons, and the dimensions include: length 63.0m (206.7ft), beam 9.3m (30.5ft) and draught 5.4m (17.7ft). The armament comprises 2 × Mk 141 quadruple container-launchers for 8 × RGM-84 Harpoon anti-ship missiles, 1 × 76mm (3in) L/62 DP in an OTO Melara Super Rapid mounting, 2 × 40mm Bofors L/70 AA in a Breda Compact twin mounting, 2 × 20mm Oerlikon AA in single mountings, and 2 × ILAS 3 triple 324mm (12.75in) mountings for ? × A 244/S anti-submarine torpedoes. The comprehensive electronic fit includes 1 × Hollandse Signaalapparaten surface search radar, 1 × navigation radar, 1 × Philips Elektronikindustrie (Bofors) fire-control system, and 1 × EDO 780 variable-depth active search and attack sonar. The propulsion arrangement is 4 × MTU 16V 538 TB93 diesels delivering 14,000kW (18,775hp) to four shafts for a maximum speed of 30kt and a range of 7,400km (4,600 miles) at 18kt. The complement is 44. It is possible that improved anti-aircraft/anti-missile armament may be retrofitted in the form of a modular Naval Crotale SAM system or a 30mm Goalkeeper CIWS mounting.

3. United Arab Emirates/Abu Dhabi ('FPB-62' class)

Name	No	Builder	Commissioned
	P6201	Lürssen	
	P6202	Lürssen	
	P6203	Lürssen	
	P6204	Lürssen	

This version of the 'FBB-62' design has a full-load displacement of about 630 tons and was delivered in the late 1980s (first pair) and early 1990s (second pair). The type lacks the helicopter of the Bahraini version, but has considerably more embarked firepower in the form of 8 × MM.40 Exocet anti-ship missiles, 1 × 76mm (3in) L/62 DP in an OTO Melara Compact single mounting, 1 × Naval Crotale launcher for ? × R.440 SAMs and 1 × SADRAL sextuple launcher for ? × Mistral SAMs. The electronics suite (including 1 × Naja optronic director, 1 × ESM system with Cutlass warning and Cygnus jamming elements, and 2 × Dagaie 'chaff'-launchers) is also highly capable, and the propulsion arrangement comprises 4 × MTU diesels delivering 14,000kW (18,775hp) for a maximum speed of 32kt and a range of 7,400km (4,600 miles) at 16kt. The complement is 43.

'Lürssen TNC-42' class
Germany/Greece

Type: fast attack craft (torpedo)
Displacement: 160 tons standard; 190 tons full load
Dimensions: length 42.5m (139.4ft); beam 7.2m (23.4ft); draught 2.4m (7.9ft)
Gun armament: 2 × 40mm Bofors L/70 AA in Bofors single mountings
Missile armament: none
Torpedo armament: 4 × single 533mm (21in) mountings for 4 × SST-4 wire-guided torpedoes
Anti-submarine armament: none
Mines: up to 8 × mines in place of torpedo tubes
Electronics: 1 × surface search and navigation radar
Propulsion: 4 × MTU 16V 538 diesels delivering 10,700kW (14,350hp) to four shafts
Performance: maximum speed 42kt; range 1,850km (1,150 miles) at 32kt or 925km (575 miles) at 40kt
Complement: 39

1. Germany (West) ('Zobel' class)

Name	No	Builder	Commissioned
Wiesel	P6093	Lürssen	Jun 1962
Dachs	P6094	Lürssen	Sep 1962
Hyane	P6099	Kröger	May 1963
Frettchen	P6100	Lürssen	Jun 1963
Ozelot	P6101	Lürssen	Oct 1963

These obsolete craft are the survivors of 40 'Jaguar' class FAC(T)s built by Lürssen (30 craft) and Kröger (10 craft), of which most have now been deleted or transferred to friendly navies. The type has a full-load displacement of 220 tons on dimensions of: length 42.6m (139.7ft), beam 7.0m (23.0ft) and draught 2.9m (9.5ft). The armament comprises two 40mm Bofors L/70 AA in Bofors single mountings and two single 533mm (21in) mountings for two Seal wire-guided torpedoes. The electronics fit includes two surface search and tracking radars used in conjunction with two WM-20 fire-control systems. The propulsion arrangement comprises four MTU diesels delivering 8,490kW (11,990hp) to four shafts for a maximum speed of 35kt+. The complement is 4+26.

2. Greece

Name	No	Builder	Commissioned
Hesperos	P50	Lürssen	Aug 1958
Kentauros	P52	Kröger	Nov 1958
Kyklon	P53	Lürssen	Mar 1959
Lelaps	P54	Lürssen	Feb 1959
Skorpios	P55	Kröger	Nov 1959
Tyfon	P56	Lürssen	Jun 1959

These Greek craft were transferred from West Germany in 1976 and 1977, together with three others to be cannibalized for spares.

3. Indonesia

Name	No	Builder	Commissioned
Beruang	652	Lürssen	1959
Harimau	654	Lürssen	1960

These Indonesian craft are the survivors of eight supplied by West Germany and are generally similar to the baseline configuration. The complement is 39. Of the eight original craft, four had wooden hulls and the other four steel hulls. The two survivors are of the wooden-hulled type. One of the class, the steel-hulled *Madjan Tutal*, was sunk by a Dutch warship off Borneo in January 1962 while trying to land infiltrators in Borneo. Of the other craft, five were deleted in the second half of the 1970s to leave the current pair used mainly for patrol and training.

4. Saudi Arabia

Name	No	Builder	Commissioned
Dammam		Lürssen	1969
Khabar		Lürssen	1969
Maccah		Lürssen	1969

These craft were ordered by West Germany during 1968, and served in the North Sea and Baltic until transferred in 1976 after extensive refitting in West German yards. The craft each have a complement of 3+30. Although they have a capability against surface ships with their torpedoes, they are used mainly for patrol and training.

5. Sweden ('Spica I' class)

Name	No	Builder	Commissioned
Spica	T121	Gotaverken	Aug 1966
Capella	T123	Gotaverken	Mar 1966
Vega	T125	Karlskrona Varvet	Nov 1967
Virgo	T126	Karlskrona Varvet	Mar 1968

This obsolescent class is based on the 'TNC-42' design and initially comprised six craft, including *Sirius* (T122) and *Castor* (T124) which have now been deleted. The remainder of the class is in the process of deletion despite its upgrade from FAC(G/T) to interim FAC(M) standard, and is used for training. The type has standard and full-load displacements of 185 and 215 tons on dimensions of: length 42.7m (140.1ft), beam 7.1m (23.3ft) and draught 2.6m (8.5ft). The armament consists of 1 × 57mm Bofors

▼ Now deleted, *Castor* was one of six 'Spica I' class FAC(G/T)s in the Swedish navy. Main armament is a single 57mm gun forward and six torpedo-launchers. [*K. AB*]

SAK 57 Mk 1 L/70 DP in a Bofors single mounting, 6 × single 533m (21in) mountings for 6 × Tp 61 wire-guided torpedoes and (if 2 or 4 × torpedo-tube mountings are unshipped) 4 or 8 × container-launchers for 4 or 8 × RBS 15M anti-ship missiles. The electronics fit includes 1 × Skanter Mk 009 surface search and navigation radar and 1 × tracking radar used in conjunction with 1 × WM-22 fire-control system. Each craft also carries 10 × illuminant launchers (4 × 103mm calibre and 6 × 57mm calibre) and 2 × Philax 'chaff'/flare-launchers. The propulsion arrangement of this licence-built series differs radically from the German norm, however, consisting of three Rolls-Royce Proteus 1274 gas turbines delivering 12,720shp (9,485kW) to three shafts for a maximum speed of 40kt. The complement is 7+21.

6. Turkey

Name	No	Builder	Commissioned
Tufan	P331	Lürssen	1962
Mizrak	P333	Lürssen	1962
Kalkan	P335	Lürssen	1959
Karayel	P336	Lürssen	1962

These are the survivors of seven 'Jaguar'-class craft transferred between late 1976 and early 1977 as operational craft together with another three non-operational craft for cannibalization as spares.

▲This view of a 'Spica I' shows the superb field of fire for the 57mm gun in its turret forward. [*MARS, London*]

◀*Meltem*, a 'Kartal'-class missile boat of the Turkish navy. [*ASKU*]

7. Turkey ('Kartal' class)

Name	No	Builder	Commissioned
Denizkusu	P321	Lürssen	1967
Atmaca	P322	Lürssen	1967
Sahin	P323	Lürssen	1967
Kartal	P324	Lürssen	1967
Pelikan	P326	Lürssen	1968
Albatros	P327	Lürssen	1968
Simsek	P328	Lürssen	1968
Kasirga	P329	Lürssen	1967

The 'Kartal' FAC(M/T) class is a variant of the 'Jaguar' class produced for the Turkish Navy. The type has standard and full-load displacements of 160 and 190 tons on dimensions of: length 42.8m (140. 5ft), beam 7.1m (23.5ft) and draught 2.2m (7.2ft). The armament is fairly impressive, comprising 4 × single container-launchers for 4 × Penguin Mk II anti-ship missiles, 2 × 40mm Bofors L/70 AA in single mountings, and 4 × single 533mm (21in) mountings for heavyweight anti-ship torpedoes. The primary electronic systems are 1 × Decca 1226 surface search and navigation radar and 1 × tracking radar used in conjunction with 1 × WM-28 fire-control system. The propulsion arrangement of 4 × MTU 16V 538 diesels delivers 8,940kW (11,990hp) to four shafts for a maximum speed of 42kt and a range of 925km (525 miles) at 40kt. The complement is 39. A ninth unit, Meltem, sank after collision with a Soviet ship in 1985 and though salved was deemed too badly damaged for economical repair.

'Lürssen FPB/TNC-45' class   Germany/United Arab Emirates

Type: fast attack craft (missile and gun)
Displacement: 235 tons standard; 260 tons full load
Dimensions: length 44.9m (147.3ft); beam 7.0m (23.0ft); draught 2.5m (8.2ft)
Gun armament: 1 × 76mm (3in) L/62 DP in an OTO Melara Compact single mounting; 2 × 40mm Bofors L/70 AA in a Breda Compact twin mounting; 2 × 7.62mm (0.3in) machine-guns in single mountings
Missile armament: 2 × twin container-launchers for 4 × MM.40 Exocet anti-ship missiles
Torpedo armament: none
Anti-submarine armament: none
Electronics: 1 × TM1226 surface search and navigation radar; 1 × 9LV 200 Mk 2 tracking radar used with; 1 × 9LV 223 fire-control system; 1 × USFA optronic director; 1 × Panda optical director; 1 × ESM system with Cutlass-E warning and Cygnus jamming elements; 1 × Dagaie 'chaff'/flare-launcher
Propulsion: 4 × MTU 16V 538 TB92 diesels delivering 11,480kW (15,395hp) to four shafts
Performance: maximum speed 41.4kt; range 2,800km

(1,740 miles) at 16kt on two engines or 925km (575 miles) at 38.5kt on four engines
Complement: 5+35 plus provision for 3 spare men

1. Argentina

Name	No	Builder	Commissioned
Intrepida	P85	Lürssen	Jul 1974
Indomita	P86	Lürssen	Dec 1974

Ordered in 1970, these Argentine craft are FAC(G/T)s. The design is modestly different from that of later 'FPB/TNC-45' craft, with slightly more length and beam. The normal and full-load displacements are 240 and 268 tons respectively on dimensions of: length 45.4m (149.0ft), beam 7.4m (24.3ft) and draught 2.3m (7.5ft). The armament consists of 1 × 76mm (3in) L/62 DP in an OTO Melara Compact single mounting and 2 × 40mm Bofors L/70 AA in Bofors single mountings, complemented by 2 × single 533mm (21in) mountings for SST-4 wire-guided torpedoes; each craft is also fitted with 2 × 81mm (3.2in) launchers for illuminants. The electronics fit includes 1 × Decca 12 navigation radar, 1 × WM-22 optronic gun fire-control system, 1 × WM-11 torpedo fire-control system, and 1 × ESM system with warning element. The propulsion arrangement comprises 4 × MTU MD 872 diesels delivering 10,400kW (13,950hp) to four shafts for a maximum speed of 40kt and a range of 2,700km (1,680 miles) at 20kt. The complement is 2+37. It had been planned to procure another two units of the same class, but the relevant financial commitment was delayed and then abandoned.

2. Bahrain

Name	No	Builder	Commissioned
Ahmed el Fateh	20	Lürssen	Feb 1983
Al Jabiri	21	Lürssen	May 1984
Abdul Rahman al Fadel	22	Lürssen	Sep 1986
Sabah	23	Lürssen	1988
	24	Lürssen	
	25	Lürssen	

These Bahraini craft are standard FAC(M/G)s basically similar to the UAE vessels. The standard and full-load displacements are 228 and 259 tons respectively on dimensions of: length 44.9m (147.3ft), beam 7.0m (23.0ft) and draught 2.5m (8.2ft). The missile armament comprises 2 × twin container-launchers for 4 × MM.40 Exocet anti-ship missiles, and the other weapons are 1 × 76mm (3in) L/62 DP in an OTO Melara Compact single mounting (250 rounds), 2 × 40mm Bofors L/70B AA in a Breda Compact twin mounting (1,800 rounds), and 3 × 7.62mm (0.3in) machine-guns in single mountings (6,000 rounds). The electronics fit includes 1 × 9LV 200 surface search and tracking radar used in conjunction with 1 × 9LV 223 fire-control system, 1 × Decca 1226 navigation radar, 1 × Panda optical director (for the 40mm guns), 1 × ESM system with Cutlass-E warning and RDL-2ABC jamming elements, and 1 × Dugaie 'chaff'/flare-launcher. The propulsion arrangement comprises 4 × MTU 16V 538 TB92 diesels delivering 11,480kW (15,395hp) to four shafts for a maximum speed of 41.5kt and a range of 2,800km (1,740 miles) at 16kt on two engines, declining to 925km (575 miles) at 38.5kt. The first pair of craft was ordered in 1979, while the slightly different second pair was ordered in 1985. These craft each have a beam of 7.3m (23.9ft) and engines delivering 11,600kw (15,560hp) for a maximum speed of 42kt. A third pair of boats was ordered in 1986, and these two boats are to the revised standard of the second pair. The complement is 6+30 plus provision for 3 spare men.

3. Chile

Name	No	Builder	Commissioned
Iquique		CMN, Cherbourg	1969
Covadonga		CMN, Cherbourg	1969

These Chilean FAC(M/G)s are the ex-Israeli 'Saar 3'-class craft *Hanit* and *Hetz* sold to Chile in December 1988. The armament comprises 6 × single container-launchers for 6 × Gabriel II anti-ship missiles, 1 × 76mm (3in) L/62 DP in an OTO Melara Compact single mounting, and 2 × 20mm Oerlikon AA in single mountings.

4. Ecuador

Name	No	Builder	Commissioned
Quito	LM24	Lürssen	Jul 1976
Guayaquil	LM25	Lürssen	Dec 1977
Cuenca	LM26	Lürssen	Jul 1977

Ordered in the early 1970s, these Ecuadorean FAC(M/G)s approximate closely to the norm at standard and full-load displacements of 250 and 265 tons respectively on dimensions of: length 45.0m (147.6ft), beam 7.0m (23.0ft) and draught 2.5m (8.2ft). The missile armament comprises 4 × single container-launchers for 4 × MM.38 Exocet anti-ship missiles, and the other weapons consist of 1 × 76mm (3in) L/62 DP in an OTO Melara Compact single mounting and 2 × 35mm Oerlikon L/90 AA in a GDM-A twin mounting. The electronics fit includes 1 × Triton air/surface search radar, 1 × Decca navigation radar, and 1 × Pollux tracking radar used in conjunction with 1 × Vega fire-control system. The propulsion arrangement comprises 4 × MTU 16V 538 diesels delivering 10,400kW (13,950hp) to four shafts for a maximum speed of 40kt and a range of 3,350km (2,080

miles) at 16kt, declining to 1,300km (810 miles) at 40kt. The complement is 35.

5. Ghana

Name	No	Builder	Commissioned
Dzata	P28	Lürssen	Jul 1980
Sebo	P29	Lürssen	Jul 1980

Ordered in 1976, these Ghanaian craft are FAC(G)s with a full-load displacement of 269 tons on dimensions of: length 44.9m (147.3ft), beam 7.0m (23.0ft) and draught 2.7m (8.9ft). The armament originally consisted of 1 × 76mm (3in) L/62 DP in an OTO Melara Compact single mounting and 1 × 40mm Bofors L/70 AA in a single mounting, but has been revised to 2 × 40mm Bofors L/70 AA in single mountings to suit the craft better for their current fishery protection role. The electronics fit includes 1 × surface search radar used in conjunction with 1 × Canopus A fire-control system, 1 × Type 978 navigation radar, and 1 × LIOD optronic director. The propulsion arrangement of 2 × MTU 16V 538 TB91 diesels delivers 5,300kW (7,110hp) to two shafts for a maximum speed of 29.5kt and a range of 4,450km (3,320 miles) at 15kt, declining to 2,050km (1,275 miles) at 25kt. The complement is 5+30 with a maximum of 55 possible.

6. Israel ('Saar 2' class)

Name	No	Builder	Commissioned
Mivtach	311	CMN, Cherbourg	1968
Miznag	312	CMN, Cherbourg	1968
Mifgav	313	CMN, Cherbourg	1968
Eilath	314	CMN, Cherbourg	1968
Haifa	315	CMN, Cherbourg	1968
Akko	316	CMN, Cherbourg	1968

Ordered in 1965, these Israeli FAC(M/G)s were built in France to avoid the political problems that might have arisen if they had been constructed in West Germany. They are exceptionally well equipped. As originally fitted out, they were 'Saar 1'-class FAC(G)s with 3 × 40mm Bofors L/70 AA in single Breda 58/11 mountings, 2 × 0.5in (12.7mm) machine-guns in single mountings and 4 × single 12.75in (324mm) Mk 32 mountings for Mk 46 anti-submarine torpedoes, but were then upgraded to the present impressive 'Saar 2'-class configuration. The standard and full-load displacements are 220 and 250 tons respectively on dimensions of: length 45.0m (147.6ft), beam 7.0m (23.0ft) and draught 2.5m (8.2ft). The missile armament comprises between 2 and 8 container-launchers for between 2 and 8 × Gabriel II anti-ship missiles (2 × trainable triple container-launchers being fitted on the after ring mountings if only 1 × 40mm gun is carried), while the other weapons consist of between 1 and 3 × 40mm Bofors L/70 AA in Breda single moun-

▶'Saar'-class FAC of the
Israeli navy.

tings, 2 or 4 × 0.5in (12.7mm) machine-guns in single mountings, and 2 × twin 12.75in (324mm) Mk 32 mountings for Mk 46 anti-submarine torpedoes if no triple missile container-launcher units are shipped. The electronics fit includes 1 × Neptune air/surface search radar, 1 × RTN 10X tracking radar used in conjunction with 1 × Argo NA10 fire-control system, 1 × EDO 780 active search and attack variable-depth sonar (not in all craft), 1 × ESM system with an Elta MN-53 warning element and a jamming element, and a combination of 6 × 24-tube and 4 × single-tube 'chaff'-launchers. The propulsion arrangement of 4 × MTU MD 871 diesels delivers 10,000kW (13,410hp) to four shafts for a maximum speed of over 40kt and a range of 4,650km (2,890 miles) at 15kt, declining to 2,950 (1,835 miles) at 20kt and finally to 1,850km (1,150 miles) at 30kt. The complement is 5+30/35.

7. Israel ('Saar 3' class)

Name	No	Builder	Commissioned
Saar	331	CMN, Cherbourg	1969
Soufa	332	CMN, Cherbourg	1969
Gaash	333	CMN, Cherbourg	1969
Herev	341	CMN, Cherbourg	1969

Ordered in 1966 as a batch of six FAC(M/G)s – of which two have now been transferred to Chile – these Israeli craft were ordered as variants of the 'Saar 1' class with 1 × 76mm (3in) L/62 DP in an OTO Melara compact single mounting and two 40mm Bofors L/70 AA in single Breda 58/11 mountings but no anti-submarine armament because of the weight and volume restrictions imposed by the 76mm (3in) gun. The craft were later upgraded to a standard comparable to that of the 'Saar 2' class. The gun armament is centred on 1 × 76mm (3in) L/62 DP located forward in an OTO Melara Compact single mounting with the option of 2 × 40mm Bofors L/70 AA generally not exercised in favour of 2 × triple container-launchers for 6 × Gabriel II anti-ship missiles aft.

8. Kuwait

Name	No	Builder	Commissioned
Al Boom	P4501	Lürssen	1983
Al Betteel	P4503	Lürssen	1983
Al Sanbouk	P4505	Lürssen	1983
Al Saadi	P4507	Lürssen	1983
Al Ahmadi	P4509	Lürssen	1984
Al Abdali	P4511	Lürssen	1984

Ordered in 1980, these Kuwaiti FAC(M/G)s have standard and full-load displacements of 255 and 275 tons respectively on dimensions of: length 44.9m (147.3ft), beam 7.0m (23.0ft) and draught 2.68m (8.8ft). The missile armament comprises 2 × twin container-launchers for 4 × MM.40 Exocet anti-ship missiles, and the other weapons consist of 1 × 76mm (3in) L/62 DP in an OTO Melara Compact single mounting, 2 × 40mm Bofors L/70 AA in a Breda Compact twin mounting, and 2 × 7.62mm (0.3in) machine-guns in single mountings. The electronics fit is 1 × S 810 surface search radar, 1 × TM1226C navigation radar, 1 × 9LV 200 tracking radar used with 1 × 9LV 228 fire-control system, 1 × Lynx optical director, 1 × ESM system with Cutlass-E/Matilda warning element, and 1 × Dagaie 'chaff'/flare-launcher. The propulsion arrangement comprises 4 × MTU 16V 956 TB92 diesels delivering 11,600kW (15,560hp) to four shafts for a maximum speed of 41.5kt and a range of 3,100km (1,925 miles) at 16kt on two engines. The complement is 5+30 plus provision for 3 spare men.

▲ *Al Betteel*, a Kuwaiti 'TNC 45'-class missile craft, in a high speed turn to port.

▶▲ P4501 is *Al Boom*, built by Lürssen for the Kuwaiti navy, and armed with two twin Exocet-launchers, a 3in L/62DP gun forward and twin 40mm Bofors aft.

▶ Kuwaiti 'TNC 45'-class FAC at sea.

9. Malaysia ('Jerong' class)

Name	No	Builder	Commissioned
Jerong	3505	Hong-Leong Lürssen	Mar 1976
Todak	3506	Hong-Leong Lürssen	Jun 1976
Paus	3507	Hong-Leong Lürssen	Aug 1976
Yu	3508	Hong-Leong Lürssen	Nov 1976
Baung	3509	Hong-Leong Lürssen	Jan 1977
Pari	3510	Hong-Leong Lürssen	Mar 1977

TNC 45

TNC 45

▲This Lürssen TNC-45 serves with the Singapore navy. Note the twin single and one triple launch containers for the Gabriel I anti-ship missile which identifies this as a Singapore FAC [M/G]

Ordered in 1973, these Malaysian craft are FAC(G)s with standard and full-load displacements of 210 and 255 tons respectively on dimensions of: length 44.9m (147.3ft), beam 7.0m (23.0ft) and draught 2.48m (8.15ft). The armament consists of 1 × 57mm SAK 57 Mk 1 L/70 DP in a Bofors single mounting, 1 × 40mm Bofors L/70 AA in a single mounting, and 2 × 7.62mm (0.3in) machine-guns in single mountings. The electronics fit includes 1 × Decca 626 surface search radar, 1 × MS 32 navigation radar, 1 × tracking radar used in conjunction with 1 × WM-28 fire-control system, 1 × Naja optronic director and 1 × Panda optical director. The propulsion arrangement of 3 × MTU MD 872 diesels delivers 7,950kW (10,665hp) to three shafts for a maximum speed of 34kt and a range of 3,700km (2,300 miles) at 15kt, declining to 1,300km (810 miles) at 31.5kt. The complement is 5+31.

10. Singapore

Name	No	Builder	Commissioned
Sea Wolf	P76	Lürssen	1972
Sea Lion	P77	Lürssen	1972
Sea Dragon	P78	Singapore SB & Eng	1974
Sea Tiger	P79	Singapore SB & Eng	1974
Sea Hawk	P80	Singapore SB & Eng	1975
Sea Scorpion	P81	Singapore SB & Eng	1975

Ordered in 1970, these Singapore FAC(M/G)s have standard and full-load displacements of 226 and 254 tons respectively on dimensions of: length 44.9m (147.3ft), beam 7.0m (23.0ft) and draught 2.3m (7.5ft). The missile armament comprises 2 × single and 1 × triple container-launchers for 5 × Gabriel I anti-ship missiles, or 2 × twin container-launchers for 4 × RGM-84 Harpoon anti-ship missiles and 2 × single container-launchers for 2 × Gabriel I anti-ship missiles, and other weapons consist of 1 × 57mm SAK 57 Mk 1 L/70 DP in a Bofors single mounting (504 rounds), and 1 × 40mm Bofors L/70 AA in a single mounting (1,008 rounds). The electronics fit includes 1 × Kelvin Hughes 17 surface search and navigation radar, 1 × tracking radar used in conjunction with the WM-28/5 fire-control system, and 1 × ESM system with warning element. The propulsion arrangement of 4 × MTU 16V 538 TB92 diesels delivers 10,740kW (14,405hp) to four shafts for a maximum speed of 38kt and a range of 3,700km (2,300 miles) at cruising speed. The complement is 5+36. It was for these craft that Israel allowed the first export order for its Gabriel anti-ship missile.

11. Thailand

Name	No	Builder	Commissioned
Prabparapak	1	Singapore SB & Eng	Jul 1976
Hanhak Sattru	2	Singapore SB & Eng	Nov 1976
Suphairin	3	Singapore SB & Eng	Feb 1977

Ordered in June 1973, these Thai FAC(M/G)s are essentially similar to the Singapore units in dimensions, weapons, electronics, propulsion and performance.

12. United Arab Emirates (Abu Dhabi)

Name	No	Builder	Commissioned
Ban Yas	P4501	Lürssen	Nov 1980
Marban	P4502	Lürssen	Nov 1980
Rodqm	P4503	Lürssen	Jul 1981
Shaheen	P4504	Lürssen	Jul 1981
Sagar	P4505	Lürssen	Sep 1981
Tarif	P4506	Lürssen	Sep 1981

Ordered in 1979, these FAC(M/G)s were the world's first operational craft with the MM.40 version of the Exocet, and it is believed that the UAE may order more of the type in the near future. Some 350 rounds are carried for the 76mm (3in) L/62 DP in an OTO Melara Compact single mounting.

'Lürssen FPB/PB-57' class   Germany/Spain

Type: fast attack craft (gun [missile])
Displacement: 275 tons standard; 393 tons full load
Dimensions: length 58.1m (190.6ft); beam 7.62m (25.0ft); draught 2.8m (9.2ft)
Gun armament: 1 × 76mm (3in) L/62 DP in an OTO Melara Compact single mounting; 1 × 40mm Bofors L/70 AA in a Breda single mounting; 2 × 20mm Oerlikon L/85 AA in GAM-B01 single mountings
Missile armament: 2 × twin container-launchers for 4 × RGM-84 Harpoon anti-ship missiles (provision for)
Torpedo armament: none
Anti-submarine armament: 2 × triple 12.75in (324mm) Mk 32 mountings for Mk 46 torpedoes (provision for); 2 × depth-charge racks
Electronics: 1 × surface search radar used in conjunction with; 1 × Raytheon TM 1620/6X navigation radar; 1 × tracking radar used in conjunction with; 1 × WM-22/41 fire-control system; 1 × HSM Mk 22 optical director; 1 × ELAC active search and attack hull sonar (provision for); 1 × ESM system with warning element

Propulsion: 2 × Bazan/MTU MA15 TB91 diesels delivering 6,000kW (8,045hp) to two shafts
Performance: maximum speed 31kt; range 12,050km (7,490 miles) at 17kt or 5,000km (3,105 miles) at 28kt
Complement: 4+26 plus provision for 2 spare men

1. Germany (West) ('Type 143A' class)

Name	No	Builder	Commissioned
Gepard	P6121	AEG/Lürssen	Dec 1982
Puma	P6122	AEG/Lürssen	Feb 1983
Hermelin	P6123	AEG/Kröger	May 1983
Nerz	P6124	AEG/Lürssen	July 1983
Zobel	P6125	AEG/Telefunken	Sep 1983
Frettchen	P6126	AEG/Telefunken	Dec 1983
Dachs	P6127	AEG/Telefunken	Mar 1984
Ozelot	P6128	AEG/Lürssen	May 1984
Wiesel	P6129	AEG/Kröger	Jul 1984
Hyane	P6130	AEG/Kröger	Nov 1984

Ordered in mid-1978 as replacements for the 'Zobel'-class FAC(T)s, these German FAC(M/G)s are to a modified 'FPB-57' design, with standard and full-load displacements of 295 and 391 tons on dimensions of: length 57.7m (189.3ft), beam 7.6m (24.9ft) and draught 2.5m (8.2ft). The missile armament comprises 2 × twin container-launchers for 4 × MM.38 Exocet anti-ship missiles, and the other weapons consist of 1 × 76mm (3in) L/62 DP in an OTO Melara Compact single mounting and (to be retrofitted) 1 × EX-31 launcher for 24 × RIM-116 RAM surface-to-air missiles; the type can also be equipped for minelaying. The electronics fit includes 1 × surface search and tracking radar used in conjunction with 1 × WM-27 fire-control system, 1 × 3RM 20 navigation radar, 1 × AGIS action information system, 1 × ESM system with FL1800 warning element, and 1 × Hot Dog/Silver Dog 'chaff'/flare-launcher. The propulsion arrangement of 4 × MTU 16V 956 SB80 diesels delivers 13,400kW (17,970hp) to four shafts for a maximum speed of 40kt and a range of 4,825km (3,000 miles) at 16kt. The complement is 4+30.

2. Germany (West) ('Type 143B' class)

Name	No	Builder	Commissioned
Albatros	P6111	Lürssen	Nov 1976
Falke	P6112	Lürssen	Apr 1976
Geier	P6113	Lürssen	Jun 1976
Bussard	P6114	Lürssen	Aug 1976
Sperber	P6115	Kröger	Sep 1976
Greif	P6116	Lürssen	Nov 1976
Kondor	P6117	Kröger	Dec 1976
Seeadler	P6118	Lürssen	Mar 1977
Habicht	P6119	Kröger	Dec 1977
Kormoran	P6120	Lürssen	Jul 1977

Ordered in 1972 as replacements for the 'Jaguar'-class FAC(T)s, these German FAC(M/G/T)s were originally of the 'Type 143' class with an armament of 2 × twin container-launchers for 4 × MM.38 Exocet anti-ship missiles, 2 × 76mm (3in) L/62 DP in two OTO Melara Compact single mountings, and 2 × single 533mm (21in) mountings for 2 × wire-guided torpedoes. The after 76mm (3in) mounting has been removed for installation on 'Type 143A'-class craft, and 1 × EX-31 launcher for 24 RIM-116 RAM SAMs is to be installed in what has now become the 'Type 143B' class. The displacement, dimensions and electronics are the same as those for the 'Type 143A' class, but the propulsion arrangement comprises 4 × MTU 16V 956 TB91 diesels delivering 16,000kW (21,460hp) to four shafts for a maximum speed of 40kt and a range of 2,400km (1,490 miles) at 30kt. The complement is 4+36.

Ordered in 1977, these Ghanaian FAC(G)s are of the original 'PB-57' type. Standard and full-load displacements are 380 and 410 tons respectively and dimensions are: length 58.1m (190.6ft), beam 7.62m (25.0ft) and draught 3.0m (9.85ft). The armament comprises one 76mm (3in) L/62 DP in an OTO Melara Compact single mounting (250 rounds) and 1 × 40mm Bofors L/70 AA in a single mounting (750 rounds). The electronics fit includes 1 × surface search, navigation and tracking radar used in conjunction with 1 × Canopus A fire-control system, 1 × Type 978 navigation radar, and 1 × LIOD optronic director. The propulsion arrangement of 3 × MTU 16V 538 TB91 diesels delivers 7,950kW (10,665hp) to three shafts for a maximum speed of 33kt and a range of 9,635km (5,985 miles) at 17kt, declining to 3,700km (2,300 miles) at 30kt. The complement is 7+38 plus provision for 2 VIPs.

3. Ghana

Name	No	Builder	Commissioned
Achimota	P28	Lürssen	Dec 1979
Yogaga	P29	Lürssen	May 1980

4. Indonesia

Name	No	Builder	Commissioned
Andau	650	Lürssen	Oct 1986

▲A clean-looking 'Lürssen FPB-57' class FAC of the Kuwait navy running trials.

Name	Pennant No	Builder	Commissioned
Singa	651	Lürssen	Oct 1987
Kakap	652	Lürssen	Apr 1988
Ajak	653	Lürssen	Oct 1988

Following a decision taken in 1982, the Indonesian Navy is procuring eight of these 'PB-57'-class craft in two variants optimized for anti-submarine warfare (two craft), gun/torpedo-armed patrol (two craft) and combat search and rescue (four craft with another eight under consideration), the last under the control of the maritime security agency rather than the Navy proper. Common features are a full-load displacement of 416 tons on dimensions of: length 58.1m (190.6ft), beam 7.62m (25.0ft) and draught 2.73m (9.0ft). The patrol version is a FAC(G) with a gun armament comprising 1 × 57mm SAK 57 Mk 2 L/70 DP in a Bofors single mounting, 1 × 40mm Bofors L/70 in a single mounting and 2 × 20mm Rheinmetall AA in S20 single mountings. The electronics fit of this variant includes 1 × Decca 2459 surface search radar, 1 × NA18 optronic director used in conjunction with 1 × WM-22 fire-control system, 1 × Thomson-CSF ESM system with warning element, and 1 × Dagaie 'chaff'/flare-launcher. The propulsion arrangement comprises 2 × MTU 16V 956 TB92 diesels delivering 6,150kW (8,250hp) to two shafts for a maximum speed of 30.5kt and a range of 11,300km (7,020 miles) at 15kt, declining to 4,075km (2,530 miles) at 28.1kt. The complement is 9+31, plus provision for 2 VIPs, 6 spare officers and, in the secondary SAR role, 9 survivors. The ASW version has 2 × single 533mm (21in) launchers for SUT wire-guided torpedoes, 1 × PHS 32 active search and attack hull sonar, and 1 × LIOD optronic director. The SAR version has a platform for one MBB (Nurtanio) BO 105 helicopter in place of the after guns and torpedo tubes. The first, second, fourth and fifth craft are of the SAR type, the second and sixth craft are of the ASW type, and the seventh and eighth craft are of the FAC(G) type.

5. Kuwait

Name	No	Builder	Commissioned
Istiqlal	P5702	Lürssen	Nov 1982
Sabhan	P5704	Lürssen	Mar 1983

Ordered in 1980, these Kuwaiti FAC(M/G)s are standard 'FPB-57'-class boats with standard and full-load displacements of 363 and 410 tons respectively on dimensions of: length 58.1m (190.6ft), beam 7.62m (25.0ft) and draught 2.78m (9.1ft). The missile armament comprises 2 × twin container-launchers for 4 × MM.40 Exocet anti-ship missiles, and other weapons consist of 1 × 76mm (3in) L/62 DP in an OTO Melara Compact single mounting, 1 × 40mm Bofors L/70 AA in a single mounting, and 2 × 7.62mm (0.3in) machine-guns in single mountings. It was originally planned that each of the two craft should also have had 4 × 30mm Oerlikon L/85 AA in 2 × twin EMERLEC-30 mountings, but topweight considerations then caused the idea to be abandoned. The electronics fit includes 1 × S 810 surface search radar, 1 × Decca 1226 navigation radar, 1 × 9LV 200 tracking radar used in conjunction with 1 × 9LV 228 fire-control system, 1 × Lynx optical director, 1 × ESM system with Cutlass-E warning and Cygnus jamming elements, and 1 × Dagaie 'chaff'/flare-launcher. The propulsion arrangement comprises 3 × MTU 16V 956 TB91 diesels delivering 8,280kW (11,105hp) to three shafts for a maximum speed of 33.5kt and a range of 6,675km (4,150 miles) at 15kt, declining to 2,780km (1,725 miles) at 31.2kt. The complement is 5+27, plus provision for 2 VIPs and 18 trainees (4 officers and 14 ratings).

6. Morocco ('Lazaga [Modified]' class)

Name	No	Builder	Commis-sioned
El Khattabi	304	Bazan	Jul 1981

Name	Pennant No	Builder	Commis-sioned
Commandant Azouggargh	305	Bazan	Aug 1982
Commandant Boutouba	306	Bazan	Nov 1981
Commandant El Harty	307	Bazan	Feb 1982

Ordered in June 1977, these Moroccan FAC(M/G)s were derived from the Spanish vessels, and have a full-load displacement of 425 tons on dimensions of: length 58.1m (190.6ft), beam 7.6m (24.9m) and draught 2.7m (8.9ft). The missile armament comprises 2 × twin container-launchers for 4 × MM.40 Exocet anti-ship missiles, and the other weapons consist of 1 × 76mm (3in) L/62 DP in an OTO Melara Compact single mounting (300 rounds), 1 × 40mm Bofors L/70 AA in a single Breda mounting (1,472 rounds), and 2 × 20mm Oerlikon L/90 AA in GAM-B01 single mountings (1,300 rounds each); there is no torpedo or anti-submarine armament. The electronics fit includes 1 × ZW-06 surface search radar, 1 × TM 1229C navigation radar, 1 × tracking radar used in conjunction with 1 × WM-25 fire-control system, and 1 × Panda optical director. The propulsion arrangement comprises 2 × MTU 16V 956 TB91 diesels delivering 6,000kW (8,050hp) to two shafts for a maximum speed of 30kt and a range of 5,500km (3,420 miles) at 15kt. The complement is 41.

▼**Damisa, a Nigerian 'FPB-57' type FAC.**

7. Nigeria

Name	No	Builder	Commissioned
Ekpe	P178	Lürssen	Aug 1981
Damisa	P179	Lürssen	Apr 1981
Agu	P180	Lürssen	Apr 1981

Ordered in November 1977, these Nigerian FAC(M/G)s are based on the standard 'FPB-57' hull with a full-load displacement of 444 tons on dimensions of: length 58.1m (190.6ft), beam 7.62m (25.0ft) and draught 3.1m (10.2ft). The missile armament comprises 4 × single container-launchers for four Otomat Mk 1 anti-ship missiles, and the other weapons consist of 1 × 76mm (3in) L/62 DP in an OTO Melara Compact single mounting (250 rounds), 2 × 40mm Bofors L/70 AA in a Breda Compact twin mounting, and 4 × 30mm Oerlikon L/85 AA in 2 × EMERLEC-30 twin mountings. It was planned at one time to ship 2 × single 533mm (21in) mountings for heavyweight Seal torpedoes, but these were never installed. The electronics fit includes 1 × Triton air/surface search radar, 1 × tracking radar used in conjunction with 1 × WM-28/41 fire-control system, and 1 × ESM system with warning and RDL-2ABC jamming elements. The propulsion arrangement comprises 4 ×

MTU 16V 956 TB92 diesels delivering 15,000kW (20,120hp) to four shafts for a maximum speed of 42kt and a range of 3,700km (2,300 miles) at 16kt, declining to 1,250km (775 miles) at 36kt. The complement is 7+45 plus provision for 2 spare officers.

8. Spain ('Lazaga' class)

Name	No	Builder	Commissioned
Lazaga	P01	Lürssen	Jul 1975
Alsedo	P02	Bazan	Feb 1977
Cadarso	P03	Bazan	Jul 1976
Villamil	P04	Bazan	Apr 1977
Bonifaz	P05	Bazan	Jul 1977
Recalde	P06	Bazan	Dec 1977

Ordered in 1972 with low performance as a result of a two-engine/two-shaft propulsion arrangement, these 'PB-57'-class craft are used mainly for patrol and training, with provision for conversion in times of crisis into anti-ship and anti-submarine FAC(M)s with additional sensors and weapons.

9. Turkey ('Dogan' class)

Name	No	Builder	Commissioned
Dogan	P340	Lürssen	Jun 1977
Marti	P341	Taskizak NY	Jul 1978

▼P340 is a 'Dogan'-class derivative of the 'PB-57' design. Note the unusual 35mm-calibre cannon at the rear and eight Harpoon missile-launchers forward of the deckhouse.

FPB 57

FPB 57

PB 57

**▲◀ Superb shot of P179
Damisa of the Nigerian navy,
at speed in a moderate sea.**

**◀P01 is *Lazaga*, the first of
the class built for the
Spanish navy.**

**▲This 'Lürssen FPB-57'
class craft of the Indonesian
navy is running builder's
trials before the armament is
shipped.**

Name	Pennant No	Builder	Commissioned
Tayfun	P342	Taskizak NY	Jul 1979
Volkan	P343	Taskizak NY	Jul 1980
Ruzgar	P344	Taskizak NY	Dec 1984
Poyraz	P345	Taskizak NY	Feb 1984
Gurbet	P346	Taskizak NY	Oct 1988
Firtina	P347	Taskizak NY	1989

These Turkish FAC(M/G)s, of which the first was ordered in August 1973, are to the standard 'FPB-57'-class specification with standard and full-load displacements of 398 tons and 436 tons respectively on dimensions of: length 58.1m (190.6ft), beam 7.62m (25.0ft) and draught 2.83m (9.3ft). The missile armament comprises 2 × quadruple container-launchers for 8 × RGM-84 Harpoon anti-ship missiles, and the other weapons consist of 1 × 76mm (3in) L/62 DP in an OTO Melara Compact single mounting, and 2 × 35mm Oerlikon L/90 AA in a GDM-A twin mounting. The electronics fit includes 1 ×

Decca 1226 surface search and navigation radar, 1 × tracking radar used in conjunction with 1 × WM-28/41 fire-control system, 1 × HSA optical director, 1 × ESM system with Susie I warning element, and 2 × multi-barrel 'chaff'/flare-launchers. The propulsion arrangement comprises 4 × MTU 16V 956 TB91 diesels delivering 13,400kW (17,970hp) to four shafts for a maximum speed of 38kt and a range of 2,400km (1,490 miles) at 26kt, declining to 1,850km (1,150 miles) at 36kt. The complement is 5+33, plus provision for 2 spare men.

'Manta' class: *see* 'Lürssen FPB-36' class

'Matka' class USSR

Type: fast attack hydrofoil (missile and gun)
Displacement: 225 tons standard; 260 tons full load
Dimensions: length 39.6m (129.9ft); beam 12.5m (41.0ft) over foils and 7.6m (24.9ft) over hull; draught 4.0m (13.1ft) foil-borne and 2.1m (6.9ft) hull-borne
Gun armament: 1 × 76mm (3in) L/60 DP in a single mounting; 1 × 30mm six-barrel rotary cannon in an ADGM-630 CIWS mounting
Missile armament: 2 × single container-launchers for 2 × SS-N-2C 'Styx' anti-ship missiles
Torpedo armament: none
Anti-submarine armament: none
Electronics: 1 × 'Plank Shave' air/surface search and tracking radar used in conjunction with; 1 × SSM fire-

control system; 1 × 'Cheese Cake' navigation radar; 1 × 'Bass Tilt' gun fire-control radar; 2 × 16-barrel 'chaff'-launchers; 1 × 'Square Head' IFF system; 1 × 'High Pole-B' or 'Salt Pot-B' IFF system

Propulsion: 3 × M 504 diesels delivering 11,250kW (15,090hp) to three shafts

Performance: maximum speed 40kt; range 2,775km (1,725 miles) at 14kt hull-borne or; 1,110km (690 miles) at 35kt foil-borne

Complement: 33

1. USSR (16 craft)

This class was built at the Kolpino yard in Leningrad between 1977 and 1983, when the type was superseded in production by the 'Tarantul' class. The basic design appears to combine the hull of the 'Osa' class with the foil system of the 'Turya' class, and is designated by the Soviets as a missile cutter.

'Minister' class: *see* 'Saar 4' class

'Muravey' class   USSR

Type: fast attack hydrofoil (gun and torpedo)

Displacement: 180 tons standard; 230 tons full load

Dimensions: length 38.6m (126.6ft); beam 7.6m (24.9ft); draught 1.9m (6.2ft)

Gun armament: 1 × 76mm (3in) L/60 DP in a single mounting; 1 × 30mm six-barrel rotary cannon in an ADGM-630 CIWS mounting

Missile armament: none

Torpedo armament: 2 × single 406mm (16in) mountings for 2 × Type 40 anti-submarine torpedoes

Anti-submarine armament: torpedoes (see above); 1 × depth-charge rack for ? depth-charges

Electronics: 1 × 'Peel Cone' surface search and navigation radar; 1 × 'Bass Tilt' gun fire-control radar; 1 × high-frequency dipping search sonar; 1 × variable-depth attack sonar

Propulsion: 2 × gas turbines delivering 13,400kW (17,970hp) to two shafts

Performance: maximum speed 40kt; range ? km (? miles)

Complement: ?

1. USSR (15 craft)

Building at Feodosiya and first seen in 1983, this is a class of impressive FAC(G/T)s used by the KGB for patrol.

'MV 400 TH' class   Italy/Thailand

Type: fast attack craft (gun)

Displacement: 400 tons standard; 450 tons full load

Dimensions: length 60.4m (198.2ft); beam 8.8m (29.0ft); draught 4.5m (14.8ft)

Gun armament: 2 × 76mm (3in) L/62 DP in OTO Melara Compact single mountings; 2 × 40mm Bofors L/70 AA in a Breda Compact twin mounting

Missile armament: provision for the retrofitting of anti-ship missiles

Torpedo armament: none

Anti-submarine armament: none

Electronics: 1 × ZW-06 surface search radar; 1 × tracking radar used in conjunction with; 1 × WM-25 fire-control system (with data provision for SSMs); 1 × 3RM 20 navigation radar; 1 × LIROD 8 optronic director; 1 × ESM system with warning element; 4 × Mk 135 'chaff'-launchers

Propulsion: 3 × MTU 20V 538 TB92 diesels delivering 11,250kW (15,090hp) to three shafts

Performance: maximum speed 30kt; range 4,600km (2,860 miles) at 18kt or 1,675km (1,040 miles) at 30kt

Complement: 6+35

1. Thailand ('Chon Buri' class)

Name	No	Builder	Commissioned
Chon Buri	1	CN Breda	Dec 1982
Songkhla	2	CN Breda	Jan 1983
Phuket	3	CN Breda	May 1983

Ordered in November 1979 (two units) and 1981 (one), these craft, with aluminium superstructures on steel hulls, are comparatively large FAC(G)s, but have the capability for easy conversion to FAC(M)s should the situation demand it.

'Nasty' class   Norway

Type: fast attack craft (torpedo)

Displacement: 70 tons standard; 82 tons full load

Dimensions: length 24.5m (80.3ft); beam 7.5m (24.5ft); draught 2.1m (6.8ft)

Gun armament: 1 × 40mm Bofors L/70 AA in a Bofors single mounting; 1 × 20mm Rheinmetall L/92 AA in an S20 single mounting

Missile armament: none

Torpedo armament: 4 × single 533mm (21in) mountings for 4 × heavyweight anti-ship torpedoes

Anti-submarine armament: none

Electronics: 1 × surface search and navigation radar

Propulsion: 2 × Napier Deltic diesels delivering 6,200hp (4,625kW) to two shafts

Performance: maximum speed 45kt; range 1,100km (685 miles) at 25kt or 835km (520 miles) at 40kt

Complement: 18

1. Greece

Name	No	Builder	Commissioned
Andromeda	P196	Batservice	Nov 1965
Kyknos	P198	Batservice	Feb 1967
Pigasos	P199	Batservice	Apr 1967
Toxotis	P228	Batservice	May 1967

▲HS *Toxotis* is a 'Nasty'-
class FAC serving with the
Greek navy.

Name	Pennant No	Builder	Commis-sioned
Lyr	P387	Batservice	Feb 1965
Delfin	P388	Batservice	Mar 1962

Five survivors of this originally six-strong class were placed in reserve during the early 1980s, but these four craft named above were refurbished and recommissioned in 1988. They have 2 × MTU MI 312 V331 diesels delivering 2,300kW (3,085hp) to two shafts for a maximum speed of 40kt and a range of 1,250km (775 miles) at 17kt. The complement is 20.

2. Norway ('Tjeld' class)

Name	No	Builder	Commis-sioned
Sel	P343	Batservice	Jun 1960
Hval	P348	Batservice	Jun 1961
Laks	P349	Batservice	Jun 1961
Knurr	P357	Batservice	Dec 1961
Skrei	P380	Batservice	Jan 1966
Hai	P381	Batservice	Jul 1964

These craft are a last legacy of the type of motor torpedo boat perfected in the Second World War, and were built on a mahogany hull. The class is now of only minimal utility except for training.

'Nanuchka I', 'Nanuchka III' and 'Nanuchka IV' classes   USSR

Type: fast attack craft (missile and gun)
Displacement: 560 tons standard; 660 tons full load
Dimensions: length 59.3m (194.6ft); beam 13.0m (42.65ft); draught 2.6m (8.5ft)
Gun armament: 2 × 57mm L/80 AA in a twin mounting, or ('Nanuchka III' and 'Nanuchka IV' class) 1 × 76mm (3in) L/60 DP in a single mounting; 1 × 30mm ADGM-630 CIWS mounting
Missile armament: 2 × triple container-launchers for 6 × SS-N-9 'Siren' anti-ship missiles or ('Nanuchka IV'

◀This Norweigan navy 'Tjeld'-class MTB is basically a 'Nasty'-class boat.

class) 2 × sextuple container-launchers for 12 × anti-ship missiles of an unknown type; 1 × twin launcher for 20 × SA-N-4 'Gecko' SAMs

Torpedo armament: none

Anti-submarine armament: none

Electronics: 1 × 'Band Stand' air/surface search and SSM fire-control radar; 1 × 'Peel Pair' surface search radar; 1 × 'Spar Stump' navigation radar; 1 × 'Pop Group' SAM fire-control radar; 1 × 'Muff Cob' or ('Nanuchka III' and 'Nanuchka IV' class) 'Bass Tilt' gun fire-control radar; 2 × 'Fish Bowl' SSM data-links; 1 × ESM system with 1 × 'Bell Tap' antenna/housing; 2 × 'chaff'-launchers; 1 × 'Square Head' IFF system; 1 × 'High Pole-B' IFF system

Propulsion: 6 × M 504 diesels delivering 22,500kW (30,175hp) to three shafts

Performance: maximum speed 36kt; range 8,350km (5,190 miles) at 15kt or 1,675km (1,040 miles) at 31kt

Complement: 10+50

1. Algeria ('Nanuchka II' class)

Name	No	Builder	Commis-sioned
Ras Hamidou	801		Jul 1980
Salah Reis	802		Feb 1981
Reis Ali	803		May 1982
	804		1989

These Algerian ships are 'Nanuchka II'-class units based on the 'Nanuchka I' class but fitted with 2 × triple container-launchers for 6 × SS-N-2C 'Styx' anti-ship missiles and search radar limited to 1 × 'Square Tie' surface search equipment supported by 1 × 'Don 2' navigation radar. The Algerians are reported to be unhappy with the Soviet diesels and are considering their replacement with German MTU engines.

2. India ('Nanuchka II' class)

Name	No	Builder	Commis-sioned
Vijay Durg	K71		Apr 1977
Sindhu Durg	K72		Sep 1977
Hos Durg	K73		Apr 1978

These Indian ships are standard 'Nanuchka II'-class units similar in all essential respects to the Algerian units, and a total of five is planned.

◀Soviet 'Nanuchka I'-class corvette. Top speed is 30kt on diesels and she is armed with two triple SS-N-9 missile-launchers and a twin 57mm gun.

3. Libya ('Nanuchka II' class)

Name	No	Builder	Commis-sioned
Ean Mara	416		Oct 1981
Ean el Gazala	417		Feb 1983
Ean Zara	418		Feb 1984

These Libyan units are standard 'Nanuchka II'-class vessels similar in all essential respects to the Algerian units. A fourth Libyan unit, Ean Zarguit [419], was sunk by US air attack in March 1986.

4. USSR (17 'Nanuchka I' class ships; 14 'Nanuchka III' class ships with 1 more building; 1 'Nanuchka IV' class ship)

The 'Nanuchka' series has been built since 1969 at Petrovsky and Leningrad, and also ('Nanuchka III' class only) in Pacific yards, the last delivering their first ship in 1978. The type offers excellent anti-ship capability on a small and speedy hull, but it is not known at present whether the single 'Nanuchka IV'-class ship is a trials unit or the first of a new sub-class.

'Nuoli' class   Finland

Type: fast attack craft (gun)

Displacement: 40 tons standard; ? tons full load

Dimensions: length 22.0m (72.2ft); beam 6.6m (21.7ft); draught 1.5m (4.9ft)

Gun armament: 1 × 40mm Bofors L/70 AA in a Bofors single mounting or 2 × 23mm L/60 AA in a twin mounting; 1 × 20mm Oerlikon AA or 1 × 12.7mm (0.5in) machine-gun in a single mounting

Missile armament: none

Torpedo armament: none

Anti-submarine armament: 4 × depth-charges

Electronics: 1 × Decca surface search and navigation radar

Propulsion: 3 × M 50 diesels delivering 2,700kW (3,620hp) to three shafts

Performance: maximum speed 40kt; range ? km (? miles) at ? kt

Complement: 15

1. Finland

Name	No	Builder	Commis-sioned
Nuoli 5	35	Laivateollisuus, Turku	Jul 1962
Nuoli 8	38	Laivateollisuus, Turku	Aug 1962
Nuoli 10	40	Laivateollisuus, Turku	May 1964
Nuoli 11	41	Laivateollisuus, Turku	May 1964
Nuoli 12	42	Laivateollisuus, Turku	Nov 1964
Nuoli 13	43	Laivateollisuus, Turku	Oct 1966

These FAC(G)s are the survivors of an original class of thirteen vessels, which were built as the 'Nuoli 1' and

'Nuoli 2' sub-classes, the latter with a lower super-structure. These six craft were modernized in the early 1980s, and the other seven were used for target practice.

'Nyayo' class: *see* 'Province' class

'Obluze (Modified)' class   Poland

Type: fast attack craft (gun)
Displacement: 150 tons standard; 170 tons full load
Dimensions: length 42.0m (137.8ft); beam 5.8m (19.0ft); draught 2.0m (6.6ft)
Gun armament: 4 × 30mm L/65 AA in 2 × twin mountings
Missile armament: none
Torpedo armament: none
Anti-submarine armament: 2 × depth-charge racks for ? depth-charges
Electronics: 1 × Tamirio RN 231 surface search and navigation radar; 1 × 'Drum Tilt' fire-control radar; 1 × hull-mounted high-frequency search and attack sonar; 2 × 'Square Head' IFF systems; 1 × 'High Pole' IFF system
Propulsion: 2 × Type 40D diesels delivering 3,700kW (4,960hp) to two shafts
Performance: maximum speed 20kt; range ? km (? miles) at ? kt
Complement: 35

1. Poland

Name	No	Builder	Commis-sioned
Grozny	351	Oksywie	1970
Wytrwaly	352	Oksywie	1970
Zawziety	353	Okyswie	1970
Zwrotny	354	Oksywie	1971
Zwinny	355	Oksywie	1971
Zreczny	356	Oksywie	1971
Nieugiety	357	Oksywie	1972
Czujny	358	Oksywie	1972

These are simple craft used for the patrol and coastal anti-submarine roles, and are the survivors of a thirteen-strong class whose five earliest members lacked anti-submarine capability.

'October' class   Egypt

Type: fast attack craft (missile)
Displacement: 71 tons standard; 82 tons full load
Dimensions: length 25.5m (84.0ft); beam 6.1m (20.0ft); draught 1.3m (5.0ft)
Gun armament: 4 × 30mm Oerlikon L/75 AA in two GCM-A03 twin mountings
Missile armament: 2 × single container-launchers for 2 × Otomat Mk 1 anti-ship missiles
Torpedo armament: none
Anti-submarine armament: none

Electronics: 1 × S 810 air/surface search radar; 1 × ST 802 tracking radar used in conjunction with; 1 × Sapphire fire-control system; 1 × optronic director; 1 × ESM system with Matilda warning element; 2 × Protean 'chaff'/flare-launchers (each with 4 × magazines each containing 36 × 'chaff' and flare grenades)
Propulsion: 4 × CRM 18V-12D/55 YE diesels delivering 4,000kW (5,365hp) to four shafts
Performance: maximum speed 40kt; range 750km (465 miles) at 30kt
Complement: 20

1. Egypt (6 craft – Nos 781, 783, 785, 787, 789 and 791)
These craft were built in Alexandria in 1975 and 1976 using a hull identical to that of the Soviet 'Komar' wooden-hulled class for a sensor and weapon fit of Western origin.

▶ **Soviet 'Osa I' fast missile attack craft seen at considerable speed in the Baltic.**

'Osa I' and 'Osa II' classes   USSR

Type: fast attack craft (missile)

Displacement: 165 tons or ('Osa II' class craft) 175 tons standard; 215 tons or ('Osa II' class craft) 230 tons full load

Dimensions: length 39.0m (127.9ft); beam 7.8m (25.6ft); draught 1.8m (5.9ft)

Gun armament: 4 × 30mm L/65 AA in two AK-230 twin mountings

Missile armament: 4 × single container-launchers for 4 × SS-N-2A 'Styx' or ('Osa II' class craft) SS-N-2B/C 'Styx' anti-ship missiles; 1 × quadruple launcher for four SA-N-5 'Grail' or SA-N-8 'Gremlin' SAMs (only in some Soviet craft)

Torpedo armament: none

Anti-submarine armament: none

Electronics: 1 × 'Square Tie' surface search and tracking radar used in conjunction with; 1 × missile fire-control system; 1 × 'Drum Tilt' gun fire-control radar; 2 × 'Square Head' IFF system; 1 × 'High Pole-A' or 'High Pole-B' IFF system

Propulsion: 3 × M 503A diesels delivering 9,000kW (12,070hp) or (in 'Osa II' class craft) 3 × M 504 diesels delivering 11,250kW (15,090hp), in each case to three shafts

Performance: maximum speed 38kt ('Osa I' class craft) or 37kt ('Osa II' class craft); range 1,500km (930 miles) at 35kt ('Osa I' class craft) or 1,675km (1,040 miles) at 34kt ('Osa II' class craft)

Complement: 5+25

1. Algeria (3 'Osa I' class – Nos 641, 642 and 643; 9 'Osa II' class – Nos 644, 645, 646, 647, 648, 649, 650, 651 and 652)
These are standard craft transferred in 1967 (three 'Osa I' craft), 1976–77 (four), September 1978 (one), December

1978 (one), 1979 (two) and December 1981 (one). It is possible that the craft may be re-engined with MTU diesels.

2. Angola (6 'Osa II' class craft)

These are standard craft transferred in pairs during September 1982, December 1982 and November 1983.

3. Bulgaria (3 'Osa I' class – Nos 103, 112 and 113; 3 'Osa II' class – Nos 101, 102 and 111)

These are standard craft, the 'Osa I' class vessels being transferred in 1971, and the 'Osa II' class ones in 1978, 1982 and 1984.

4. China (100+ 'Huangfen' class craft)

The 'Huangfen'-class craft are 'Osa Is' built in China. The type entered production in 1985 after the Chinese Navy had gained experience with such FAC(M)s via seven 'Osa I' craft supplied by the USSR but now deleted. The Chinese variant has standard and full-load displacements of 165 and 205 tons respectively on dimensions of: length 38.8m (127.3ft), beam 7.6m (24.9ft) and draught 1.5m (4.9ft). The missile armament comprises 4 × single container-launchers for 4 × HY-2 or (in later craft and as a retrofit in earlier craft) 6 or 8 × single container-launchers for 6 or 8 × C-801 anti-ship missiles. The other weapons consist of 4 × 25mm L/60 or (in later craft and as a retrofit in earlier craft) 4 × 30mm L/65 in 2 × twin mountings. The electronics fit includes 1 × 'Square Tie' surface search radar, 1 × 'Round Ball' fire-control radar in those craft fitted with 30mm cannon, 2 × 'Square Head' IFF systems, and 1 × 'High Pole-A' IFF system. The propulsion arrangement comprises 3 × M 503A diesels for a speed of 41kt and a range of 1,500km (930 miles) at 30kt.

5. Cuba (5 'Osa I' class, 13 'Osa II' class craft)

These are standard craft and of the original strength of six 'Osa Is' one has been deleted. The 'Osa I'-class vessels were transferred between 1972 and 1976, while the 'Osa IIs' were transferred between 1976 and 1982.

6. Egypt (7 'Osa I' class – named *631, 633, 635, 637, 639, 641* and *643*)

These are standard craft, and another six were sunk in the 1973 'Yom Kippur' War or have since been deleted. The craft were transferred between 1966 and 1968. At least some of the current vessels have been re-engined with MTU diesels and had their armament bolstered with two heavy machine-guns.

7. Ethiopia (4 'Osa II' class – named *FMB 160*, *FMB 161*, *FMB 162* and *FMB 163*)

These are standard craft transferred in January 1978 (one), September 1980 (one) and January 1981 (two).

8. Finland (4 'Tuima' class craft)

These are of Soviet 'Osa II'-class construction, purchased between 1974 and 1976 for completion with Finnish electronics and Western navigation radar. The craft are named *Tuima* (11), *Tuisku* (12), *Tuuli* (14) and *Tyrsky* (15).

9. Germany (East) (12 'Osa I'-class craft)

These are standard craft transferred in 1966, and are named *Max Reichpietsch* (711), *Heinrich Dorrenbach* (712), *Richard Sorge* (713), *Walter Kramer* (714), *Otto Tost* (731), *Karl Meseberg* (732), *August Luttgens* (733), *Anton Saefkow* (734), *Josef Schares* (751), *Paul Schulz* (752), *Paul Wieczorek* (753) and *Fritz Gast* (754). Three other craft have been deleted.

10. India (6 'Osa I' class craft; 8 'Osa II' class craft)

The former were delivered between January and April 1971, and are named *Vidyut* (K83), *Vijeta* (K84), *Vinash* (K85), *Nipat* (K86), *Nashat* (K87) and *Nirghat* (K89), of which K84 and K87 are used in the patrol role with their missiles removed. The latter were delivered between January 1976 and September 1977, and are *Prachand* (K90), *Pralaya* (K91), *Pratap* (K92), *Prabal* (K93), *Chapal* (K94), *Chamak* (K95), *Chatak* (K96) and *Charag* (K97)

11. Iraq (2 'Osa I' class; 5 'Osa II' class craft)

Delivered between July 1972 and February 1983, the former are *Nisan* (R14) and *Hazirani* (R15), and another two were lost in the Iraq–Iran War. Delivered between April 1974 and February 1977, the latter are *Khalid ibn Ali Walid* (R18), *Said* (R19), (R21), (R22) and (R23), and another three were lost in the war with Iran.

12. Libya (12 'Osa II'-class craft)

Delivered between October 1976 and July 1980, these are *Al Katum* (511), *Al Zuara* (513), *Al Ruha* (515), *Al Baida* (517), *Al Nabha* (519), *Al Safhra* (521), *Al Fikah* (523), *Al Sakab* (525), *Al Mosha* (527), *Al Mathur* (529), *Al Bitar* (531) and *Al Sadad* (533).

13. North Korea (8 'Osa I' class craft; 4 'Huangfen' class craft; 10 locally built 'Soju' class craft with another 2 building)

These are standard craft, the 'Osa Is' being survivors of sixteen transferred between 1968 and 1973, the 'Huangfens' being transferred in 1982, and the 'Soju'-class craft

◄This 'Tuima'-class missile boat serves in the Finnish navy but is based on the Soviet 'Osa' class.

►'Osa II'-class fast missile boats.

being built between 1981 and 1985. The 'Soju'-class vessels are to a revised 'Osa I' design with a full-load displacement of 220 tons on dimensions of: length 43.0m (141.1ft), beam 7.5m (24.6ft) and draught 1.7m (5.6ft). The standard propulsion arrangement of 3 × M 504A diesels allows a maximum speed of 34kt.

14. Pakistan (4 'Huangfen'-class craft – named P1025, P1026, P1027 and P1028)
These are standard craft transferred in April 1984.

15. Poland (12 'Osa I' class craft – named *422, 423, 424, 425, 426, 427, 428, 429, 430, 431, 432* and *433*)
These are standard craft of which seven were built in Poland between the early and mid-1960s.

16. Romania (5 'Osa I' class craft – named *194, 195, 196, 197* and *198*)
These are standard craft, and from the original strength of six transferred in 1964 one was deleted in 1988.

17. Somalia (2 'Osa II' class aircraft)
These are standard craft transferred in September 1975 and January 1976.

18. South Yemen (6 'Osa II'-class craft – named *116, 117, 118, 119, 120* and *121*)
These are standard craft, and from the original strength of eight transferred between February 1979 and September 1983, two were sunk during 1987.

19. Syria (6 'Osa I' class craft – named *21, 22, 23, 24, 25* and *26*; 6 'Osa II'-class craft)
These are standard craft. The 'Osa Is' were transferred between December 1972 and December 1973, while the 'Osa IIs' were transferred between September 1978 and May 1984. Some of the vessels may already have been deleted, with others to follow in the near future.

20. USSR (50 'Osa I'-class craft; 30 'Osa II'-class craft)
These are standard craft, some of them with SAM armament.

21. Vietnam (8 'Osa II'-class craft)
These are standard craft transferred between October 1979 and February 1981.

22. Yugoslavia (10 'Osa I'-class craft)
Transferred between 1965 and 1969, these are named *Mitar Acev* (RC301), *Vlado Bagat* (RC302), *Petar Drapsin* (RC303), *Stevo Filipovic* (RC304), *Zikica Jovanovic Spanac* (RC305), *Nikola Martinovic* (RC306), *Josip Mazar Sosa* (RC307), *Karlo Rojc* (RC308), *Franc Rozman Stanec* (RC309) and *Velimir Skorpik* (RC310).

General note
The 'Osa I' class was the first purpose-built type of Soviet FAC(M), and was evolved as successor to the 'Komar'

class with double the missile armament and a considerably more seaworthy hull design. The class was built between 1959 and 1965 to the extent of some 175 craft. The design features a steel hull with a steel and aluminium superstructure, flat-sided missile container-launchers, a new type of twin 30mm mounting later adopted for a large number of larger surface combatants, and citadel-type protection against NBC hazards. Built to the extent of some 114 craft between 1966 and 1970, the 'Osa II' class has longer-ranged missiles in cylindrical rather than flat-sided container-launchers, a more powerful and reliable propulsion system, and slightly greater fuel capacity. Many yards were involved. The type is now obsolescent but still in very widespread service, and is designated by the Soviets as a missile cutter.

'Osprey 55' class   Denmark/Greece

Type: fast attack craft (missile and gun)
Displacement: 400 tons standard; 475 tons full load
Dimensions: length 54.8m (179.8ft); beam 10.3m (33.8ft); draught 2.6m (8.5ft)
Gun armament: 1 × 76mm (3in) L/62 DP in an OTO Melara single mounting; 2 × 40mm Bofors L/70 AA in a Breda Fast Forty twin mounting
Missile armament: 2 × twin Mk 141 container-launchers for 4 × RGM-84 Harpoon anti-ship missiles
Torpedo armament: none
Anti-submarine armament: none
Mines: fitted with two rails
Electronics: 1 × Plessey surface search and navigation radar; 1 × tracking radar used in conjunction with; 1 × fire-control system; 1 × Plessey action information system; 1 × ESM system; ? × 'chaff'/flare-launchers
Propulsion: 2 × MTU 16V 396 diesels delivering ? kW (? hp) to two shafts
Performance: maximum speed 24kt+; range ? km (? miles)
Complement: about 20

1. Greece

Name	No	Builder	Commissioned
Armatolos		Hellenic Shipyards	Mar 1990
		Hellenic Shipyards	Jul 1990

The contract for the licensed production of these two craft was signed with Danyard in July 1987, the object being the construction of two large FAC(M/G)s of limited performance but high capabilities in the anti-ship and patrol roles. The planned total is ten units.

▶ *Njambuur* is the Senegambian navy's most powerful unit, a 'PR 72S' class FAC(G).

2. Senegambia ('Osprey [Improved]' class)

Name	No	Builder	Commis-sioned
Fouta		Danyard	Jun 1987

This unit is designed for patrol rather than offensive operations as a true FAC, and this is reflected in the armament and sensors. The former comprise 2 × 30mm Hispano–Suiza cannon, and the latter 1 × FR 1411 surface search radar and 1 × FR 1221 navigation radar. The propulsion arrangement comprises 2 × Burmeister & Wain/MAN Alpha 12V 23/30-DVO diesels delivering 3,700kW (4,960hp) to two shafts for a maximum speed of 20kt. The complement is 4+34 with provision for 8 passengers.

'P 4' class   USSR

Type: fast attack craft (torpedo)
Displacement: 22.5 tons standard; 25 tons full load
Dimensions: length 19.0m (62.3ft); beam 3.3m (10.8ft); draught 1.0m (3.3ft)

Gun armament: 2 or 4 × 14.5mm (0.57in) L/90 machine-guns in 1 or 2 × twin mountings
Missile armament: none
Torpedo armament: 2 × single 457mm (18in) mountings for 2 × Type 45 medium-weight anti-ship torpedoes
Anti-submarine armament: 8 × depth-charges
Mines: can be carried in place of depth-charges
Electronics: 1 × 'Skin Head' surface search and navigation radar
Propulsion: 2 × M 50-F4 diesels delivering 1,800kW (2,415hp) to two shafts
Performance: maximum speed 50kt; range 760km (470 miles) at 30kt
Complement: 12

1. Bangladesh (4 'Type 123K' class craft)
These are standard Chinese-built craft transferred in April 1983.

2. Benin (2 craft)
These are standard craft transferred from North Korea in 1979.

3. China (80 'Type 123K'-class craft)

These are to a Chinese revision of the Soviet design with an aluminium rather than wooden hull, and it is thought that about half are in reserve.

General note

About 200 of this simple FAC(T) class were built between 1950 and 1956 in the USSR, but only a few examples now remain apart from the Chinese-built derivative.

▲▲A rare photograph of a Soviet 'P4'-class torpedo boat. The crew have clearly been caught unawares.

◀Despite its poor quality this photogaph demonstrates the small size and high speed of the 'P4' class to good effect.

▶The 'P6' class is a larger torpedo boat with better AA armament fore and aft. This one serves in the Cuban navy.

'P 6' class   USSR

Type: fast attack craft (torpedo)
Displacement: 64 tons standard; 73 tons full load
Dimensions: length 26.0m (85.3ft); beam 6.1m (20.0ft);
    draught 1.5m (4.9ft)
Gun armament: 4 × 25mm L/80 AA in 2 × twin
    mountings
Missile armament: none
Torpedo armament: 2 × single 533mm (21in) mountings
    for 2 × Type 53 heavyweight anti-ship torpedoes
Anti-submarine armament: 8 or 12 × depth-charges
Mines: can be carried in place of depth-charges
Electronics: 1 × 'Skin Head' or 'Pot Head' surface
    search and navigation radar; 1 × 'Dead Duck' IFF
    system; 1 × 'High Pole' IFF system
Propulsion: 4 × M 50-F4 diesels delivering 3,600kW
    (4,830hp) to four shafts
Performance: maximum speed 45kt; range 1,100km (685
    miles) at 15kt or 825km (515 miles) at 30kt
Complement: 15

1. China (69 craft)

These are standard craft and some of them were built in
Chinese yards in the period up to 1966. It is thought that
perhaps half of the current total is in reserve.

2. Iraq (8 craft)

These are standard craft transferred between 1959 and
1961. The original total was twelve units, of which four
were sunk in the war with Iran during the 1980s. The
current craft are named *14 Tamouz* (212), *Al Adrisi* (213),
Al Taqi (214), *Al Shulab* (216), *14 Ramadan* (217), *Alef*
(220), *Ghazi* (221) and *Ibn Said* (222).

3. North Korea (32 'P 6'-class craft; 12 'Sinpo'-class craft)

Operating with pennant numbers in the 400 series, the
baseline craft are the survivors of 42 'P 6'-class units
transferred by the USSR (27 craft) and China (15 craft);
some of them have been modified with a gun armament of
2 × 37mm L/70 AA in single mountings. The locally
produced 'Sinpo' class has a steel rather than wooden
hull, and is replacing the original craft. It is a FAC(G)
type used for the patrol role with an armament of 6 ×
14.5in (0.57in) machine-guns in 3 × twin mountings.

General note

Produced from 1953 to the late 1960s to the extent of
some 500 craft, the 'P 6' class was widely used by the
USSR and a large number of allies and clients. The design
is thought to have been derived from the US Elco type of
the Second World War and used a wooden hull.

'P 48S' class
France/Cameroun

Type: fast attack craft (missile)
Displacement: ? tons standard; 308 tons full load
Dimensions: length 52.6m (172.5ft); beam 7.2m (23.6ft);
   draught 2.4m (7.9ft)
Gun armament: 2 × 40mm Bofors L/70 AA in single
   mountings
Missile armament: 2 × quadruple container-launchers for
   8 × MM.40 Exocet anti-ship missiles
Torpedo armament: none
Anti-submarine armament: none
Electronics: 2 × Decca 1226 surface search and
   navigation radars; 2 × Naja optronic directors; 1 ×
   Decca Cane 100 action information system
Propulsion: 2 × SACM/AGO 195 V16 CZSHR diesels
   delivering 4,800kW (6,440hp) to two shafts
Performance: maximum speed 25kt; range, 3,700km
   (2,300 miles) at 16kt
Complement: 6+33

▲ *Bakassi* is a 'P 48S'-class
FAC(M) serving in the
Cameroun navy.

1. Cameroun

Name	No	Builder	Commissioned
Bakassi	P104	SFCN	Jan 1984

Though comparatively slow and possessing only limited electronic capability, this large FAC(M/G) has particularly potent anti-ship missile armament.

'P400' class
France

Type: fast attack craft (missile)
Displacement: 406 tons standard; 454 tons full load
Dimensions: length 54.5m (178.6ft); beam 8.0m (26.2ft);
   draught 2.5m (8.3ft)

Gun armament: 1 × 40mm Bofors L/60 AA in a single
   mounting; 1 × 20mm GIAT L/103 AA in a DCN Type
   A single mounting; 1 × 7.62mm (0.3in) machine-gun
Missile armament: 2 × single container-launchers for two
   MM.38 Exocet anti-ship missiles (provision for); 1 ×
   sextuple SADRAL launcher for Mistral SAMs
   (replacing 20mm cannon mounting)
Torpedo armament: none
Anti-submarine armament: none
Electronics: 1 × Decca 1226 surface search and
   navigation radar
Propulsion: 2 × SEMT-Pielstick 16 PA4-V200 VGDS
   diesels delivering 6,000kW (8,045hp) to two shafts
Performance: maximum speed 24.5kt; range 7,800km
   (4,845 miles) at 15kt
Complement: 3+21 plus berthing and stores provision for
   the accommodation of 20 troops in the overseas
   transport role

1. France

Name	No	Builder	Commis-sioned
L'Audacieuse	P682	CMN, Cherbourg	Sep 1986
La Boudeuse	P683	CMN, Cherbourg	Jan 1987
La Capricieuse	P684	CMN, Cherbourg	Mar 1987
La Fougeuse	P685	CMN, Cherbourg	Mar 1987
La Glorieuse	P686	CMN, Cherbourg	Apr 1987
La Gracieuse	P687	CMN, Cherbourg	Jul 1987
La Moqueuse	P688	CMN, Cherbourg	Apr 1987
La Railleuse	P689	CMN, Cherbourg	May 1987

Name	Pennant No	Builder	Commis-sioned
La Rieuse	P690	CMN, Cherbourg	Jun 1987
La Tapageuse	P691	CMN, Cherbourg	Jan 1988

Ordered in May 1982 (six craft) and March 1984 (four
craft), these simple FACs are generally disposed in pairs
in four of France's overseas territories, while the remaining pair is kept in home waters.

2. Gabon

Name	No	Builder	Commis-sioned
General B.A. Oumar	P07	CMN, Cherbourg	Jun 1988
	P08	CMN, Cherbourg	1990

Ordered in May 1985, these two Gabonaise units are
generally similar to the French craft, but the primary
armament of each is 1 × 57mm SAK 57 Mk 2 L/70 DP in a
Bofors single mounting, supported by 1 or 2 × 20mm
Oerlikon AA in a single or twin mounting.

'Patra' class   France

Type: fast attack craft (gun)
Displacement: 115 tons standard; 147.5 tons full load
Dimensions: length 37.0m (121.4ft); beam 5.5m (18.0ft);
   draught 1.6m (5.2ft)
Gun armament: 1 × 40mm Bofors L/60 AA in a single
   mounting; 1 or 2 × 12.7mm (0.5in) machine-guns in
   single mountings

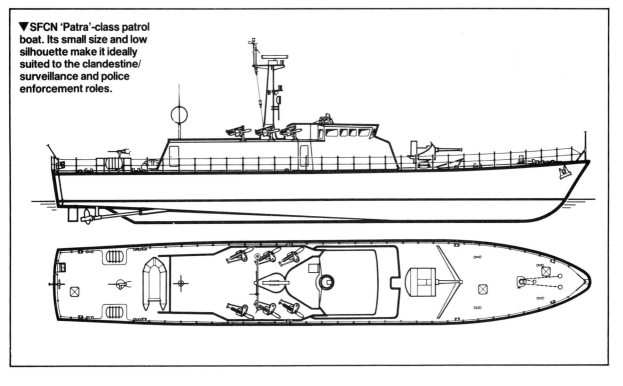

▼ SFCN 'Patra'-class patrol
boat. Its small size and low
silhouette make it ideally
suited to the clandestine/
surveillance and police
enforcement roles.

Missile armament: none
Torpedo armament: none
Anti-submarine armament: none
Electronics: 1 × surface search and navigation radar
Propulsion: 2 × AGO 195 V12 CZSHR diesels delivering
3,000kW (4,025hp) to two shafts
Performance: maximum speed 26kt; range 3,250km (2,020
miles) at 10kt or 1,400km (870 miles) at 20kt
Complement: 1+17

1. France

Name	No	Builder	Commis-sioned
Trident	P670	Auroux	Dec 1976
Glaive	P671	Auroux	Apr 1977
Epée	P672	CMN, Cherbourg	Oct 1976
Pertuisane	P673	CMN, Cherbourg	Jan 1977

These French craft are simple FAC(G)s whose low-powered engines and indifferent performance suit them to the patrol rather than combat role.

2. Ivory Coast

Name	No	Builder	Commis-sioned
L'Ardent		Auroux	Oct 1978
L'Intrepide		Auroux	Oct 1978

These Ivory Coast units are similar to the French craft but are limited-capability FAC(M)s with an indifferent missile armament of 4 × SS.12 anti-ship missiles.

3. Mauritania

Name	No	Builder	Commis-sioned
Le Dix Juillet	P411	Auroux	May 1982

This was the private-venture prototype for the 'Patra' class, subsequently bought by Mauritania and used as a basic FAC(G) with an armament of 1 × 40mm Bofors L/60 AA, 1 × 20mm Oerlikon AA and 2 × 0.5in (12.7mm) machine-guns. It was reported in the early 1980s that the SS.12 installation was to be replaced by 1 × quadruple container-launchers for four MM.38 Exocet anti-ship missiles, but this plan was later cancelled.

'Pauk' class   USSR

Type: fast attack craft (gun)
Displacement: ? tons standard; 580 tons full load
Dimensions: length 58.0m (190.3ft); beam 10.5m (34.4ft);
draught 2.5m (8.2ft)

Gun armament: 1 × 76mm (3in) L/60 DP in a single
mounting; 1 × 30mm ADGM-630 CIWS mounting
Missile armament: 1 × quadruple launcher for 8 × SA-N-
5 'Grail' SAMs
Torpedo armament: see below
Anti-submarine armament: 2 × RBU 1200 five-barrel
rocket-launchers; 4 × single 406mm (16in) mountings
for ? × Type 40 torpedoes; 2 × two racks for 12 ×
depth-charges
Electronics: 1 × 'Peel Cone' air/surface search radar; 1 ×
'Spin Trough' surface search and navigation radar; 1 ×
'Bass Tilt' gun fire-control radar; 1 × medium-
frequency active search and attack hull sonar; 1 ×
medium-frequency variable-depth active search sonar;
1 × ESM system with warning element; 2 × 'chaff'-
launchers; 1 × 'Square Head' IFF system; 1 × 'High
Pole-B' IFF system
Propulsion: 4 × M 504 diesels delivering 12,000kW
(16,095hp) to two shafts
Performance: maximum speed 34kt; range not revealed
Complement: 40

1. USSR (30 craft with more 3 more building and more planned)
Designed as replacement for the 'Poti' class, this useful patrol and anti-submarine type is derived from the 'Tarantul' class. The first unit was delivered in 1979 and the building programme continues.

'Pegasus' class   USA

Type: fast attack hydrofoil (missile and gun)
Displacement: ? tons standard; 240 tons full load
Dimensions: length 132.9ft (40.5m) with foils extended
and 145.3ft (44.3m) with foils retracted; beam 47.5ft
(14.5m) with foils extended and 28.2ft (8.6m) with foils
retracted; draught 23.2ft (7.1m) with foils extended and
6.2ft (1.9m) with foils retracted
Gun armament: 1 × 76mm (3in) L/62 DP in a Mk 75
(OTO Melara Compact) single mounting
Missile armament: 2 × quadruple Mk 141 container-
launchers for 8 × RGM-84 Harpoon anti-ship missiles
Torpedo armament: none
Anti-submarine armament: none
Electronics: 1 × SPS-64 surface search and navigation
radar; 1 × tracking radar used in conjunction with; 1 ×
WM-28 (in PHM-1) or Mk 92/94 (in others) gun and
SSM fire-control system; 1 × SWG-1A(V)4 launch and
control system; 1 × ESM system with SLQ-650
warning and jamming element; 2 × Mk 34 RBOC
'chaff'/flare-launchers; 1 × OE-82 satellite
communication system; 1 × WSC-3 satellite
communication transceiver; 1 × SRR-1 satellite
communication receiver
Propulsion: 2 × MTU 8V 331 TC81 diesels delivering
1,220kW (1,635hp) to two waterjets for hull-borne
operation, and one General Electric LM2500 gas

▶USS *Pegasus* is a guided-missile hydrofoil seen cruising normally off Port Hueheme, California, during Harpoon missile tests.

▼*Pegasus* is hosed down to remove sea water prior to her launch at Reston, Washington. This picture shows clearly the hydraulic workings of the hydrofoil astern and the waterjet propulsion system.

turbine delivering 18,000shp (13,420kW) to two
waterjets for foil-borne operation
Performance: maximum speed 48kt foil-borne or 12kt
hull-borne; range 1,950 miles (3,140km) at 9kt or 800
miles (1,285km) at 40kt
Complement: 4+20

1. USA

Name	No	Builder	Commissioned
Pegasus	PHM1	Boeing	Jul 1977
Hercules	PHM2	Boeing	Jul 1982
Taurus	PHM3	Boeing	Oct 1981
Aquila	PHM4	Boeing	Dec 1981
Aries	PHM5	Boeing	Apr 1982
Gemini	PHM6	Boeing	Jun 1982

These are capable FAH(M)s with advanced sensors and
weapons, but do not really fit into the US Navy's
operational scheme. *Pegasus* was completed in February
1975, but the whole programme was cancelled in February 1977. In August of the same year, Congressional
pressure forced a revival of the rest of the programme and
the other five craft were reordered.

'Perdana' class: *see* 'La Combattante II' class

'Poti' class   USSR

Type: fast attack craft (gun)
Displacement: 500 tons standard; 580 tons full load
Dimensions: length 60.0m (196.8ft); beam 8.0m (26.2ft);
draught 2.8m (9.2ft)
Armament: 2 × 57mm L/80 DP in a twin mounting
Missile armament: none
Torpedo armament: see below
Anti-submarine armament: 2 × RBU 6000 12-barrel
rocket-launchers; 4 × single 406mm (16in) mountings
for ? × Type 40 torpedoes
Electronics: 1 × 'Strut Curve' air search radar; 1 × 'Spin
Trough' surface search and navigation radar; 1 × 'Muff
Cob' gun fire-control radar; 1 × high frequency
variable-depth active search and attack sonar; 1 ×
ESM system with 2 × 'Watch Dog' antennae/housings;
1 × 'High Pole-B' IFF system
Propulsion: CODOG arrangement with 2 × gas turbines
delivering 22,400kW (30,045hp) or two M 503A
diesels delivering 6,000kW (8,065hp) to two shafts
Performance: maximum speed 38kt; range 11,130km
(6,915 miles) at 10kt or 925km (575 miles) at 34kt
Comlement: 80

1. Bulgaria (3 ships)
These craft were delivered in the mid-1970s.

2. Romania (3 ships)
These craft were delivered in the late 1960s.

3. USSR (55 ships)
Built between 1961 and 1968 at Khabarovsk and Zelenodolsk, this is an obsolescent coastal anti-submarine type.

'PR 72P' class   France/Peru

Type: fast attack craft (missile and gun)
Displacement: 470 tons standard; 560 tons full load
Dimensions: length 64.0m (210.0ft); beam 8.35m (27.4ft);
draught 1.6m (5.2ft)
Gun armament: 1 × 76mm (3in) L/62 DP in an OTO
Melara Compact single mounting; 2 × 40mm Bofors
L/70 AA in a Breda Compact twin mounting; 2 × 20mm
AA in single mountings
Missile armament: 2 × twin container-launchers for 4 ×
MM.38 Exocet anti-ship missiles
Torpedo armament: none
Anti-submarine armament: none
Electronics: 1 × Triton surface search radar; 1 × TM1226
navigation radar; 1 × Castor II tracking radar used in
conjunction with; 1 × Vega fire-control system; 1 ×
Panda optical director
Propulsion: 4 × SACM/AGO 240 V16 diesels delivering
16,400kW (21,995hp) to four shafts
Performance: maximum speed 34kt; range 4,625km (2,875
miles) at 16kt or 1,300km (810 miles) at 30kt
Complement: 36 with a maximum of 46 possible

1. Morocco ('PR 72M' class)

Name	No	Builder	Commissioned
Okba	33	SFCN	Dec 1976
Triki	34	SFCN	Jul 1977

Ordered in June 1973, these Moroccan FAC(G)s are
smaller than the Peruvian units, with standard and full-
load displacements of 375 and 445 tons on dimensions of:
length 57.5m (188.8ft), beam 7.6m (24.9ft) and draught
2.1m (7.1ft). The craft have an armament of 1 × 76mm
(3in) L/62 DP in an OTO Melara Compact single
mounting and 1 × 40mm Bofors L/70 AA in single
mounting, but there is provision for their conversion into
FAC(M/G)s by the installation of 2 × twin container-
launchers for 4 × MM.38 Exocet anti-ship missiles used
in conjunction with 1 × Vega fire-control system; each
vessel has 1 × search and navigation radar and 2 × Panda
optical directors. The powerplant comprises 4 × AGO
V16 ASHR diesels delivering 8,200kW (11,000hp) for a
maximum speed of 28kt and a range of 4,600km (2,860
miles) at 16kt; endurance is 20 days. The complement is
5+48.

▲ *Herrera* is a Peruvian 'PR
72P'-class FAC(G/M).

2. Peru ('PR 72P' class)

Name	No	Builder	Commis-sioned
Velarde	P21	SFCN	Jul 1980
Santillana	P22	SFCN	Jul 1980
De Los Heros	P23	SFCN	Nov 1980
Herrera	P24	SFCN	Feb 1981
Larrea	P25	SFCN	Jun 1981
Sanchez Carrion	P26	SFCN	Sep 1981

Ordered in late 1976, these large FAC(M/G)s are by local standards powerful craft with good missile and gun armament.

3. Senegambia ('PR 72S' class)

Name	No	Builder	Commis-sioned
Njambur	P773	SFCN	1982

Ordered in 1978, this Senegambian unit is a FAC(G)

similar to the Moroccan ship. The vessel has standard and full-load displacements of 375 and 450 tons respectively on dimensions of: length 58.7m (192.5ft), beam 7.6m (24.9ft) and draught 2.2m (7.2ft). The armament comprises 2 × 76mm (3in) L/62 DP in two OTO Melara Compact single mountings and 2 × 20mm AA in single mountings. The electronics fit is more capable than that of the Moroccan craft with 1 × Decca 1226 surface search and navigation radar, plus 2 × Naja optronic directors. The powerplant of 4 × AGO V16 RVR diesels delivers 9,600kW (12,875hp) to four shafts for a maximum speed of 29kt and a range of 4,600km (2,860 miles) at 16kt. The complement is 39, with provision for 7 passengers.

'Province' class
UK/Oman

Type: fast attack craft (missile and gun)
Displacement: 310 tons standard; 395 tons full load
Dimensions: length 186.0ft (56.7m); beam 26.9ft (8.2m); draught 8.9ft (2.7m)
Gun armament: 1 × 76mm (3in) L/62 DP in an OTO Melara Compact single mounting; 2 × 40mm Bofors L/70 AA in a Breda Compact twin mounting
Missile armament: 2 × triple or (in B11, 12 and 14) quadruple container-launchers for 6 or (in B11, 12 and 14) 8 × MM.40 Exocet anti-ship missiles
Torpedo armament: none

◀SNV *Dhofar* is a 'Province'-class FAC(M) serving in the Oman navy.

Anti-submarine armament: none

Electronics: 1 × AWS 4 or (in B11, 12 and 14) TM1226C surface search and tracking radar used in conjunction with; 1 × Sea Archer or (in B11, 12 and 14) Philips 307 fire-control system; 1 × optronic director; 1 × ESM system with Cutlass warning and Scorpion jamming elements; 2 × Barricade four-barrel 'chaff'/flare-launchers

Propulsion: 4 × Paxman Valenta 18RP-200 diesels delivering 18,200hp (13,570kW) to four shafts

Performance: maximum speed 40kt; range 2,300 miles (3,700km) at 18kt

Complement: 5+40 plus provision for 14 trainees

1. Kenya ('Nyayo' class)

Name	No	Builder	Commissioned
Nyayo	P3126	Vosper Thornycroft	Jul 1987
Umoja	P3127	Vosper Thornycroft	Sep 1987

Ordered in late 1984, these Kenyan FAC(M/G)s have standard and full-load displacements of 310 and 400 tons on dimensions of: length 186.0ft (56.7m), beam 26.9ft (8.2m) and draught 7.9ft (2.4m). The missile armament comprises 2 × twin container-launchers for 4 × Otomat Mk 2 anti-ship missiles and the other weapons consist of 1 × 76mm (3in) L/62 DP in an OTO Melara Compact single mounting, 2 × 30mm Oerlikon L/85 AA in a GCM-AO3-2 twin mounting, and 2 × 20mm Oerlikon L/75 AA in two A41A single mountings. The electronics fit includes 1 × AWS 4 surface search radar, 1 × AC1226 navigation radar used in conjunction with 1 × fire-control system, plus 1 × CAAIS 450 action information system, 1 × ESM system with warning element, and 2 × Barricade 18-barrel 'chaff'/flare-launchers. The powerplant comprises 4 × Paxman Valenta 18RP-200CM diesels delivering 18,200hp (13,570kW) to four shafts for a maximum speed

▼A fine three-quarter view of *Dhofar*, the first Oman navy boat of the 'Province' class.

of 40kt, and there are also two 100hp (76kW) electric motors for slow-speed cruising at a very low noise level. The complement is 40.

2. Oman

Name	No	Builder	Commissioned
Dhofar	B10	Vosper Thornycroft	Aug 1982
Al Sharqiyah	B11	Vosper Thornycroft	Nov 1983
Al Bat'nah	B12	Vosper Thornycroft	Jan 1984
Musandam	B14	Vosper Thornycroft	Mar 1989

These are large and powerful FAC(M/G)s with a potent missile armament plus the barrelled weapons for effective operations against smaller craft in confined waters. The craft were ordered in 1980 (one), 1981 (two) and 1986 (one), and the Vosper Thornycroft design is a development of that used for the Egyptian 'Ramadan'-class FAC(M)s.

'PSMM Mk 5' class   USA/South Korea

Type: fast attack craft (missile and gun)
Displacement: 240 tons standard; 268 tons full load
Dimensions: length 176.2ft (53.7m); beam 23.9ft (7.3m); draught 9.5ft (2.9m)
Gun armament: 1 × 3in (76mm) L/50 DP in a Mk 34 single mounting (in PGM352-355) or 1 × 76mm (3in) L/62 DP in an OTO Melara Compact single mounting; 2 × 30mm Oerlikon L/85 AA in an EMERLEC-30 twin mounting; 2 × 0.5in (12.7mm) machine-guns in single mountings
Missile armament: 4 × Standard launchers for 8 × RIM-66 ARM anti-ship missiles (only in PGM352, 353 and 355) or 2 × twin container-launchers for 4 × RGM-84 Harpoon anti-ship missiles (in other craft)
Torpedo armament: none
Anti-submarine armament: none
Electronics: 1 × SPS-58 air search radar; 1 × HC-75 surface search and navigation radar; 1 × SPG-50 or (in PGM356 onward) Westinghouse W-120 tracking radar used in conjunction with; 1 × Mk 63 gun or (in PGM356 onward) H 930 gun/SSM fire-control system or; 1 × ESM system with warning element; 2 × Mk 33 RBOC 'chaff'/flare-launchers
Propulsion: COGOG arrangement of 6 × Avco Lycoming TF35 gas turbines delivering 16,800shp (12,525kW) to two shafts
Performance: maximum speed 40kt+; range 2,750 miles (4,425km) at 18kt
Complement: 5+27

1. Indonesia ('Dagger' class)

Name	No	Builder	Commissioned
Mandau	621	Korea–Tacoma	Oct 1979
Rencong	622	Korea–Tacoma	Oct 1979
Badik	623	Korea–Tacoma	Feb 1980
Keris	624	Korea–Tacoma	Feb 1980

These Indonesian FAC(M/G)s differ somewhat from the South Korean units, having a full-load displacement of 270 tons on dimensions of: length 50.2m (164.7ft), beam 7.3m (23.9ft) and draught 2.3m (7.5ft). The missile armament comprises 2 × twin container-launchers for 4 × MM.38 Exocet anti-ship missiles, and the other weapons consist of 1 × 57mm SAK 57 Mk 1 L/70 DP in a Bofors single mounting, 1 × 40mm Bofors L/70 AA in a single mounting and 2 × 20mm Rheinmetall AA in S20 single mountings. The missiles are used in conjunction with the radar of 1 × WM-28 fire-control system, and the 76mm (3in) and 40mm guns are used in conjunction with 1 × NA18 optronic director; each vessel also possesses 1 × Decca 1226 surface search and navigation radar. The powerplant is a CODOG arrangement of 1 × General Electric LM2500 gas turbine or 2 × MTU 12V 331 TC81 diesels delivering 25,000shp (18,640kW) and 1,670kW (2,240hp) respectively to two shafts for speeds of 41kt on the gas turbine or 17kt on the diesels, while the range is 3,700km (2,300 miles) at 17kt. The complement is 7+36. Indonesia originally intended to procure eight of this class, but the plan seems to have been curtailed at the four current units.

2. South Korea

Name	No	Builder	Commissioned
Paek Ku 52	PGM352	Tacoma BB	Mar 1975
Paek Ku 53	PGM353	Tacoma BB	Mar 1975
Paek Ku 55	PGM355	Tacoma BB	Feb 1976
Paek Ku 56	PGM356	Tacoma BB	Feb 1976
Paek Ku 57	PGM357	Korea–Tacoma	1977
Paek Ku 58	PGM358	Korea–Tacoma	1977
Paek Ku 59	PGM359	Korea–Tacoma	1977
Paek Ku 61	PGM361	Korea–Tacoma	1978

The first three of this FAC(M/G) class are unusual in being armed with the radar-homing anti-ship version of the Standard SAM.

3. Taiwan ('Lung Chiang' class)

Name	No	Builder	Commissioned
Lung Chiang	PCG581	Tacoma BB	May 1978
Sui Chiang	PGG582	China SB	1982

These Taiwanese FAC(M/G)s are similar to the South Korean units, but possess standard and full-load displacements of 220 and 250 tons respectively on dimensions of:

length 164.5ft (50.2m), beam 23.9ft (7.3m) and draught 7.5ft (2.3m). The craft each have a missile armament of 4 × single container-launchers for 4 × Hsiung Feng I anti-ship missiles, and the other weapons consist of 1 × 76mm (3in) L/62 DP in an OTO Melara Compact single mounting, 2 × 30mm Oerlikon L/85 AA in an EMERLEC-30 twin mounting, and 2 × 0.5in/12.7mm machine-guns in single mountings. The electronics include 1 × RAN 11L/X air/surface search radar, 1 × tracking radar used in conjunction with 1 × Argo NA10 fire-control system, 1 × HR 76 tracking radar used in conjunction with 1 × H 930 missile fire-control system (in PGG582 only), 1 × IPN 10 action information system, and 4 × 'chaff'/flare-launchers. The powerplant is a CODOG arrangement of 3 × Avco Lycoming TF35 gas turbines delivering 13,800shp (10,290kW) or three General Motors 12V 149TI diesels delivering 2,880hp (2,145kW), in each case to three shafts, for maximum speeds of 40 or 20kt respectively; the range is 5,000km (3,105 miles) at 12kt on one diesel, declining to 1,300km (805 miles) at 40kt on three gas turbines. The complement is 5+29. The Taiwanese had planned to produce a large class whose later units would have had RGM-84 Harpoon anti-ship missiles and the RCA R76 C5 fire-control system, but the USA's refusal of an export licence for the Harpoon led to cancellation of the plan as the type has suspect stability with the Hsiung Feng missiles.

4. Thailand ('Sattahip' class)

Name	No	Builder	Commis-sioned
Sattahip	4	Ital–Thai (Samutprakarn)	Sep 1983
Klongyai	5	Ital–Thai (Samutprakarn)	May 1984
Takbai	6	Ital–Thai (Samutprakarn)	Jul 1984
Kantang	7	Ital–Thai (Samutprakarn)	Oct 1985
Thepha	8	Ital–Thai (Samutprakarn)	Apr 1986
Taimuang	9	Ital–Thai (Samutprakarn)	Apr 1986

Ordered in September 1981 (first four units), December 1983 and August 1984, these Thai craft are considerably less capable than their counterparts, and are FAC(G)s with standard and full-load displacements of 270 and 300 tons respectively on dimensions of: length 50.1m (164.5ft), beam 7.3m (23.9ft) and draught 1.8m (5.9ft). The type lacks missile armament, and the weapons therefore consist of 1 × 3in (76mm) L/50 DP in a single mounting, 1 × 40mm Bofors L/70 AA in a single mounting and 2 × 0.5in (12.7mm) machine-guns in single mountings. The 3in (76mm) and 40mm guns are used in conjunction with 1 × NA18 optronic director (in three craft), and each vessel possesses 1 × Decca surface search and navigation radar. The powerplant is 2 × MTU 16V 538 TB91-2 diesels delivering 5,100kW (6,840hp) to two shafts for a speed of 22kt and a range of 4,600km (2,860 miles) at 15kt. The complement is 56.

General note
The 'PSSM Mk 5' design is the Patrol Ship Multi-Mission Mk 5 derivative of the 'Asheville'-class FAC(G). Seventeen of this type were built for the US Navy between 1966 and 1971 for coastal patrol and blockade, but were not extensively used. The class has a full-load displacement of 245 tons on dimensions of: length 164.5ft (50.1m), beam 23.8ft (7.3m) and draught 9.5ft (2.9m) for a speed of 38kt on the CODOG arrangement of 2 × Cummins diesels delivering 3,500hp (2,610kW) and 1 × General Electric gas turbine delivering 13,300shp (9,915kW) to two shafts. The standard armament is 1 × 3in (76mm) gun in a Mk 76 single mounting, 1 × 40mm Bofors L/60 AA in a Mk 3 single mounting, and 2 × 0.5in (12.7mm) machine-guns in a twin mounting. The craft are now out of US service and either exported as one to South Korea as a FAC(M) with two Standard ARM anti-ship missiles, and two each to Colombia, Taiwan (now deleted) and Turkey as FAC(G)s or awaiting transfer.

'PT 11' class   Japan

Type: fast attack craft (gun and torpedo)
Displacement: 100 tons standard; 125 tons full load
Dimensions: length 35.0m (114.8ft); beam 9.2m (30.2ft); draught 1.2m (3.9ft)
Gun armament: 4 × 40mm Bofors L/70 AA in 2 × Mk 3 single mountings
Missile armament: none
Torpedo armament: 4 × single 533mm (21in) mountings for 4 × heavyweight anti-ship torpedoes
Anti-submarine armament: none
Electronics: 1 × OPS-19 surface search and navigation radar
Propulsion: CODAG arrangement of 2 × Ishikawajima–Harima IM-300 gas turbines and 2 × Mitsubishi 24 WZ-31MZ diesels delivering 8,200kW (11,000shp) to three shafts
Performance: maximum speed 40kt; range 1,850km (1,150 miles) at 18kt or 555km (345 miles) at 40kt
Complement: ?

1. Japan

Name	No	Builder	Commis-sioned
PT 11	PT811	Mitsubishi, Shimonoseki	Mar 1971
PT 12	PT812	Mitsubishi, Shimonoseki	Mar 1972
PT 13	PT813	Mitsubishi, Shimonoseki	Dec 1972
PT 14	PT814	Mitsubishi, Shimonoseki	Feb 1974
PT 15	PT815	Mitsubishi, Shimonoseki	Jul 1975

These are limited but still useful anti-ship FAC(T)s for use in Japan's coastal waters.

'Rade Koncar' or 'Type 211' class   Yugoslavia

Type: fast attack craft (missile and gun)

Displacement: ? tons standard; 240 tons full load

Dimensions: length 45.0m (147.6ft); beam 8.4m (27.6ft); draught 2.5m (8.2ft)

Gun armament: 2 × 57mm SAK 57 Mk 1 L/70 DP in Bofors single mountings

Missile armament: 2 × twin container-launchers for 4 × SS-N-2B 'Styx' anti-ship missiles

Torpedo armament: none

Anti-submarine armament: none

Electronics: 1 × Decca 1226 surface search and navigation radar; 1 × Philips TAB tracking radar used in conjunction with; 1 × 9LV 200 fire-control system

Propulsion: CODAG arrangement of 2 × Rolls-Royce Proteus gas turbines delivering 11,600shp (8,650kW) and two MTU 20V 538 TB92 diesels delivering 5,400kW (7,240hp) to four shafts

Performance: maximum speed 40kt; range 1,850km (1,150 miles) at 20kt or 925km (575 miles) at 35kt

Complement: 5+25

1. Libya

Name	No	Builder	Commissioned
		Tito Shipyard	
		Tito Shipyard	
		Tito Shipyard	
		Tito Shipyard	

Ordered in 1985, these are unexceptional FAC(M/G)s probably making use of weapons and sensors already available to Libya. The gun armament is 1 × 76mm (3in) L/62 DP in an OTO Melara Compact single mounting, 1 × 40mm Bofors L/70 AA in a Breda single mounting, 2 × 30mm Oerlikon L/85 AA in a GCM-A03 twin mounting, and 2 × 12.7mm (0.5in) machine-guns. The missile armament comprises 2 × twin container-launchers for 4 × SS-N-2C 'Styx' anti-ship missiles. The fact that the craft have not yet been delivered may mean that the programme is in abeyance, probably because of the Western embargo on the supply of military equipment (including engines) to Libya.

2. Yugoslavia

Name	No	Builder	Commissioned
Rade Koncar	RT401	Tito Shipyard	Apr 1977
Vlado Cetkovic	RT402	Tito Shipyard	Mar 1978
Ramiz Sadiko	RT403	Tito Shipyard	Aug 1978
Hasan Zahirovic-Laca	RT404	Tito Shipyard	Dec 1978
Orce Nikolov	RT405	Tito Shipyard	Aug 1979
Ante Banina	RT406	Tito Shipyard	Nov 1980

▼'PT11'-class fast torpedo boat serving in the Japanese navy.

These Yugoslav FAC(M/G)s are based on the hull of the Swedish 'Spica II' class with the amidships bridge of the Malaysian 'Spica II-M' class, simple electronics of Western origin, a propulsion arrangement of Western origin, and a mix of Soviet and Swedish armament.

'Ramadan' class

UK/Egypt

Type: fast attack craft (missile and gun)
Displacement: 258 tons standard; 310 tons full load
Dimensions: length 170.6ft (52.0m); beam 25.0ft (7.6m);

◄'Ramadan'-class missile craft of the Egyptian navy.

▼'Ratcharit'-class FAC of the Thai navy.

draught 6.6ft (2.0m)

Gun armament: 1 × 76mm (3in) L/62 DP in an OTO Melara Compact single mounting; 2 × two 40mm Bofors L/70 AA in a Breda Compact twin mounting

Missile armament: 2 × twin container-launchers for 4 × Otomat Mk 1 anti-ship missiles

Torpedo armament: none

Anti-submarine armament: none

Electronics: 1 × S 820 surface search radar; 1 × S 810 navigation radar; 2 × ST 802 tracking radars used in conjunction with; 1 × Sapphire fire-control system; 2 × optronic directors; 2 × optical directors; 1 × CAAIS action information system; 1 × ESM system with Cutlass warning and Cygnus jamming elements; 2 × Protean 'chaff'/flare-launchers each with 4 × magazines carrying 36 × 'chaff'/flare grenades

Propulsion: 4 × MTU 20V 538 TB91 diesels delivering 12,800kW (17,170hp) to four shafts

Performance: maximum speed 40kt; range 3,700km (2,300 miles) at 16kt

Complement: 4+26

1. Egypt

Name	No	Builder	Commissioned
Ramadan	670	Vosper Thornycroft	Jul 1981
Khyber	672	Vosper Thornycroft	Sep 1981
El Kadesseya	674	Vosper Thornycroft	Apr 1982

Name	Pennant No	Builder	Commissioned
El Yarmouk	676	Vosper Thornycroft	May 1982
Badr	678	Vosper Thornycroft	Jun 1982
Hettein	680	Vosper Thornycroft	Oct 1982

This powerful FAC(M/G) class features a nicely balanced sensor and armament combination optimized for the anti-ship role.

'Ratcharit' class   Italy/Thailand

Type: fast attack craft (missile and gun)

Displacement: 235 tons standard; 270 tons full load

Dimensions: length 49.8m (163.4ft); beam 7.5m (24.6ft); draught 2.3m (7.5ft)

Gun armament: 1 × 76mm (3in) L/62 DP in an OTO Melara Compact single mounting; 1 × 40mm Bofors L/70 AA in a Breda single mounting

Missile armament: 2 × twin container-launchers for 4 × MM.38 Exocet anti-ship missiles

Torpedo armament: none

Anti-submarine armament: none

Electronics: 1 × Decca surface search and navigation radar; 1 × tracking radar used in conjunction with; 1 × WM-25 fire-control system; 1 × ESM system with warning element

Propulsion: 3 × MTU 20V 538 TB91 diesels delivering 10,050kW (13,480hp) to three shafts

Performance: maximum speed 37kt; range 3,700km (2,300 miles) at 15kt or 1,200km (745 miles) at 36kt
Complement: 7+38

1. Thailand

Name	No	Builder	Commissioned
Ratcharit	4	CNR, Breda	Aug 1979
Witthayakhom	5	CNR, Breda	Nov 1979
Udomdet	6	CNR, Breda	Feb 1980

Ordered in July 1976, these are medium-sized FAC(M/G)s with modest missile armament and the standard combination of one 76mm (3in) DP and one 40mm AA guns.

'Reshef' class: *see* 'Saar 4' class
'Ramat' class: *see* 'Saar 4.5' class
'Saar 2' class: *see* 'Lürssen FPB/TNC-45' class
'Saar 3' class: *see* 'Lürssen FPB/TNC-45' class

'Saar 4' or 'Reshef' class   Israel

Type: fast attack craft (missile and gun)
Displacement: 415 tons standard; 450 tons full load
Dimensions: length 58.0m (190.6ft); beam 7.8m (25.6ft); draught 2.4m (8.0ft)

Gun armament: 1 × 76mm (3in) L/62 DP in an OTO Melara Compact single mounting (not in *Tarshish*); 1 × 20mm six-barrel rotary cannon in a Phalanx Mk 15 CIWS mounting; 2 × 20mm Oerlikon L/75 AA in A41A single mountings; 2 × 0.5in (12.7mm) machine-guns in single mountings
Missile armament: 1 × twin or quadruple Mk 141 container-launcher for 2 or 4 × RGM-84 Harpoon anti-ship missiles, or 4 or 6 × single container-launchers for 4 or 6 × Gabriel II or III anti-ship missiles (or a mix of the two missile types)
Torpedo armament: none
Anti-submarine armament: none
Aircraft: 1 × IAI/Mata Hellstar light remotely piloted helicopter on a platfrom aft (on *Tarshish* only)
Electronics: 1 × Neptune air/surface search radar; 1 × RTN 10X tracking radar used in conjunction with; 1 × Argo NA10 fire-control system; 1 × ELAC active

▼'Minister'-class FAC(M/G) serving with the South African navy. The type is an exceptional design combining long range, excellent sea-keeping qualities and devastating six Skorpioen missile armament.

search and attack hull sonar (not in *Yaffo*); 1 × ESM system with MN-53 warning and jamming elements; 9 or 11 × 'chaff'-launchers (1 × 45-tube, 4 or 6 × 24-tube and 4 × 1-tube)

Propulsion: 4 × MTU 16V 956 TB91 diesels delivering 10,400kW (13,950hp) to four shafts

Performance: maximum speed 32kt; range 7,400km (4,600 miles) at 17.5kt or 3,075km (1,910 miles) at 30kt

Complement: 45

1. Chile

Name	No	Builder	Commis-sioned
Casma	30	Haifa Shipyard	May 1974
Chipana	31	Haifa Shipyard	Oct 1973

These Chilean FAC(M/G)s are similar to the original Israeli norm, but have a missile armament of 4 × single container-launchers for 4 × Gabriel anti-ship missiles, while the other weapons consist of 2 × 76mm (3in) L/62 DP in OTO Melara Compact single mountings and 2 × 20mm Oerlikon L/75 AA in A41A single mountings, and a less sophisticated sensor fit based on 1 × Neptune surface search and navigation radar used in conjunction with 1 × EL/M 2221 fire-control system; each vessel also possesses 4 × Israeli 'chaff'-launchers. The craft (ex-*Romat* and ex-*Keshet*) were transferred to Chile in 1979 and 1981 respectively. Chile planned to build more of the type under licence, but the normalization of relations with Argentina after the Vatican's settlement of the Beagle Channel dispute may have caused the cancellation of the notion, especially as the country brought two 'Saar 3'-class FACs from Israel in 1989.

2. Israel

Name	No	Builder	Commis-sioned
Reshef		Haifa Shipyard	Apr 1973
Kidon		Haifa Shipyard	Sep 1974
Tarshish		Haifa Shipyard	Mar 1975
Yaffo		Haifa Shipyard	Apr 1975
Nitzhon		Haifa Shipyard	Sep 1978
Atsmout		Haifa Shipyard	Feb 1979
Moledet		Haifa Shipyard	May 1979
Komemiut		Haifa Shipyard	Aug 1980

These are in every way exceptional FAC(M/G)s, built to a basic design from Lürssen but adapted to Israeli requirements to produce long-range craft of very good sea-keeping qualities and devastating missile armament. The extension of this armament has led to the modification of the original gun armament, which is reflected in the fit carried by the Chilean craft. Israel plans to replace the CIWS mounting with a vertical-launch syusystem for Barak 1 SAMs.

3. South Africa ('Minister' class)

Name	No	Builder	Commis-sioned
Jan Smuts	P1561	Haifa Shipyard	Sep 1977
P.W. Botha	P1562	Haifa Shipyard	Dec 1977
Frederic Cresswell	P1563	Haifa Shipyard	May 1978
Jim Fouche	P1564	Sandock Austral	Dec 1978
Frans Erasmus	P1565	Sandock Austral	Jul 1979
Oswald Pirow	P1566	Sandock Austral	Mar 1980
Hendrik Mentz	P1567	Sandock Austral	Sep 1982
Kobie Coetzee	P1568	Sandock Austral	Mar 1983
Magnus Malan	P1569	Sandock Austral	Jul 1986
	P1571	Sandock Austral	1989
	P1572	Sandock Austral	1990
	P1573	Sandock Austral	1990

Ordered in late 1974, these South African FAC(M/G)s are a variation on the Israeli norm, with a full-load displacement of 430 tons on dimensions of: length 62.2m (204.0ft), beam 7.8m (25.6ft) and draught 2.4m (8.0ft). The missile armament comprises 6 × single container-launchers for 6 × Skorpioen (Gabriel II) anti-ship missiles, and the other weapons consist of 2 × 76mm (3in) L/62 DP in OTO Melara Compact single mountings, 2 × 20mm Oerlikon L/75 AA in A41A single mountings and 2 × 0.5in (12.7mm) machine-guns in single mountings. The electronics fit, propulsion and performance are similar to those of the Israeli craft, and the complement is 7+40. It is reported that another three units are to be built to an improved standard.

'Saar 4.5' or 'Aliya/Romat' class   Israel

Type: fast attack craft (missile and gun)

Displacement: 490 tons standard; ? tons full load

Dimensions: length 61.7m (202.4ft); beam 7.6m (24.9ft); draught 2.5m (8.2ft)

Gun armament: 1 × 76mm (3in) L/62 DP in an OTO Melara Compact single mounting (not in *Alia* and *Geoula*); 1 × 20mm six-barrel rotary cannon in a Phalanx Mk 15 CIWS mounting; 2 × 20mm Oerlikon AA in single mountings: 2 or 4 × 0.5in (12.7mm) machine-guns in a twin or quadruple mounting

Missile armament: 1 or (in *Romat* and *Keshet*) 2 × quadruple Mk 141 container-launchers for 4 × 8 RGM-84 Harpoon anti-ship missiles, and 4 or (in *Romat* and *Keshet*) 8 × single container-launchers for 4 or 8 × Gabriel II or III anti-ship missiles

Torpedo armament: none

Anti-submarine armament: helicopter-launched weapons (see below)

Aircraft: 1 × Agusta (Bell) AB.206 helicopter or Mata Hellstar light remotely piloted helicopter in a hangar amidships (in *Alia* and *Geoula* only)

Electronics: 1 × Neptune air/surface search radar; 1 ×

RTN 10X tracking radar used in conjunction with; 1 × Argo NA10 fire-control system; 1 × ELAC hull-mounted sonar; 1 × Elta ESM system with MN-53 warning and jamming elements; 6 × 'chaff'/flare-launchers (1 × 45-tube, 1 × 24-tube and 4 × 1-tube)

Propulsion: 4 × MTU 16V 956 TB91 diesels delivering 10,400kW (13,950hp) to four shafts

Performance: maximum speed 31kt; range 7,400km (4,600 miles) at 17kt or 2,800km (1,740 miles) at 30kt

Complement: 53 or (in *Romat* and *Keshet*) 45

1. Israel

Name	No	Builder	Commis-sioned
Aliya		Haifa Shipyard	Aug 1980
Geoula		Haifa Shipyard	Dec 1980
Romat		Haifa Shipyard	Oct 1981
Keshet		Haifa Shipyard	1982

These large FAC(M/G)s were designed as leaders for flotillas of smaller craft, and have quite exceptional missile firepower, even in *Aliya* and *Geoula*, which have a small helicopter for the mid-course guidance update of long-range anti-ship missiles and, as a secondary task, anti-submarine defence.

'Saettia' class   Italy

Type: fast attack craft (missile and gun)

Displacement: 360 tons standard; 400 tons full load

Dimensions: length 51.7m (169.6ft); beam 8.1m (26.6ft); draught ? m (? ft)

Gun armament: 1 × 76mm (3in) L/62 DP in an OTO Melara Compact single mounting; 2 × 30mm Breda L/82 DP in a Breda Twin 30 Compact twin mounting

Missile armament: 2 × twin Teseo 2 container-launchers for 4 × Otomat Mk 2 anti-ship missiles

Torpedo armament: none

Anti-submarine armament: none

Electronics: 1 × RAN 11L/X air/surface search radar; 1 × RAN-series navigation radar; 1 × RTN-20 tracking radar used in conjunction with; 1 × Argo NA21 fire-control system; 1 × NA18 optronic director (provision for); 1 × IPN 10 action information system; 1 × Elettronica ESM system with warning element; 2 × SCLAR 'chaff'/flare-launchers

Propulsion: 4 × MTU 16V 538 TB93 diesels delivering 13,120kW (17,600hp) to two shafts

Performance: maximum speed 40kt; range 4,450km (2,765 miles) at 16kt or 960km (595 miles) at 37kt

Complement: 4+29

1. Italy

Name	No	Builder	Commis-sioned
Saettia	920	Fincantieri	

This comparatively large FAC(M/G) is designed for operational compatibility with the same builder's range of missile-armed corvettes, and offers a high level of seakeeping and survivability married to a potent weapon system (missiles, guns and sensors) and a low radar signature.

▼Side view of the Italian *Saettia* small missile craft.

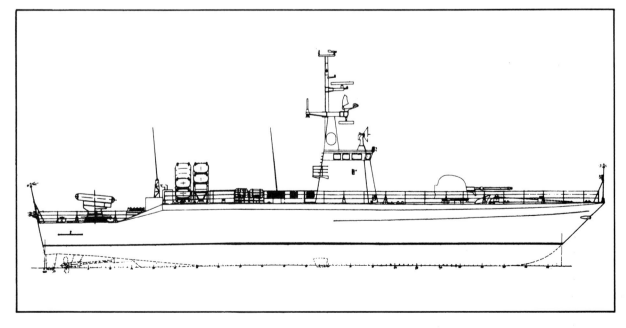

'SAR 33' class
Germany/Libya

Type: fast attack craft (gun)
Displacement: 140 tons standard; 170 tons full load
Dimensions: length 33.0m (108.3ft); beam 8.6m (28.2ft); draught 3.0m (9.8ft)
Gun armament: 2 × 40mm Bofors L/70 AA in a twin mounting; 2 × 12.7mm (0.5in) machine-guns in single mountings
Missile armament: none
Torpedo armament: none
Anti-submarine armament: none
Electronics: 1 × surface search and navigation radar
Propulsion: 3 × SACM AGO V16 CSHR diesels delivering 9,000kW (12,070hp) to three shafts
Performance: maximum speed 40kt; range 1,850km (1,150 miles) at 20kt or 825km (515 miles) at 35kt
Complement: 23

1. Libya (14 craft)
Ordered in 1980, designed in Germany by Abeking und Rasmussen of Lemwerder and built in Turkey by the Taskizak Navy Yard of Istanbul, these craft were delivered in 1986 (twelve units) and (1987 two units). The design allows for these comparatively simple FAC(G)s to be upgraded to FAC(M/G) standard with anti-ship missiles, 1 × 76mm (3in) L/62 DP in an OTO Melara Compact single mounting and 2 × 35mm Oerlikon L/90 AA in a twin mounting.

2. Turkey (10 craft)
Ordered in May 1976 in the form of one German-built prototype, with another nine units later built under licence in Turkey, these are simple FAC(G)s named *SG61* to *SG70*. They are operated by the Turkish Coast Guard and are basically similar to those in service with Libya except in their armament, which comprises 1 × 40mm Bofors L/70 AA in a single mounting and 2 × 7.62mm (0.3in) machine-guns in single mountings.

'Sattahip' class: *see* 'PSMM Mk 5' class

'SBD Mk 2' class
India

Type: fast attack craft (gun)
Displacement: 140 tons standard; 170 tons full load
Dimensions: length 37.5m (123.0ft); beam 7.5m (24.6ft); draught 1.8m (5.9ft)
Gun armament: 1 × 40mm Bofors L/60 AA in a single mounting
Missile armament: none
Torpedo armament: none
Anti-submarine armament: 28 × depth-charges (18 × Mk 7 and 10 × Mk 12)
Electronics: 1 × surface search and navigation radar; 1 × hull-mounted active search and attack sonar

Propulsion: 2 × Paxman Deltic diesels delivering 6,880hp (5,130kW) to two shafts; 1 × Kirloskar-Cummins auxiliary diesel delivering 165hp (123kW)
Performance: maximum speed 29kt on main diesels or 4kt on auxiliary diesel; range 2,600km (1,615 miles) at 14kt
Complement: 4+26

1. India (5 'SBD Mk 2'-class craft)
Numbered 51 to 55, these craft were built by Garden Reach Ship Yard in Calcutta and commissioned between 1977 and 1982. They are simple FAC(G)s and although they are used mainly for patrol, they also possess a limited anti-submarine capability.

2. India (7 'SBD Mk 3'-class craft)
Four of this class were built by the Garden Reach Ship Yard in Calcutta and the other three by Mazagon in Goa, and the class was commissioned between 1984 and 1986. The type is slightly larger than the 'SBD Mk 2' with a full-load displacement of 210 tons on dimensions of: length 37.8m (124.0ft), beam 7.6m (25.0ft) and draught 1.5m (4.9ft). The type has the same armament as the 'SBD Mk 2' class, but the propulsion arrangement comprises 2 × MTU diesels delivering 6,850kW (9,185hp) to two shafts for a maximum speed of 34kt. The complement is 31.

'Sea Dolphin' class
South Korea

Type: fast attack craft (gun)
Displacement: ? tons standard; 170 tons full load
Dimensions: length 33.1m (108.6ft); beam 6.9m (22.6ft); draught 2.5m (8.2ft)
Gun armament: 1 × 40mm Bofors L/60 AA in a single mounting; 4 × 30mm Oerlikon L/85 AA in 2 × EMERLEC-30 twin mountings; 2 × 20mm Oerlikon AA in a twin mounting; 2 × 0.5in (12.7mm) machine-guns in a twin mounting
Missile armament: none
Torpedo armament: none
Anti-submarine armament: none
Electronics: 1 × surface search and navigation radar
Propulsion: 2 × MTU 16V 538 TB90 diesels delivering 8,050kW (10,795hp) to two shafts
Performance: maximum speed 38kt; range 1,300km (810 miles) at 20kt
Complement: 31

1. South Korea (32 craft)
Ordered in 1978, the vessels of this last FAC(G) class were built by Korea SEC and Korea–Tacoma at Masan. The armament is very good for the patrol role, and although the performance is generally good, the range is notably low.

'Shanghai II, III and IV' classes   China

Type: fast attack craft (gun)
Displacement: 120 tons standard; 155 tons full load
Dimensions: length 39.0m (128.0ft); beam 5.5m (18.0ft);
    draught 1.7m (5.5ft)
Gun armament:
'Shanghai II' class craft: 4 × 37mm L/63 AA in 2 × twin
    mountings; 4 × 25mm AA in 2 × twin mountings
'Shanghai III and IV' class craft: 2 × 57mm L/70 AA in a
    twin mounting; 1 × 25mm AA in a single mounting; 2 ×
    75mm (2.95in) Type 56 recoilless rifles in a twin
    mounting (in some craft only)
Missile armament: none
Torpedo armament: none
Anti-submarine armament: 2 × throwers for 8 × depth-
    charges
Mines: up to 10
Electronics: 1 × 'Skin Head' or 'Pot Head' surface
    search radar; 1 × hull-mounted sonar; 1 × variable-
    depth sonar (in some craft only); 1 × 'High Pole-A' IFF
    system
Propulsion: 2 × M 50F diesels delivering 1,800kW
    (2,415hp) and 2 × Type 12D6 diesels delivering
    1,350kW (1,810hp) to four shafts
Performance: maximum speed 30kt; range 1,500km (930
    miles) at 17kt
Complement: 6+30

1. Albania (6 'Shanghai II'-class craft – Nos 541, 542, 543, 544, 545 and 546)
These are standard craft transferred in mid-1974 (four)
and 1975 (two).

2. Bangladesh (8 'Shanghai II'-class craft)
Transferred in groups of four during March 1980 and
1982, these are *Shaheet Daulat* (P411), *Shaheed Farid*
(P412), *Shaheed Mohobullah* (P413), *Shaheed Akhtar-
ruddin* (P414), *Tahweed* (P611), *Tawfiq* (P612), *Tamjeed*
(P613) and *Tanveer* (P614).

3. China (290+ 'Shanghai II, III and IV'-class craft)
These serve from ports all along the Chinese coast.

4. Congo (3 'Shanghai II' class craft – Nos 201, 202 and 203)
These are standard craft transferred in 1975.

5. Egypt (4 'Shanghai II'-class craft – Nos 793, 795, 797 and 799)
These are standard craft transferred in 1984.

6. Guinea (6 'Shanghai II'-class craft – Nos P733, P734, P735, P736, P737 and P738)
These are standard craft transferred as a group of four in
1973–74 and two in 1976.

7. North Korea (15 'Shanghai II'-class craft)
These are standard craft transferred since 1967.

8. Pakistan (12 'Shanghai II'-class craft)
These are *Quetta* (P141), *Lahore* (P142), *Marden* (P143),
Gilgit (P144), *Pishin* (P145), *Sukkur* (P146), *Sehwan*
(P147), *Bahawalpur* (P149), *Banum* (P154), *Kalat* (P156),
Larkana (P157) and *Sahiwal* (P160). The first eight craft
were transferred in 1972 and the last four in 1973.

9. Romania (27 'Shanghai II'-class craft)
These are *Saturn* and *Venus* for harbour security, VP20
to VP40 for maritime border patrol, and VS41 to VS44 for
anti-submarine patrol with a high-frequency search and
attack hull sonar and two racks of depth-charges. These
are all locally built craft produced at Mangalia from 1973.

10. Sri Lanka (6 'Shanghai II'-class craft)
These are known locally as the 'Sooraya' class and are
named *Sooraya* (P3140), *Weeraya* (P3141), *Ranakami*
(P3142), *Balawatha* (P3144), *Jagatha* (P3145) and *Rak-
shaka* (P3146). The craft originally numbered seven, and
were transferred in February 1972 (two), July 1972 (two),
December 1972 (one) and November 1980 (two). *Daksaya*
(P3143) was deleted in 1983.

11. Tanzania (6 'Shanghai II'-class craft – Nos JW9841, JW9842, JW9843, JW9844, JW9845 and JW9846)
These are standard craft transferred in 1975.

12. Tunisia (2 'Shanghai II'-class craft)
These are *Gafsah* (P305) and *Amilcar* (P306) transferred
in April 1977.

13. Zaire (4 'Shanghai II'-class craft)
These are standard craft, the survivors of four transferred
in 1976–78 and two transferred in February 1967.

General note
These are simple and very economical craft, and production began at Shanghai in 1961. Other yards now build
the type, with construction continuing at about ten units
per year for later variants with revised bridge arrangements and different armament. The original type was the
'Shanghai I' class (about 25 built) with a standard
displacement of 100 tons on a hull only 36.6m (120.0ft)
long, and was armed with 2 × 57mm AA in a twin
mounting forward, two 37mm AA in a twin mounting aft,
and (later removed) 2 × 457mm (18in) tubes in a twin
mounting for 2 × anti-ship torpedoes. There is a con-
sistent turnover in the class, numbers remaining roughly
constant as deletions are balanced by new construction.

'Shantou' class   China

Type: fast attack craft (gun)
Displacement: 60 tons standard; 80 tons full load

Dimensions: lenght 25.5m (83.7ft); beam 5.8m (19.0ft); draught 2.0m (6.6ft)

Gun armament: 4 × 37mm L/63 AA in 2 × twin mountings; 2 × 12.7mm (0.5in) machine-guns in a twin mounting or (in some craft only) 2 × 75mm (2.95in) recoilless rifles in a twin mounting

Missile armament: none

Torpedo armament: none

Anti-submarine armament: 8 × depth-charges

Electronics: 1 × 'Skin Head' surface search radar

Propulsion: 2 × Type 3D12 diesels delivering 450kW (605hp) and 2 × M 50L diesels delivering 1,800kW (2,415hp) to four shafts

Performance: maximum speed 28kt; range 1,400km (870 miles) at 15kt or 925km (575 miles) at 28kt

Complement: 17

1. China (50 craft)

Built from 1958 at Luda, Guangzhou and Shanghai, this FAC(G) class was initially known in the West as the 'Swatow' class. The type is based on the hull of the 'P 6'-class FAC(T) revised in steel.

2. Equatorial Guinea (2 craft)

These are standard craft transferred in 1983.

3. Guinea-Bissau (4 craft)

These are standard craft transferred in pairs during 1983 and March 1986.

4. North Korea (4 craft)

These are standard craft transferred in 1968.

'Shershen' and 'Mol' classes   USSR

Type: fast attack craft (torpedo)

Displacement: ('Shershen' class) 145 tons standard; 175 tons full load; ('Mol' class) 160 tons standard; 200 tons full load

Dimensions: ('Shershen' class) length 34.7m (113.8ft); beam 6.7m (22.0ft); draught 1.5m (4.9ft); ('Mol' class) length 39.0m (127.9ft); beam 8.1m (26.6ft); draught 1.8m (5.9ft)

Gun armament: 4 × 30mm L/65 AA in 2 × twin mountings

Missile armament: none

Torpedo armament: 4 × single 533mm (21in) mountings for 4 × Type 53 torpedoes

Anti-submarine armament: 2 × racks for 12 × depth-charges

Electronics: 1 × 'Pot Drum' surface search radar; 1 × 'Drum Tilt' gun-control radar; 1 × 'Square Head' IFF system; 1 × 'High Pole-A' IFF system

Propulsion: ('Shershen' class) 3 × M 503A diesels delivering 9,000kW (12,070hp) to three shafts; ('Mol' class) 3 × M 504 diesels delivering 11,250kW (15,090hp) to three shafts

Performance: maximum speed ('Shershen' class) 47kt; ('Mol' class) 36kt; range 1,500km (930 miles) at 30kt; 850km (530 miles) at 42kt

Complement: ('Shershen' class) 23; ('Mol' class) 25

1. Angola (4 'Shershen'-class craft)

These are standard craft transferred between December 1977 and early 1983.

2. Bulgaria (6 'Shershen'-class craft – Nos 104, 105, 106, 114, 115 and 116)

These are standard craft transferred in 1970.

3. Cape Verde (2 'Shershen'-class craft – Nos 451 and 452)

These craft were transferred in March and July 1979 without torpedo armament.

4. Congo (1 'Shershen'-class craft)

This is the sole survivor of three vessels transferred in December 1979. It has had its torpedo armament removed.

5. Egypt (6 'Shershen'-class craft – Nos 751, 753, 755, 757, 759 and 761)

These are the survivors of seven standard craft transferred between 1967 and 1968. They were refitted in 1987 and 1988, and four have had their torpedo armament removed to make way for 1 × 122mm (4.82in) BM-21 Grad 20-tube rocket launcher and 1 × container-launcher for ? SA-N-5 'Grail' surface-to-air missiles.

6. Ethiopia (2 'Mol'-class craft – Nos FTB110 and FTB111)

These are standard craft transferred in January 1978.

7. Germany (East) (6 'Shershen'-class craft)

These are *Wilhelm Florin, Fritz Behn, Willi Brezdel, Walte Huesman, Edgar Andre* and *Ernst Grube*. They are the survivors of eighteen craft transferred between 1968 (first four) and 1976 (last three).

8. Guinea (3 'Shershen'-class craft)

These craft were transferred in December 1978, and have had their torpedo armament removed.

9. North Korea (3 'Shershen'-class craft)

These are standard craft transferred in 1968.

10. Somalia (4 'Mol'-class craft)

These are standard craft transferred between December 1976 and February 1977. Two have been stripped of their torpedo armament.

11. USSR (7 'Shershen'-class craft)

These are standard craft.

13. Vietnam (16 'Shershen'-class craft)

These are standard craft transferred between 1973 and June 1983. Some of them have been stripped of their torpedo armament and now serve in the training and patrol roles.

14. Yugoslavia (14 'Shershen'-class craft)

These are *Pionir* (TC211), *Partizan* (TC212), *Proleter* (TC213), *Topcider* (TC214), *Ivan* (TC215), *Jadran* (TC216), *Kornat* (TC217), *Biokovak* (TC218), *Streljko* (TC219), *Crvena Zvijezda* (TC220), *Partizan III* (TC221), *Partizan II* (TC222), *Napredak* (TC223) and *Pionir II* (TC224). After three or four craft had been obtained in 1965 directly from the USSR, the rest were built under licence at the Tito Shipyard at Kraljevica between 1966 and 1971. The Yugoslav-built vessels lack depth-charge racks.

General note

These are obsolete FAC(T)s built from 1962 in a number of Soviet yards to the extent of some 80 craft up to 1970. They are contemporaries of the 'Osa'-class FAC(M)s, and have the same propulsion arrangement in a slightly smaller hull. Notable features compared with the preceding 'P 6'-class FAC(T)s are two rather than four tube mountings, and the new 30mm gun armament. The 'Mol' is essentially an enlarged version of the 'Shershen' specifically for export. The Soviets classify both classes as torpedo cutters.

'Sin-hung' class: *see* 'Ku-song' class
'Sinpo' class: *see* 'P6' class

'Snogg' class   Norway

Type: fast attack craft (missile and torpedo)
Displacement: 100 tons standard; 135 tons full load
Dimensions: length 36.5m (119.8ft); beam 6.1m (20.0ft); draught 1.5m (5.0ft)
Gun armament: 1 × 40mm Bofors L/70 AA in a Bofors single mounting
Missile armament: 4 × single container-launchers for 4 × Penguin anti-ship missiles
Torpedo armament: 4 × single 533mm (21in) mountings for 4 × Tp 61 wire-guided torpedoes
Anti-submarine armament: none
Electronics: 1 × TM626 surface search and navigation radar; 1 × MSI-80S fire-control system (with 1 × TVT-300 optronic tracker and 1 × laser rangefinder); 1 × TORC1 torpedo fire-control system
Propulsion: 2 × MTU 16V TB92 diesels delivering 5,400kW (7,240hp) to two shafts
Performance: maximum speed 32kt; range 1,000km (620 miles) at 32kt
Complement: 3+16

◀ **'Snogg'-class fast missile and torpedo boat of the Norwegian navy.**

1. Norway

Name	No	Builder	Commis-sioned
Snogg	P980	Batservice	1970
Rapp	P981	Batservice	1970
Snar	P982	Batservice	1970
Rask	P983	Batservice	1971
Kvikk	P984	Batservice	1971
Kjapp	P985	Batservice	1971

Based on the same steel hull as that of the 'Storm'-class FAC(M), these FAC(M/T)s have been modernized with better electronics, but can only be regarded as obsolescent.

'SO 1' class   USSR

Type: fast attack craft (gun and torpedo)
Displacement: 170 tons standard; 215 tons full load
Dimensions: length 42.0m (137.8ft); beam 6.0m (19.7ft); draught 1.8m (5.9ft)
Gun armament: 4 × 25mm L/80 AA in 2 × 2-M-3 110PM twin mountings
Missile armament: none
Torpedo armament: 2 × single 406mm (16in) mountings for 2 × Type 40 anti-submarine torpedoes (in some craft only)
Anti-submarine armament: torpedoes (see above); 4 × RBU-1200 five-barrel rocket-launchers; 2 × depth-charge racks for ? × depth-charges

▲'SO1'-class large patrol craft serving in the North Korean navy.

Mines: provision for 10 × mines
Electronics: 1 × 'Pot Head' surface search and navigation radar; 1 × Tamir 2 hull-mounted high-frequency search and attack sonar; 1 × 'High Pole-A/B' IFF system; 1 × 'Dead Duck' IFF system
Propulsion: 3 × Type 40D diesels delivering 5,550kW (7,445hp) to three shafts
Performance: maximum speed 28kt; range 2,000km (1,245 miles) at 13kt or 650km (405 miles) at 28kt
Complement: 31

1. Bulgaria (2 craft – Nos 45 and 46)
These are standard craft transferred in 1963, and are the survivors of six craft originally supplied.

2. Cuba (2 craft)
These are standard craft, and are the survivors of twelve originally supplied in groups of six during September 1964 and 1967.

3. Iraq (3 craft – Nos 310, 311 and 312)
These are standard craft transferred in May 1962.

4. Mozambique (2 craft)
These are standard craft transferred in June 1985.

5. North Korea (20 craft)

Eight of these are standard craft transferred in the early 1960s, and the rest were built locally in North Korean yards. In their current form, these vessels carry an armament of 1 × 85mm (3.35in) L/52 DP in a single mounting, 2 × 37mm L/63 AA in a twin mounting, 4 × 25mm L/60 AA in 2 × 2-M-3 110PM twin mountings, and 4 × 14.5mm (0.57in) machine-guns in single mountings.

6. USSR (13 craft)

Some of these craft are fitted with 1 × 57mm L/77 AA in a single mounting and 2 × 25mm L/80 AA in a 2 × 2-M-3 110PM twin mounting. Vessels with anti-submarine armament generally carry only 2 × 25mm L/80 AA in a 2 × 2-M-3 110PM twin mounting.

7. Vietnam (8 craft)

These are standard craft transferred between March 1980 and September 1983, and are the survivors of twelve originally supplied from 1960.

'Sohung' class: *see* 'Komar' class
'Soju' class: *see* 'Osa I' and 'Osa II' classes

General note

Built at Zelenodolsk and Khabarov between 1957 and the late 1960s, these FAC(G)s are obsolete patrol craft and relatively few now survive, from an original total of about 150.

'Søløven' class   Denmark

Type: fast attack craft (torpedo)
Displacement: 95 tons standard; 120 tons full load
Dimensions: length 99.4ft (30.3m); beam 26.25ft (8.0m); draught 8.2ft (2.5m)
Gun armament: 1 × 40mm Bofors L/70 AA in a Bofors single mounting; 1 × 20mm Oerlikon AA in a single mounting
Missile armament: none
Torpedo armament: 2 or 4 × single 533mm (21in) mountings for 2 or 4 × Tp 61 wire-guided heavyweight torpedoes
Anti-submarine armament: none
Electronics: 1 × Terma NWS 1 surface search and navigation radar; 1 × Radamec Type 409 optronic director; 1 × torpedo fire-control system
Propulsion: 3 × Rolls-Royce Proteus gas turbines

▼Libyan 'Susa'-class FAC(G) built to the same specifications as the Danish 'Søløven' class, and mounting twin 40mm Bofors guns and eight SS.12M light missiles.

delivering 12,750shp (9,505kW) to three shafts, and 2 × General Motors 6V-71 cruising diesels delivering 300hp (225kW) to the two wing shafts

Performance: maximum speed 54kt on gas turbines or 10kt on diesels; range 460 miles (740km) at 46kt

Complement: 4+21

1. Denmark

Name	No	Builder	Commissioned
Søløven	P510	Vosper, Gosport	Feb 1965
Søridderen	P511	Vosper, Gosport	Feb 1965
Søbjørnen	P512	Royal Dockyard, Copenhagen	Oct 1965
Søhesten	P513	Royal Dockyard, Copenhagen	Jun 1966
Søhunden	P514	Royal Dockyard, Copenhagen	Dec 1966
Søulven	P515	Royal Dockyard, Copenhagen	May 1967

▼Test-firing an SS.12M short-range anti-ship missile.

These FAC(T)s are based on the British 'Brave' class but are obsolete and due for replacement by the 'Flyvevisken' class.

2. Libya ('Susa' class)

Name	No	Builder	Commissioned
Susa	512	Vosper, Portsmouth	Jan 1969
Sirte	513	Vosper, Portsmouth	Jan 1969
Sebha	514	Vosper, Portsmouth	Jan 1969

Ordered in October 1966, this is essentially a FAC(G) version of the 'Søløven' class with the same propulsion arrangement and similar performance, but standard and full-load displacements of 95 and 114 tons respectively on dimensions of: length 100.1ft (30.5m), beam 25.5ft (7.8m) and draught 7.0ft (2.1m). The missile armament is limited by modern standards, and comprises 8 × single container-launchers for 8 × SS.12M short-range anti-ship missiles; the other weapons consist of 2 × 40mm Bofors L/70 AA in single mountings. The electronics fit includes 1 × surface search and navigation radar and 1 × Aérospatiale SSM fire-control system. The complement is 20. The craft were refitted in 1984 with more modern electronics.

'Sparviero' class   Italy

Type: fast attack hydrofoil (missile and gun)
Displacement: 60 tons standard; 62.5 tons full load
Dimensions: length 24.6m (80.7ft) with foils retracted and
    23.0m (75.4ft) with foils extended; beam 12.0m (39.4ft)
    with foils retracted, 10.8m (35.4ft) with foils extended
    and 7.0m (22.9ft) for hull; draught 4.3m (14.1ft) hull-
    borne with foils extended and 1.8m (5.9ft) foil-borne
Gun armament: 1 × 76mm (3in) L/62 DP in an OTO
    Melara Compact single mounting
Missile armament: 2 × single container-launchers for 2 ×
    Otomat Mk 2 anti-ship missiles
Torpedo armament: none
Anti-submarine armament: none
Electronics: 1 × 3RM 7-250 surface search and navigation
    radar; 1 × RTN 10X tracking radar used in conjunction
    with; 1 × Argo NA10 fire-control system; 1 × Farad A
    ESM system with warning element
Propulsion: CODOG arrangement of 1 × Isotta Fraschini
    ID 38 N6V diesel delivering 120kW (161hp) to one
    retractable propeller for hull-borne operation or 1 ×
    Rolls-Royce Proteus 15M560 gas turbine delivering
    5,000shp (3,728kW) to one waterjet for foil-borne
    operation

Performance: maximum speed 50kt foil-borne or 8kt hull-
    borne; range 2,225km (1,385 miles) at 8kt or 740km
    (460 miles) at 45kt
Complement: 2+8

1. Italy

Name	No	Builder	Commis-sioned
Sparviero	P420	Alinavi	Jul 1974
Nibbio	P421	CNR, Muggiano	Mar 1982
Falcone	P422	CNR, Muggiano	Mar 1982
Astore	P423	CNR, Muggiano	Feb 1983
Grifone	P424	CNR, Muggiano	Feb 1983
Gheppio	P425	CNR, Muggiano	Jan 1983
Condor	P426	CNR, Muggiano	Jan 1984

These small daylight-only FAC(M/G)s pack considerable firepower in a small hull, the two missiles being powerful types usable to best effect with the capable electronics system of these craft.

2. Japan

Name	No	Builder	Commis-sioned

These three craft are to be built under licence in Japan to a standard generally similar to the Italian baseline configuration, but will have a primary armament of SSM-1B anti-ship missiles developed from the coast-launched SSM-1.

'Spica I' class: see 'Lürssen TNC-42' class

'Spica II' class   Sweden

Type: fast attack craft (missile, gun and torpedo)
Displacement: 190 tons standard; 230 tons full load
Dimensions: length 43.6m (143.0ft); beam 7.1m (23.3ft);
    draught 2.4m (7.4ft)
Gun armament: 1 × 57mm SAK 57 Mk 2 L/70 DP in a
    Bofors single mounting
Missile armament: 8 × single container-launchers for 8 ×
    RBS 15M anti-ship missiles
Torpedo armament: 6 × single 533mm (21in) mountings
    for 6 × Tp 61 wire-guided torpedoes (up to this total in
    place of the missiles)
Anti-submarine armament: none
Mines: fitted for minelaying
Electronics: 1 × Sea Giraffe air/surface search radar; 1 ×
    9LV 200 Mk 2 tracking radar used in conjunction with;
    1 × 9LV 228 fire-control system; 1 × action
    information system; 1 × ESM system with EWS 905
    warning element; 2 × Philax 'chaff'/flare-launchers
Propulsion: 3 × Rolls-Royce Proteus gas turbines
    delivering 12,900hp (9,620kW) to three shafts

▼The Italian CNR firm has also developed the hydrofoil into an operational service weapon. This is *Sparviero*, a 50kt missile and gun attack boat which gave its name to this modern and potent class.

Performance: maximum speed 40.5kt; range ? km (? miles) at ? kt

Complement: 7+20

1. Malaysia ('Spica-M' class)

Name	No	Builder	Commissioned
Handalan	5311	Karlskrona Varvet	Aug 1979
Perkasa	5312	Karlskrona Varvet	Aug 1979
Pendekar	5313	Karlskrona Varvet	Aug 1979
Gempita	5314	Karlskrona Varvet	Aug 1979

Ordered in October 1976 as replacements for the original 'Perkasa' class of FAC(T)s based on the British 'Brave' class, these Malaysian FAC(M)s are essentially diesel-engined versions of the Swedish 'Spica II' class, with 3 × MTU 16V 538 TB91 diesels delivering 8,100kW (10,865hp) to three shafts for a maximum speed of 34.5kt and a range of 3,425km (2,130 miles) at 14kt. The standard and full-load displacements are 240 and 268 tons respectively on dimensions of: length 42.6m (139.75ft), beam 7.0m (23.0ft) and draught 2.3m (7.5ft). The missile armament comprises 2 × twin container-launchers for 4 × MM.38 Exocet anti-ship missiles, and the other weapons consist of 1 × 57mm SAK 57 Mk 2 L/70 DP in a single mounting and 1 × 40mm Bofors L/70 AA in a single mounting. The electronics fit includes 1 × 9GR 600 surface radar, 1 × Decca 616 navigation radar, 1 × 9LV 212 radar used with 1 × 9LV 228 Mk 2 fire-control system, 1 × optronic AA fire-control system and 1 × ESM system with a Susie warning element. The complement is 6+34. The craft have provision for the installation of 12.75in (324mm) tubes for Mk 46 or Stingray anti-submarine torpedoes, and there are plans to procure an additional four units when funding permits.

2. Sweden

Name	No	Builder	Commissioned
Norrköping	R131	Karlskrona Varvet	May 1973
Nynashamn	R132	Karlskrona Varvet	Sep 1973
Norrtalje	R133	Karlksrona Varvet	Feb 1974
Varberg	R134	Karlskrona Varvet	Jun 1974
Vasterås	R135	Karlskrona Varvet	Oct 1974
Vastervik	R136	Karlskrona Varvet	Jan 1975
Umea	R137	Karlskrona Varvet	May 1975
Pitea	R138	Karlskrona Varvet	Sep 1975
Lulea	R139	Karlskrona Varvet	Nov 1975
Halmstad	R140	Karlskrona Varvet	Apr 1976
Stromstad	R141	Karlksrona Varvet	Sep 1976
Ystad	R142	Karlskrona Varvet	Jan 1976

This is an impressive class with missile and/or torpedo capability and a powerful DP gun. Laid down between 1971 and 1975, the class was rebuilt from 1982 with provision for 4 × tube mountings to be replaced by 8 × container-launchers for 8 × RBS 15M anti-ship missiles, and with revised electronics.

'Sri Kedah' class: *see* 'Kris' class

'Stenka' class   USSR

Type: fast attack craft (torpedo)

Displacement: 170 tons standard; 210 tons full load

Dimensions: length 39.0m (127.9ft); beam 7.8m (25.6ft); draught 1.8m (5.9ft)

Gun armament: 4 × 30mm L/65 AA in 2 × twin mountings

Missile armament: none

Torpedo armament: none

Anti-submarine armament: 4 × single 406mm (16in) mountings for 4 × Type 40 torpedoes; 2 × depth-charge racks for ? × depth-charges

Electronics: 1 × 'Pot Drum' or 'Peel Cone' surface search radar; 1 × 'Drum Tilt' gun fire-control radar; 1 × high-frequency active search variable-depth sonar; 2

▼'Spica II'-class torpedo attack boat, showing the characteristic long forward section and single 57mm gun forward.

× 'Square Head' IFF systems; 1 × 'High Pole' IFF systems

Propulsion: 3 × M 503A diesels delivering 9,000kW (12,070hp) to three shafts

Performance: maximum speed 36kt; range 1,500km (930 miles) at 24kt or 925km (575 miles) at 35kt

Complement: 30

1. Cambodia (4 craft)

These craft were transferred in November 1987 and are of the limited type for export without torpedo armament or sonar.

2. Cuba (3 craft)

These craft were transferred in 1985 and are of the limited type for export without torpedo armament or sonar.

3. USSR (114 craft with more building and planned)

Several units of this important class are used for trials with armament planned for other Soviet light force classes.

General note

The 'Stenka' class is based on the hull and propulsion arrangement of the 'Osa' class, and is now building at the rate of about five craft per year at Petrovsky, Leningrad and Vladivostok. The programme was launched in 1967, and the Soviets classify these craft as border patrol ships. The design features a larger superstructure than that of the 'Osa' class, and completely revised armament suiting the type for the patrol role.

'Stockholm' class   Sweden

Type: fast attack craft (missile, gun and torpedo)

Displacement: 310 tons standard; 335 tons full load

Dimensions: length 50.0m (164.0ft); beam 6.8m (22.3ft); draught 1.9m (6.2ft)

Gun armament: 1 × 57mm L/70 SAK 57 Mk 2 L/70 DP in a Bofors single mounting; 1 × 40mm Bofors L/70 AA in a Bofors single mounting

Missile armament: 4 × twin container-launchers for 8 × RBS 15M anti-ship missiles

Torpedo armament: 2 × single 533mm (21in) mountings for 2 × Tp 613 wire-guided torpedoes, or 2 × twin 400mm (15.75in) mountings for 4 × Tp 42 wire-guided torpedoes

Anti-submarine armament: 1 × Elma grenade system with 4 × LLS-920 nine-barrel launchers; 4 × Tp 42 torpedoes (see above); 2 × depth-charge racks for ? × depth-charges

Mines: has laying capability

Electronics: 1 × Sea Giraffe air/surface search radar; 1 × navigation radar; 1 × 9LV 200 Mk 3 tracking radar used in conjunction with; 1 × Maril fire-control system; 1 × 9LV 300 gun fire-control system (with 1 × 90LV 100 optronic director); 1 × TSM 2642 Salmon active search

variable-depth sonar; 1 × Simrad SS 304 active attack hull sonar; 1 × ESM system with EWS 905 warning element; 2 × Philax 'chaff'/flare-launchers

Propulsion: CODAG arrangement of 1 × Allison 570KLF gas turbine delivering 6,000shp (4,475kW) and 2 × MTU 16V 396 TB93 diesels delivering 3,150kW (4,225hp) to three shafts

Performance: maximum speed 32kt on gas turbine and diesels or 20kt on diesels; range 1,850km (1,150 miles) at 20kt

Complement: 30

1. Sweden

Name	No	Builder	Commis-sioned
Stockholm	K11	Karlskrona Varvet	Feb 1985
Malmö	K12	Karlskrona Varvet	May 1985

Ordered in September 1981, these are potent craft despite their comparatively small size and act as flotilla leaders for Sweden's smaller FAC types. These vessels have also been tested with Plessey variable-depth sonar to improve their already useful anti-submarine capability.

'Storm' class   Norway

Type: fast attack craft (missile and gun)

Displacement: 100 tons standard; 135 tons full load

Dimensions: length 36.5m (119.8ft); beam 6.1m (20.0ft); draught 1.5m (4.9ft)

Gun armament: 1 × 76mm (3in) L/50 in a Bofors single mounting; 1 × 40mm Bofors L/70 AA in a Bofors single mounting

Missile armament: 6 × single container-launchers for 6 × Penguin Mk II anti-ship missiles

Torpedo armament: none

Anti-submarine armament: none

Electronics: 1 × TM1226 surface search and navigation radar; 1 × tracking radar used in conjunction with; 1 × WM-26 fire-control system; 1 × MSI-80S fire-control system (with 1 × TVT-300 optronic tracker and 1 × laser rangefinder)

Propulsion: 2 × MTU 872A diesels delivering 5,400kW (7,240hp) to two shafts

Performance: maximum speed 32kt; range ? km (? miles) at ? kt

Complement: 4+15

1. Norway

Name	No	Builder	Commis-sioned
Blink	P961	Bergens Mek	1965
Glimt	P962	Bergens Mek	1966
Skjold	P963	Westermoen	1966

Name	Pennant No	Builder	Commis-sioned
Trygg	P964	Bergens Mek	1966
Kjekk	P965	Bergens Mek	1966
Djerv	P966	Westermoen	1966
Skudd	P967	Bergens Mek	1966
Arg	P968	Bergens Mek	1966
Steil	P969	Westermoen	1967
Brann	P970	Bergens Mek	1967
Tross	P971	Bergens Mek	1967
Hvass	P972	Westermoen	1967
Traust	P973	Bergens Mek	1967
Brott	P974	Bergens Mek	1967
Odd	P975	Westermoen	1967
Brask	P977	Bergens Mek	1967
Rokk	P978	Westermoen	1968
Gnist	P979	Bergens Mek	1968

▲Impressive close-range head-on photograph of a 'Storm'-class fast missile boat serving in the Norwegian navy.

These are small but agile FAC(M/G)s designed specifically for the particular operational conditions faced by the Norwegian Navy in countering maritime incursions along the country's very long coastline. The hull is basically that of the 'Snogg'-class FAC.

'Super Dvora' class: *see* 'Dvora' class
'Susa' class: *see* 'Søløren' class

'Tarantul I', 'Tarantul II' and 'Tarantul III' classes
USSR

Type: fast attack craft (missile and gun)
Displacement: 480 tons standard; 580 tons full load

Dimensions: length 56.0m (183.7ft); beam 10.5m (34.4ft); draught 2.5m (8.2ft)

Gun armament: 1 × 76mm (3in) L/60 DP in a single mounting; 2 × 30mm ADGM-630 CIWS mountings

Missile armament: 2 × twin container-launchers for 4 × SS-N-2C 'Styx' anti-ship missiles or ('Tarantul III' class) 2 or 1 × twin container-launcher for 4 or 2 × SS-N-22 'Sunburn' anti-ship missiles; 1 × quadruple launcher for 16 × SA-N-5 'Grail' surface-to-air missiles

Torpedo armament: none

Anti-submarine armament: none

Electronics: 1 × 'Plank Shave' or ('Tarantul II' and 'Tarantul III' class) 'Light Bulb' air/surface search and SSM fire-control radar; 1 × 'Band Stand' surface search radar (not 'Tarantual I' class); 1 × 'Spin Trough' navigation radar; 1 × 'Bass Tilt' gun fire-control radar; 1 × ESM system with four antennae/housings; 2 × 'chaff'-launchers; 1 × 'Square Head' IFF system; 1 × 'High Pole-B' IFF system

Propulsion: CODOG or COGOG arrangement with 2 × NK-12M gas turbines delivering 18,000kW (24,140hp) and/or two diesels or gas turbines delivering between 3,000 and 4,500kW (4,025 and 6,035hp) to two shafts

Performance: maximum speed 36kt; range 3,700km (2,300 miles) at 20kt or 740km (460 miles) at 36kt

Complement: 50

1. Germany (East)

Name	No	Builder	Commissioned
Albin Koebis	571	Petrovsky	Sep 1984
Rudolf Egelhofer	572	Petrovsky	Dec 1985
Fritz Globig	573	Petrovsky	Sep 1985
Paul Eisenschneider	574	Petrovsky	Jan 1986
Hans Beimler	575	Petrovsky	Nov 1986

These are 'Tarantul I'-class ships, and more were to have been delivered as replacements for East Germany's 'Osa I'-class FACs.

2. India ('Veer' class)

Name	No	Builder	Commissioned
Veer	K40	Petrovsky	May 1987
Nirbhik	K41	Petrovsky	Jan 1988
Nipat	K42	Petrovsky	Jan 1989
Vibhuti	K43	Mazagon Dock	1991

India plans to acquire a total of 35 of these 'Tarantul I'-class ships, 20 of them directly from the USSR and the other fifteen from two Indian yards, namely Mazagon Dock and Goa Shipyard. It is thought that the Indian-built ships are to an improved standard, but it has not yet been revealed what this standard comprises.

3. Poland

Name	No	Builder	Commissioned
Gornik	434	Petrovsky	Dec 1983
Hutnik	435	Petrovsky	Apr 1984
Stozniowiec	436	Petrovsky	Jan 1988

These 'Tarantul I'-class ships were to have been joined by at least one and possibly nine more units.

4. USSR (2 'Tarantul I'-class ships; 20 'Tarantul II'-class ships; 10 'Tarantul III'-class ships with 3 more building and more planned)

The 'Tarantul' classes use basically the same hull as the 'Pauk' class without the latter's extended transom for the accommodation of variable-depth sonar. The first 'Tarantul I'-class ship was delivered from Petrovsky in 1978, deliveries from this source being complemented from Kolpino and Pacific coast yards. The 'Tarantul II' class was built between 1980 and 1986, and the current variant is the 'Tarantul III'.

'Taechong' class   North Korea

Type: fast attack craft (gun)

Displacement: 140 tons standard; 165 tons full load

Dimensions: length 44.2m (145.0ft); beam 5.5m (18.0ft); draught 2.4m (7.8ft)

Gun armament: 2 × 57mm L/70 AA in a twin mounting; 1 × 37mm L/63 in a single mounting; 2 × 25mm L/60 AA in a twin mounting; 4 × 14.5mm (0.57in) machine-guns in 2 × twin mountings

Missile armament: none

Torpedo armament: none

Anti-submarine armament: 2 × RBU-1200 five-barrel rocket-launchers; 2 × depth-charge racks for ? × depth-charges

Electronics: 1 × 'Pot Head' surface search and navigation radar; 1 × Tamir 2 hull-mounted high-frequency search and attack sonar; 1 × 'High Pole-A' IFF system; 1 × 'Square Head' IFF system

Propulsion: 2 × diesels delivering ? kW (hp) to two shafts

Performance: maximum speed ? kt; range ? km (? miles) at ? kt

Complement: ?

1. North Korea (10 craft)

Still being built after a start in the mid-1970s, this is a class of simple FAC(G)s used mainly for patrol and coastal anti-submarine operations.

'Tjeld' class: see 'Nasty' class

'Turya' class   USSR

Type: fast attack hydrofoil (torpedo)
Displacement: 190 tons standard; 250 tons full load
Dimensions: length 39.6m (129.9ft); beam 12.5m (41.0ft)
    over foils and 7.6m (25.0ft) for hull; draught 4.0m
    (13.1ft) over foils and 1.8m (5.9ft) for hull
Gun armament: 2 × 57mm L/80 AA in a SIF-31B twin
    mounting; 2 × 25mm L/80 AA in a 2-M-3 110PM twin
    mounting; 1 × 14.5mm (0.57in) machine-gun
Missile armament: none
Torpedo armament: 4 × single 533mm (21in) mountings
    for 4 × Type 53 dual-role torpedoes
Anti-submarine armament: 4 × Type 53 torpedoes (see
    above); 1 × depth-charge rack for ? × depth-charges
Electronics: 1 × 'Pot Drum' surface search radar; 1 ×
    'Muff Cob' gun fire-control radar; 1 × high-frequency
    active search and attacks variable-depth sonar; 1 ×
    'Square Head' IFF system; 1 × 'High Pole' IFF system
Propulsion: 3 × M 504 diesels delivering 11,250kW
    (15,090hp) to three shafts
Performance: maximum speed 40kt foil-borne; range
    2,700km (1,680 miles) at 14kt hull-borne or 1,100km
    (685 miles) at 35kt foil-borne
Complement: 30

1. Cambodia (2 craft)
Transferred in March 1984 and February 1985, these are
downgraded craft without dipping sonar and torpedo
tubes.

2. Cuba (9 craft)
These are standard craft transferred between February
1979 and November 1983. Some of them may carry 1 ×
quadruple container-launcher for ? × SA-N-5 'Grail'
surface-to-air missiles.

3. Ethiopia (2 craft – Nos HTB112 and HTB113)
These are standard craft transferred in March 1985 and
March 1986.

4. Seychelles (1 craft)
Named *Zoroaster*, this unit was transferred in June 1986
and is of the downgraded type without sonar and torpedo
armament.

5. USSR (30 craft)
These are standard craft delivered between 1972 and
1978.

6. Vietnam (5 craft)
These craft were transferred between mid-1984 to January 1986, and two are of the downgraded type without
sonar and torpedo armament.

General note
Based on the hull and propulsion arrangement of the 'Osa
II'-class FAC(M) with a single forward hydrofoil (and a
planing after hull trimmed by an adjustable flap on the
transom), this FAH(T) class has been built since 1972 at
Petrovsky, Leningrad and Vladivostok. Since 1978 pro-

duction has been for export only. The Soviets classify the
type as a torpedo cutter.

'Type 024' class: *see* 'Komar' class
'Type 123' class: *see* 'P4' class
'Type 143' class: *see* 'Lürssen FPB/PB-57' class
'Type 148' class: *see* 'La Combattante II' class
'Type 211' class: *see* 'Rode Koucar' class
'Veer' class: *see* 'Tarantul' class

'Vigilante' class   France/Venezuela

Type: fast attack craft (gun)
Displacement: ? tons standard; 190 tons full load
Dimensions: length 41.8m (137.1ft); beam 6.8m (22.3ft);
    draught 1.6m (5.25ft)
Gun armament: 1 × 40mm Bofors L/70 AA in a single
    mounting
Missile armament: none
Torpedo armament: none
Anti-submarine armament: none
Electronics: 1 × TM 1226C surface search and navigation
    radar; 1 × Naja optronic director
Propulsion: 2 × MTU 12V 538 TB91 diesels delivering
    4,000kW (5,365hp) to two shafts
Performance: maximum speed 28kt; range 4,450km (2,765
    miles) at 15kt
Complement: 5+23

1. Venezuela

Name	No	Builder	Commis- sioned
15 de Noviembre	5	CMN, Cherbourg	Mar 1981
25 de Agosto	6	CMN, Cherbourg	Mar 1981
Comodoro Coe	7	CMN, Cherbourg	Mar 1981

Ordered in 1979, these are simple FAC(G)s of only the
most limited capability and therefore more useful as
training and patrol craft than as fully operational vessels.

'Vosper Thornycroft 110ft' class   UK/Singapore

Type: fast attack craft (gun)
Displacement: 112 tons standard; 142 tons full load
Dimensions: length 109.6ft (33.5m); beam 21.0ft (6.4m);
    draught 5.6ft (1.8m)
Gun armament: 1 × 76mm (3in) Bofors L/50 in a single
    mounting ('Type B' class craft), or 1 × 40mm Bofors
    L/70 AA in a single mounting ('Type A' craft); 1 ×
    20mm Oerlikon L/75 AA in an A41A single mounting
Missile armament: none
Torpedo armament: none
Anti-submarine armament: none
Electronics: 1 × MS 32 surface search radar; 1 × Decca
    626 navigation radar; 1 × tracking radar (only in 'Type
    B' class craft) used in conjunction with; 1 × WM-26

◀RSS *Independence* is a
'Type A' fast attack boat of
the Singapore navy.

fire-control system (only in 'Type B' class craft)
Propulsion: 2 × MTU 16V 538 diesels delivering 5,400kW
(7,240hp) to two shafts
Performance: maximum speed 32kt; range 1,275 miles
(2,050km) at 14kt
Complement: 3+19/22

1. Singapore

Name	No	Builder	Commis-sioned
Independence	P69	Vosper, Thornycroft	Jul 1970
Freedom	P70	Vosper, Singapore	Jan 1971
Justice	P71	Vosper, Singapore	Apr 1971
Sovereignty*	P72	Vosper Thornycroft	Feb 1971
Daring*	P73	Vosper, Singapore	Sep 1971
Dauntless*	P74	Vosper, Singapore	1971

*'Vosper Thornycroft 110ft Type B'-class craft

Ordered in May 1968, this is a simple (FAC)G type
produced in two forms with the lead boat of each sub-
class from the UK and the other from Vosper Thornycroft's Singapore subsidiary.

2. United Arab Emirates (Abu Dhabi)

Name	No	Builder	Commis-sioned
Ardhana	P1101	Vosper Thornycroft	Jun 1975
Zurara	P1102	Vosper Thornycroft	Aug 1975
Murban	P1103	Vosper Thornycroft	Sep 1975
Al Ghullan	P1104	Vosper Thornycroft	Sep 1975
Radoom	P1105	Vosper Thornycroft	Jul 1976
Ghanadhah	P1106	Vosper Thornycroft	Jul 1976

These FAC(G)s are used mainly for patrol, but at
standard and full-load displacements of 110 and 175 tons
respectively on a length of 109.9ft (33.5m) they have a
useful gun armament comprising 2 × 30mm Oerlikon L/85
AA in a GCM-A twin mounting and 1 × 20mm Oerlikon
L/75 AA in an A41A single mounting. Electronics are
limited to 1 × TM1626 surface search and navigation
radar. The propulsion comprises 2 × Paxman Valenta
16RP-200M diesels delivering 5,400hp (4,025kW) to two
shafts for a maximum speed of 30kt, and the range is
2,100 miles (3,380km) at 14kt. The complement is 26.

◀RSS *Justice*, a 'Type B'
FAC of the Singapore navy.
Note the unusual forward
76mm gun turret mounting.

▲P1101 is *Ardhana*, a 'Vosper 110ft'-class gunboat serving in the United Arab Emirates navy and mounting useful twin 30mm Oerlikon and single 20mm Oerlikon cannon.

These medium-sized FAC(M)s are ideally suited to the coastal requirement of Brunei. In 1988 they were committed to an upgrade programme designed to improve the fire-control and ESM systems because of political problems in this volatile region.

'Vosper Thornycroft 121ft' class   UK/Brunei

Type: fast attack craft (missile)
Displacement: ? tons standard; 206 tons full load
Dimensions: length 121.0ft (36.9m); beam 23.5ft (7.2m); draught 6.0ft (1.8m)
Gun armament: 2 × 30mm Oerlikon L/85 AA in a GCM-A03 single mounting; 2 × 7.62mm (0.3in) machine-guns in single mountings
Missile armament: 2 × single container-launchers for 2 × MM.38 Exocet anti-ship missiles
Torpedo armament: none
Anti-submarine armament: none
Electronics: 1 × TM1229 surface search and navigation radar; 1 × tracking radar used in conjunction with; 1 × Sea Archer fire-control system; 1 × ESM system with RDL warning element
Propulsion: 2 × MTU 20V 538 TB91 diesels delivering 6,700kW (8,985hp) to two shafts
Performance: maximum speed 32kt; range 1,380 miles (2,220km) at 14kt
Complement: 4+20

1. Brunei ('Waspada' class)

Name	No	Builder	Commissioned
Waspada	P02	Vosper (Singapore)	1978
Pejuang	P03	Vosper (Singapore)	1979
Seteria	P04	Vosper (Singapore)	1979

2. Venezuela ('Constitucion' class)

Name	No	Builder	Commissioned
Constitucion	PC11	Vosper Thornycroft	Aug 1974
Federacion	PC12	Vosper Thornycroft	Mar 1975
Independencia	PC13	Vosper Thornycroft	Sep 1974
Libertad	PC14	Vosper Thornycroft	Jun 1975
Patria	PC15	Vosper Thornycroft	Jan 1975
Victoria	PC16	Vosper Thornycroft	Sep 1975

These are comparatively light FACs of which three are equipped with gun armament as FAC(G)s and the other three with anti-ship missiles as FAC(M/G)s. They are based on the same hull and superstructure as the 'Waspada' class, and have a full-load displacement of 170 tons on dimensions of: length 121.0ft (36.9m), beam 23.3ft (7.1m) and draught 6.0ft (1.8m). The three FAC(G)s are PC11, 13 and 15, and these have an armament of 1 × 76mm (3in) L/62 DP in an OTO Melara Compact single mounting and 1 × 40mm Bofors L/70 AA in a Breda single mounting. The FAC(M)s are PC12, 14 and 16, and in addition to 1 × 40mm gun they have 2 × single Teseo container-launchers for 2 × Otomat anti-ship missiles. The electronics fit includes 1 × SPQ 2D surface search radar, 1 × RTN 10X tracking radar (only in PC11, 13 and 15) used in conjunction with 1 × Argo NA10 gun fire-control system. The propulsion arrangement comprises 2 × MTU 16V 538 TB90 diesels delivering 5,400kW (7,240hp) to two shafts for a maximum speed of 31kt and a range of 2,500km (1,555 miles) at 16kt. The complement is

3+14. All the craft are being modernized, the three FAC(G)s being turned into FAC(M)s by the replacement of the 76mm (3in) gun with RGM-84 Harpoon anti-ship missiles. It is likely that the three current FAC(M)s will then receive the same missile type in place of their Otomat weapons.

'Waspada' class: *see* 'Vosper Thornycroft 121ft' class

'Wildcat' class

South Korea

Type: fast attack craft (missile)
Displacement: ? tons standard; 150 tons full load
Dimensions: length 33.9m (108.9ft); beam 6.9m (22.6ft); draught 2.4m (7.9ft)
Gun armament: 2 × 40mm Bofors L/60 AA in single mountings; 2 × two 0.5in (12.7mm) machine-guns
Missile armament: 2 × single container-launchers for 2 × MM.38 Exocet anti-ship missiles
Torpedo armament: none
Anti-submarine armament: none
Electronics: 1 × Raytheon 1645 surface search and navigation radar
Propulsion: 2 × MTU 518D diesels delivering 7,400kW (9,925hp) to two shafts, or (only in PKM272) 3 × MTU 16V 536 TB90 diesels delivering 8,100kW (10,865hp) to three shafts
Performance: maximum speed 40kt; range 1,500km (930 miles) at 17kt
Complement: 5+24

1. South Korea

Name	No	Builder	Commis- sioned
	PKM271	Korea–Tacoma	1972
	PKM272	Korea–Tacoma	1972

These are elderly and obsolescent FAC(M)s now useful mainly for training and patrol.

'Willemoes' class

Denmark

Type: fast attack craft (missile, gun and torpedo)
Displacement: ? tons standard; 260 tons full load
Dimensions: length 46.0m (150.9ft); beam 7.4m (24.0ft); draught 2.5m (8.2ft)
Gun armament: 1 × 76mm (3in) L/62 DP in an OTO Melara Compact single mounting
Missile armament: 2 × single or twin Mk 141 container-launchers for 2 or 4 × RGM-84 Harpoon anti-ship missiles
Torpedo armament: 2 or 4 × single 533mm (21in) mountings for 2 or 4 × Tp 61 wire-guided torpedoes
Anti-submarine armament: none
Electronics: 1 × 9GR 208 surface search radar; 1 × Terma 20T 48 Super navigation radar; 1 × 9LV 200 tracking radar used in conjunction with; 1 × 9LV 228 fire-control system; 1 × EPLO action information system; 1 × ESM system with Cutlass warning element
Propulsion: CODOG arrangement of 3 × Rolls-Royce Proteus 52M/544 gas tubines delivering 12,750shp (9,510kW) and 2 × General Motors 8V-71 diesels delivering 1,600hp (1,195kW) to three shafts
Performance: maximum speed 38kt on gas tubines or 12kt on diesels; range ? km (? miles) at ? kt
Complement: 5+20

▼ *Bille* **is the first ship of the 'Willemoes'-class FACs in the Danish navy, mounting missiles, guns and torpedoes.**

Name	No	Builder	Commis-sioned
Bille	P540	Frederikshavn Vaerft	Oct 1976
Bredal	P541	Frederikshavn Vaerft	Jan 1977
Hammer	P542	Frederikshavn Vaerft	Apr 1977
Huitfeld	P543	Frederikshavn Vaerft	Jun 1977
Krieger	P544	Frederikshavn Vaerft	Sep 1977
Norby	P545	Frederikshavn Vaerft	Nov 1977
Rodsteen	P546	Frederikshavn Vaerft	Feb 1978
Sehested	P547	Frederikshavn Vaerft	May 1978
Suenson	P548	Frederikshavn Vaerft	Aug 1978
Willemoes	P549	Frederikshavn Vaerft	Jun 1976

This FAC(M/G/T) class is similar to the Swedish 'Spica II' design, and was prepared by Lürssen in West Germany. In general, the craft each carry 2 × missiles and 2 × torpedoes.

'Wisla' class   Poland

Type: fast attack craft (torpedo)
Displacement: ? tons standard; 70 tons full load
Dimensions: length 25.0m (82.0ft); beam 5.5m (18.05ft); draught 1.8m (5.9ft)

Gun armament: 2 × 30mm L/65 DP in a twin mounting
Missile armament: none
Torpedo armament: 4 × 533mm (21in) mountings for 4 × Type 53 torpedoes
Anti-submarine armament: none
Electronics: 1 × 'Pot Drum' surface search radar; 1 × 'High Pole-A' IFF system
Propulsion: CODAG arrangement, with 2 × M50-FA diesels delivering 1,800kW (2,415hp) and 2 × gas turbines delivering 7,150kW (9,590hp) to four shafts
Performance: maximum speed 50kt; range 925km (575 miles) at 20kt or 185km (115 miles) at 50kt
Complement: not revealed

1. Poland (15+ craft)

Initial work on this FAC(T) type began in the early 1960s and production began about ten years later on the basis of an aluminium-alloy hull surmounted by a somewhat large superstructure of the same material. The units of this class are notable for their high level of automation, by communist bloc standards, but the craft are at best obsolescent despite their high speed.

'Zobel' class: *see* 'Lürssen TNC-42' class

◀'Wisla'-class FAC ploughing through heavy seas while serving in the Polish navy.